Cities and Development in the Third World

edited by
Robert B. Potter and
Ademola T. Salau

Published in association with

The
Commonwealth
Foundation

MANSELL

LONDON AND NEW YORK

First published 1990 by Mansell Publishing Limited
A Cassell imprint
Villiers House, 41/47 Strand, London WC2N 5JE, England
125 East 23rd Street, Suite 300, New York 10010, USA

Reprinted 1992

British Library Cataloguing in Publication Data
Cities and development in the Third World.
  1. Developing countries. Cities
  I. Potter, Robert B.   II. Salau, A.T.
  III. Commonwealth Foundation
  307 .76091724

  ISBN 0-7201-2066-7

Library of Congress Cataloging-in-Publication Data
applied for

Printed and bound in Great Britain by
Short Run Press Ltd, Exeter

Contents

Preface

The aim of this edited volume is to make available first-hand authorita-
tive accounts of contemporary patterns and processes of urbanization
in developing countries, and to dovetail these with new thinking about
the roles that cities play in the contemporary Third World development
process. As such, the focus is most definitely on actual examples, experiences and policies set within their relevant theoretical contexts, and not
on theory *per se*.

Although the literature on Third World cities is burgeoning, relatively
few volumes attempt to cover the full scale of consideration, which extends
from global political economy perspectives to detailed local circumstances
within particular towns and cities. Further, the scale and pace of change
in Third World urban areas is such that there is constant need for fresh
empirical accounts from those commentators who possess first-hand
experience. In this respect, we hope it will not go unnoticed that at the
time of writing, eight of the ten authors contributing to this volume were
to be found residing and teaching in developing countries. In contrast
to many volumes of this type, this book really does present perspectives
from developing countries, and not just *about* developing countries.

The book is based on a selection of papers originally presented at a
workshop dealing with urbanization in developing countries which was
held in Delhi, India. The meeting was organized by the Commonwealth
Geographical Bureau with funding from the Commonwealth Foundation.
Following the workshop, the papers selected for inclusion in this volume
were revised and rewritten during 1989. The original meeting attracted
a total of thirty-five participants from various areas of the Commonwealth
and twenty-seven papers were presented during the five-day research
workshop. One set of papers focused on problems of housing, services
and welfare at the local scale, while another group concentrated on the
urbanization process at the national and regional scales. This division
is broadly maintained in the present volume, with Chapters 2–6 covering

conditions within cities, and Chapters 7–11 dealing with inter-urban considerations. The first chapter endeavours to examine changing ideas relating to the relationship between cities and development within the Third World, while the ways in which the essays contained in the volume relate to these themes are drawn out in a brief concluding chapter.

In order to provide greater balance, one invited contribution is included here which did not form part of the original workshop. Subsequent to the meeting in Delhi, Chapter 5 in the present volume was published in the *Geographical Journal* (vol. 155, part 2, 1989. pp. 81–93) and appears here in slightly modified form by kind permission of the journal's editor and the Royal Geographical Society.

We feel sure that the contributors to the volume, along with the original participants, would certainly not wish to see this opportunity pass without their gratitude being recorded for the hospitality shown by the geographers at the University of Delhi, especially Dr Chandra Pal Singh, who hosted the Delhi meeting.

Robert B. Potter
Englefield Green, Surrey, England

Ademola T. Salau
Port Harcourt, Nigeria

Contributors

Jenny J. Bryant, Senior Lecturer in Geography, University of the South Pacific, Suva, Fiji.

M. Chatterjee, Lecturer in Geography, Mithibai College, Bombay.

Sioux D. Cumming, Lecturer in Geography, University of Zimbabwe.

Graham M. S. Dann, Senior Lecturer in Sociology, University of the West Indies, Cave Hill, Barbados.

David Drakakis-Smith, Professor of Development Studies, University of Keele.

H. A. C. Main, formerly Senior Lecturer in Geography, Bayero University, Nigeria and presently Temporary Lecturer in Geography and Recreation Studies, Staffordshire Polytechnic.

Sulong Mohamad, Associate Professor of Geography and Regional Planning, National University of Malaysia.

Robert B. Potter, Reader in Geography, Royal Holloway & Bedford New College, University of London.

Ademola T. Salau, Professor of Geography, University of Port Harcourt, Nigeria.

K. Sita, Reader in Geography, University of Bombay.

[1]

Cities, Convergence, Divergence and Third World Development

Robert B. Potter

Introduction: Cities and Development

The past ten years have seen fundamental changes in thinking about the roles that urban settlements play in the processes of development and change in Third World societies. Specifically, new approaches have looked more critically upon the assumed function of large cities as the generators of modernization and development. In addition, the role of cities has come increasingly to be viewed as part of a wider array of factors which affect development at all levels, from that of the global economy to the individual locality. The essays in this book seek to provide first-hand and detailed empirical evidence of the need for these reappraisals in thinking about the role of cities in the development process.

In the period immediately after the Second World War, cities were almost without exception seen as the agents of development – as the spatial oases from which progress would eventually be spread; first, from the rich countries of the world to the poorer ones, and then inexorably from relatively prosperous areas to lagging regions within these poorer countries. Impediments to this process of development were seen as transitional – merely involving temporal lags in the inescapable spread of more efficient techniques of production, higher standards of living and new ways of life. This process, referred to as *modernization*, was envisaged as one involving the primarily hierarchical diffusion of growth-inducing innovation and change, whereby development was transmitted from the largest urban place down through the successively lower levels of the national urban settlement system (Hudson, 1969; Pederson, 1970; Berry, 1972). At the same time modernization would be spread outward from the national capital to the rural, peripheral and underdeveloped regions of the national space. As this pattern of urban-centred spatial transformation had characterized growth and industrial change in eighteenth- and nineteenth-century Britain and the United States, there appeared to be few who seriously doubted its applicability to the newly decolonized nations which made up the Third World.

But the experiences of the postwar decades now point to the idealized nature of this picture of progressive, albeit gradual, change and socio-economic betterment. Despite development programmes and development decades, the majority of Third World countries have shown only moderate rates of economic development in the postwar period. But more saliently, even where economic growth has occurred, evidence suggests that its products have been far from equitably distributed – either in spatial or in social terms. Towns and cities and their proximate regions have done disproportionately well, in so far as they show average wage levels which are closely positively related to urban size (Hoch, 1972), as well as relatively low average price levels (Gwynne, 1978). A number of countries have managed to expand their productive industrial sectors, and the existing major urban places with their attendant infrastructures have been the points of concentration of such developments in newly industrializing countries (NICs).

But little seems to have happened to raise the overall standard of living and quality of life of the rural majority. In fact, in many instances, with global economic recession and high levels of debt, it is the rural poor who are feeling the effects of structural adjustments made to secure financial assistance from international organizations. Rather than growth spreading from urban to rural areas, in hard times, the rural areas seem to have been paying a high price for the essentially polarized urban forms of development which have characterized the past. This is in addition to the longstanding mechanisms of unequal exchange between the urban and rural sectors whereby the latter provides the former with food at cheap procurement prices (see Harriss, 1989), and a ready supply of cheap reserve labour at the lowest social reproduction cost. All of these criticisms of the major perspective on growth come together under the accusation that, for a multiplicity of reasons, the development efforts of Third World countries have suffered from rampant and persistent *urban bias* (Lipton, 1977; 1982).

In addition to this realization concerning the efficacy of modes and models of development based on large urban places, in the past twenty years there has been a re-evaluation of the meaning and scope of the process of development itself. Rather than being equated with economic growth, as connoted by increasing Gross Domestic Product and the immutable and essentially linear path to development envisaged by writers such as Rostow (1960) and Hirschman (1958) in the postwar period, a new paradigm has emerged which stresses the importance of social and humanitarian aspects of development. In particular, the salience of quality of life, including liberty and basic human rights, as the criterion of development has been stressed. Development should not be more of everything (or at least material goods) per head of the population – but rather more of the things that make for a fulfilling and satisfactory life, and these should be expressly targeted at those in the population who have little in the first place. Many of the changes in perspective concerning cities and development can be viewed in parallel with these changing views on the process of development itself.

New Approaches to the Study of Cities and Development

The new paradigm of development theory and practice is one which rejects a series of false schisms in thinking about socio-economic change. Specifically, the conditions of development and underdevelopment (Frank, 1969; 1980; Beckford, 1972; Wallerstein, 1974), the apparent geographical contrasts between urban and rural (Potter and Unwin, 1989; Dixon, 1987), and the socio-economic gradations between rich and poor are all to be viewed as symbiotic conditions and not polar opposites. The existence of underdevelopment, of poverty and rural backwardness cannot be treated as unfortunate failures to achieve some rightful state, but rather as the direct corollary of development, wealth and urbanization elsewhere.

Some of the most important aspects of the changes in thinking about cities and development have recently been cogently summarized in Armstrong and McGee's (1985) book *Theatres of Accumulation*. In this work, four new approaches which have infused work since the 1970s are identified.

The first is the rise of the *world political economy approach*, which sees cities as centres of capitalist accumulation. The approach stresses that cities and sets of cities have been the mechanisms for the incorporation of countries into the international economic system. The dominant view argues that this mechanism has basically been exploitative, witnessing the accumulation of capital in Third World cities and its draining off into the major centres of developing countries (Frank, 1969; 1980; Amin, 1974; 1976). For others, especially Warren (1973; 1980), the process has been interpreted far more favourably, and the incipient spread of industrialization in urban areas is regarded as the positive outcome. Others have covered the important criticism that historical internationalist explanations cannot account entirely for patterns of development. Dependence also relates to the internal mechanisms of class division within a particular society (Dos Santos, 1973). It is very tempting to argue that the greatest contribution of *dependency* approaches is that they have served to emphasize the need to re-evaluate the role of cities in the contemporary development process at all levels. A practical policy-oriented implication suggests the need to close dependent countries and dependent cities to outside influences, to some degree or another, depending, of course, on local conditions, the size of the nation, its resource base and the like.

The second theme, alluded to previously in this account, has been the recognition given to the existence of enduring poverty among large sections of the population of Third World countries, especially that part of the citizenry not enjoying the fruits of concentrated development in the largest cities and towns. This reflects the principle of urban bias in development with all its connotations of the importation of foreign technology and ways of doing things. Since the late 1970s, the need to satisfy the *basic needs* of the less well off has been the clarion call from development experts. This has gone hand in hand with the argument that the case for the growth-inducing efficiency of large cities has not been proven. For every set of statistics and for every argument suggesting the developmental efficiency of very large cities due to economies of scale (Richardson, 1976), the argument is forwarded that this efficiency merely reflects the massive concentration of capital that has occurred in these areas in the past. Thus cities are efficient because we have assumed without question that they are efficient. Many geographers, Gilbert (1976; 1977) among them, have argued that if comparable investment in infrastructure and social overhead capital were to have been provided in small urban nodes – or even rural locales – they too would now be showing good returns. The need, it is argued, is to establish indigenous forms of development which are pro-rural and which serve to stress the vital importance of bottom-up and participatory codes of planning and development practice. Such a stance has focused attention on the need for the creation of small (Hardoy and Satterthwaite, 1986) and intermediate-sized urban places (Rondinelli, 1982; 1983a; 1983b), a theme which is highly germane to the present volume.

A greater awareness of the sophistication and complexity of patterns of rural-to-urban migration represents a third strand in the new wave of thinking concerning Third World urban development. Previously viewed as rushing headlong directly from rural poverty to urban hope, it has come to be increasingly appreciated that rural denizens who are unemployed, underemployed or misemployed frequently move to the city as part of a gradual sequence of chain migration. Further, the salience of circulatory migration, whereby new urbanites return to their rural origin either seasonally or once and for all, has come to be recognized. The implication is that if intervening opportunities of consequence existed, then many people would not find their way to the capital city. Urban bias is once again seen to be leading to a literally circular argument about change and development. This approach also relates to the generic point that just as development can only be understood in relation to underdevelopment elsewhere, so urban conditions can only be appreciated if their close functional interrelation with rural conditions is fully appreciated (Potter and Unwin, 1989). The two are opposite sides of the same coin.

The fourth strand in this new set of ideas relating to cities and Third World development concerns the role and contribution of the informal sector of the economy. This component of cities in the less developed world was at first viewed in negative and basically pejorative terms, as providing poor and low-paid jobs, and implicitly accepting low productivity levels, and thereby sanctioning poverty. However, the sheer range and volume of informal sector jobs, covering all aspects of consumption, production and exchange, have forced a gradual re-evaluation. Thus, the family small-scale sector is now looked upon more favourably as providing jobs where the state appears to be powerless to do the same. The fact that the informal sector has strong links with the formal sector has increasingly been recognized as having 'buttressed arguments that policy-makers should adopt policies that would encourage entrepreneurial activity and capital accumulation in the informal sector' (Armstrong and McGee, 1985: 13). The occurrence of the two circuits of the economy in Third World cities has also served to emphasize the salience of people-oriented forms of development and change. This is as true of people's efforts to provide their own housing by means of self-help as it is of those who are providing their own gainful employment in a context of hard-pressed economic circumstances (Potter, 1991).

The Thesis of Convergence and Divergence

It has already been noted how the dominant view held in the 1950s was that large cities played a generative role in what were regarded as peripheral regions and territories (Hoselitz, 1955; Hirschman, 1958). Cities were viewed as centres from which growth was diffused, and regional imbalances were regarded as merely transitional.

But surely cities concentrate some developments and spread others? Pred (1973; 1977), working in the context of the United States, argued that new growth-inducing productive techniques appear to be bounced around between large urban places, with multinational corporations playing a crucial role in this process. Productive capacity is thereby being channelled more and more into selected urban nodes. This process has recently been referred to by Armstrong and McGee (1985) as one of *divergence*. The countries of the world – including poor countries – are showing increasing heterogeneity with respect to the economic activities that they carry out. Most notably, in the Third World itself, one can distinguish between export-oriented industrializing countries such as Taiwan, Hong Kong, Singapore, large inward-looking industrializing countries such as Brazil, India and Mexico, raw-material exporters like

Nigeria, and low-income agricultural exporters such as Bangladesh (Armstrong and McGee, 1985). Thus, the division of labour at the international level is resulting in increasing divergence between countries in terms of patterns of capital accumulation and their productive capabilities.

In contrast, Third World nations and their cities may be regarded as being rendered more homogeneous by virtue of the lifestyles enjoyed by some of their residents. In particular, this is witnessed in the possession of consumer goods by the elite and middle-class groups. This involves a process of the *convergence* of consumption on Western capitalist norms. This is also reflected in the built form of cities with respect to modern architecture, and the use of land and transport facilities (see Roberts, 1978; Browning and Roberts, 1980; and also Potter, 1989a; 1989b). As Armstrong and McGee (1985: 4) wryly observe, it is in this sense that 'Donald Duck, Coca Cola and Tupperware have become ubiquitous items of consumption throughout the Third World'.

The role of cities is obviously central to the processes of both convergence and divergence. Large cities are spreading the norms of global consumption within their national territories, but are acting as agents for the concentration of capital and productive activities into a relatively few large urban places. This thesis is, of course, closely related to dependency theory, and seems to further stress that 'Third World cities play a crucial role in the underdevelopment of the Third World' (Armstrong and McGee, 1985: 11). Top-down forms of change, predicated on existing large cities and/or on newly planned urban growth poles and centres, are increasingly questioned as the invariant path to development, especially in a contemporary context of increasing capital articulation. It is argued that the imperatives of basically top-down forms of planning have failed to live up to their promise. This is because they have merely involved the dispersal of the dominant form of polarized development at the national and international scales and not its alleviation.

The Role of Cities Reassessed: Large and Small

Related to such thinking, a major new paradigm has emerged since the mid-1970s. This is associated with the concept of rural–urban development and involves more fundamental change than has hitherto been envisaged. It is frequently referred to as bottom-up planning but is also described as agropolitan development or urban-based rural development (see Friedmann and Douglas, 1978). A principal objective of the approach is, of course, to reduce dependency. Rather than the emphasis of development being placed on a nexus of urban industrialization, the accent is placed on the creation of rural employment. Rather than prizing imported foreign ways of life, local indigenous modes of production are valued and encouraged. Rather than pure economic factors forming the criteria for change, social considerations are seen as salient. Instead of the consumption of goods being all-important, the emphasis is placed firmly on the production of the things that are required by all: expressly the *basic needs* of food, clothing and shelter. Thus, the ethos of development is based firmly on territorial needs and not the dictates of functional efficiency (see Friedmann and Weaver, 1979).

This, it is argued, can only be achieved by the commercialization of productive wealth and the closing of regions to trade to some degree or another. This strategy – known as selective regional closure – is designed to extricate Third World countries from the the process of unequal exchange which is involved in the state of surplus accumulation and dependent development. The only way around this is to increase self-sufficiency and reliance. Although the approach stresses the importance of agriculture and rural areas to begin with, it is envisaged that later the economy will be diversified and non-agricultural activities introduced. But it is argued that at this stage urban locations are not mandatory. Equally it is recognized that cities can be based on agriculture and agro-industries, just as many were in earlier times. Thus, Friedmann and Weaver (1979: 200) aver that 'large cities will lose their present overwhelming advantage'. Clearly the approach is inspired by, if not entirely based upon, the communalization of production (Stöhr, 1981) and may be dovetailed with the need for the establishment of sustainable forms of development (Redclift, 1987).

These approaches are not to be interpreted as anti-urban, but ones which are increasingly serving to emphasize the development efficacy of small and medium-sized urban places. Frequently these are conceptualized at the 10,000 to 25,000 population level, acting as the centres of units of local government which are based on agricultural regions. Although advocating urban settlements of a somewhat lower level of population, this dovetails with Rondinelli's call for secondary or intermediate cities of more than 100,000 people but with a population considerably less than that of the capital city. It is envisaged that these secondary cities will act as key agents in establishing a more equitable distribution of population and economic activities, with these settlements being based on agribusiness rather than heavy industrialization *per se*.

The Structure and Contribution of the Present Volume

This chapter has outlined the comprehensive reappraisal that perspectives on cities and development in Third World nations have undergone during the last ten to fifteen years. In the majority of circumstances – both with regard to theoretical standpoints and applied practice in the field – the developmental efficacy of a large number of smaller urban places is stressed, rather than the smaller number of larger ones invariably adopted in the past.

Coupled with this, it is now recognized that there is pressing need for the close integration of urban and rural forms of development, with the accent being tipped some way toward the latter, in a direct effort to counter the effects of decades of uncritical urban bias in past planning and development. The terms of trade between rural and urban areas within countries are as much in need of change as those existing between rich and poor countries viewed at the global scale. It is only in this manner that there is any real chance that the patterns and processes of unequal exchange that have existed for hundreds of years in the past will be gradually modified and ameliorated. The provision of basic needs is increasingly being accorded the highest priority among developmental criteria. Stemming from these broad changes in philosophy and practice, fresh perspectives are currently being adopted concerning the role that is played by the informal sector, both in relation to housing and to jobs, within Third World towns and cities.

The essays making up this volume focus attention upon changes in perspective concerning the relations between cities and development in the Third World. They provide first-hand contemporary accounts by academic geographers who are actively working in developing countries. The book provides empirical accounts concerning cities, change and development set within their respective conceptual frameworks. In collecting together these essays the aim was most definitely not to dwell on theory *per se*.

As was stressed in the Preface, the rate and magnitude of the changes occurring in Third World societies are such that there is constant need for fresh empirical accounts. Following this introductory chapter overviewing changing perspectives on cities and development at the world scale, the chapters encompass two broad scales of consideration. In Chapters 2–6 the focus is on issues of urban housing, services and welfare, primarily at the level of individual urban areas. Geographically the chapters cover Kano, Nigeria; Harare, Zimbabwe; urban Nigeria; metropolitan Bridgetown, Barbados; and Suva, Fiji. The second set of chapters focus on case studies of urban structure and development at the inter-urban scale. Chapters 7–11 deal with Asia and Africa in general; Malaysia; India; West Africa; and Barbados, respectively. Finally, the ways in which these case studies relate to the themes enumerated in this introductory essay are briefly summarized in the concluding chapter, 12.

We are living at the end of a long era during which development has been directly associated, both normatively and positively, with Western patterns of urbanization and change. Any such simple conceptualization of the association existing between cities and the development process is of little or no relevance today. In the past decade new perspectives concerning the role of urban areas in socio-economic and political change have started to emerge. It is intended that the chapters contained in this volume will provide much-needed updated empirical material and debate, drawn from the experiences of a variety of Third World countries, which will be of interest to all those concerned with these rapid and fundamental changes in development thinking and practice.

REFERENCES

Amin, S. (1974) *Accumulation on a World Scale: A Critique of the Theory of Underdevelopment*, 2 vols. New York: Monthly Review Press.

Amin, S. (1976) *Unequal Development*. New York: Monthly Review Press.

Armstrong, W. and McGee, T.G. (1985) *Theatres of Accumulation: Studies in Asian and Latin American Urbanization*. London and New York: Methuen.

Beckford, G.L. (1972) *Persistent Poverty: Underdevelopment in Plantation Economies of the Third World*. New York: Oxford University Press.

Berry, B.J.L. (1972) 'Hierarchical diffusion: the basis of development filtering and spread in a system of growth centres', in: Hanson, N.M. (ed.) *Growth Centres in Regional Economic Development*. New York: Free Press.

Browning, H. and Roberts, B. (1980) 'Urbanization, sectoral transformation and the utilization of labor in Latin America'. *Comparative Urban Research*, 8, 86–103.

Dixon, C. (ed.) (1987) *Rural–Urban Interaction in the Third World*. London: Developing Areas Research Group, Institute of British Geographers.

Dos Santos, T. (1973) 'The crisis of development theory and the problem of dependence in Latin America', in: Bernstein, H. (ed.) *Underdevelopment and Development in the Third World Today*. Harmondsworth: Penguin.

Frank, A.G. (1969) *Capitalism and Underdevelopment in Latin America*. New York: Monthly Review Press.

Frank, A.G. (1980) *Crisis in the World Economy*. New York: Holmes & Meier.

Friedmann, J. and Douglas, M. (1978) 'Agropolitan development: toward a new strategy for regional planning in Asia', in: Lo, F.C. and Salih, K. (eds) *Growth Pole Strategy and Regional Development Policy: Asian Experience and Alternative Approaches*. Oxford: Pergamon Press.

Friedmann, J. and Weaver, C. (1979) *Territory and Function: The Evolution of Regional Planning*. London: Edward Arnold.

Gilbert, A.G. (1976) 'The argument for very large cities reconsidered'. *Urban Studies*, 13, 27–34.

Gilbert, A.G. (1977) 'The argument for very large cities reconsidered: a reply'. *Urban Studies*, 14, 225–7.

Gwynne, R.N. (1978) 'City size and retail prices in less-developed countries: an insight into primacy'. *Area*, 10, 136–40.

Hardoy, J.E. and Satterthwaite, D. (eds) (1986) *Small and Intermediate Urban Centres: Their Role in National and Regional Development in the Third World*. London: Hodder & Stoughton.

Harriss, B. (1989) 'Commercialisation, distribution and consumption: rural–urban grain and resource transfers in peasant society', in: Potter, R.B. and Unwin, P.T.H. (eds) *The Geography of Urban–Rural Interaction in Developing Countries: Essays for Alan B. Mountjoy*. London and New York: Routledge.

Hirschman, A.O. (1958) *The Strategy of Economic Development*. New Haven, Connecticut: Yale University Press.

Hoch, I. (1972) 'Income and city size'. *Urban Studies*, 9, 299–328.

Hoselitz, B.F. (1955) 'Generative and parasitic cities'. *Economic Development and Cultural Change*, 3, 278–94.

Hudson, J.C. (1969) 'Diffusion in a central place system'. *Geographical Analysis*, 1, 45–58.

Lipton, M. (1977) *Why Poor People Stay Poor: Urban Bias in World Development*. London: Temple Smith.

Lipton, M. (1982) 'Why poor people stay poor', in: Harriss, J. (ed.) *Rural Development: Theories of Peasant Economy and Agrarian Change*. London: Hutchinson.

Pederson, P.O. (1970) 'Innovation diffusion within and between national urban systems'. *Geographical Analysis*, 2, 203–54.

Potter, R.B. (1989a) 'Urbanization, planning and development in the Caribbean: an introduction', in: Potter, R.B. (ed.) *Urbanization, Planning and Development in the Caribbean*. London and New York: Mansell.

Potter, R.B. (1989b) 'Caribbean urban development and planning: conclusions', in: Potter, R.B. (ed.) *Urbanization, Planning and Development in the Caribbean*. London and New York: Mansell.

Potter, R.B. (1991) *Third World Urbanization: Contemporary Issues in Geography*. Oxford and New York: Oxford University Press.

Potter, R.B. and Unwin, T. (eds) (1989) *The Geography of Urban–Rural Interaction in Developing Countries: Essays for Alan B. Mountjoy*. London and New York: Routledge.

Pred, A. (1973) 'The growth and development of systems of cities in advanced economies', in: Pred, A.R. and Tornquist, G., *Systems of Cities and Information Flows: Two Essays*, Lund Series in Geography, Series B, 38, 9–82.

Pred, A. (1977) *City-Systems in Advanced Economies*. London: Hutchinson.

Redclift, M. (1987) *Sustainable Development: Exploring the Contradictions*. London and New York: Methuen.

Richardson, H.W. (1976) 'The argument for very large cities reconsidered: a comment'. *Urban Studies*, 13, 307–10.

Roberts, B. (1978) *Cities of Peasants: The Political Economy of Urbanization in the Third World*. London: Edward Arnold.

Rondinelli, D.A. (1982) 'Intermediate cities in developing countries'. *Third World Planning Review*, 4, 357–86.

Rondinelli, D.A. (1983a) *Secondary Cities in Developing Countries: Policies for Diffusing Urbanization*. New York: Sage.

Rondinelli, D.A. (1983b) 'Dynamics of growth of secondary cities in developing countries'. *Geographical Review*, 73, 42–57.

Rostow, W.W. (1960) *The Stages of Economic Growth: A Non-Communist Manifesto*. Cambridge: Cambridge University Press.

Stöhr, W.B. (1981) 'Development from below: the bottom up and periphery–inward development paradigm', in: Stöhr, W.B. and Taylor, D.R.F. (eds) *Development from Above or Below?*. Chichester: Wiley.

Wallerstein, I. (1974) *The Modern World-System*. New York: Academic Press.

Warren, B. (1973) 'Imperialism and capitalist industrialisation'. *New Left Review*, **81**, 3–44.

Warren, B. (1980) *Imperialism: Pioneer of Capitalism*. London: Verso.

[2]
Housing Problems and Squatting Solutions in Metropolitan Kano

H. A. C. Main

Introduction

Much has been written in the past twenty years on squatting in Third World cities, and on overlapping or associated housing subjects including spontaneous housing and slums. This chapter focuses on one aspect of squatting: the role of government authorities in the creation and maintenance of illegal residential neighbourhoods. Following Collier (1976), Peattie (1979) and others, it is argued that squatter settlements are features of cities throughout almost the entire Third World primarily because their presence serves class interests represented by those in power; and that ambiguous land and housing policies, and the ambivalent implementation of these policies, are useful in ensuring the continuing existence of such neighbourhoods. The first three sections of the chapter focus on why this is so, with particular reference to Africa. The remainder of the chapter seeks to illustrate how it has been achieved in metropolitan Kano.

Processes of Squatter Settlement Formation in the Third World

In the Third World, squatting usually refers to the illegal occupation of land, rather than of existing housing as is normally the case in the First World. Three major processes of squatter settlement formation in the Third World have been identified by McAuslan (1985: 49–58): mass invasion, pirate subdivision, and infiltration.

Mass invasions of land belonging to private landowners, who have not given their permission for squatter occupation, are usually well-organized and are often achieved literally overnight. Settlements created in this way exist in many Latin American and Asian cities: among them are the *barrios paracaidistas* or 'parachutists' neighbourhoods' of Mexico

City, the *barriadas* of Lima, and the 'built overnight' *gecekondu* of Ankara. Far more common in Africa are squatters who have bought or who rent land from landowners who have no quarrel with them; they are squatters because they have not obtained the papers, or met the building or amenity standards, deemed necessary by the authorities. Such unauthorized settlements are typically located around the urban periphery, where farmland has been subdivided without planning approval for residential plots. These 'private subdivisions' are also identified by distinctive terms peculiar to given societies in many parts of the Third World: the *mercado pirata* of Bogotá, some of the *barrios clandestinos* of Mexico City and the *juggi jhompri* of Delhi. Less spectacular is the 'slow, almost invisible spillage onto land' (McAuslan, 1985: 56), with or without permission, by which squatters infiltrate unoccupied land. Infiltration, common in many parts of the Third World, including Africa, does not seem to attract the vivid terminology of other squatter processes.

Squatter occupation processes have occurred during the past thirty years in cities practically throughout Africa (Obudho and Mhlanga, 1988), and even earlier in some countries, such as Zambia (Van Velsen, 1975: 298). It appears that almost all these processes have comprised either pirate subdivision or infiltration. Reasons for the lack of squatter invasions in Africa have been the subject of some debate (Peil, 1976). Cultural distinctions in the history of urbanism and community access to land, and geographical differences in land quality and population density, are clearly relevant in understanding variations in squatting circumstances. It is also pertinent to consider who benefits and who loses from given squatter strategies, and from the implementation of given government policies regarding squatters. Whereas land invasions represent the most direct threat to capitalist principles of private property, unauthorized infiltration and pirate subdivision are something of a compromise. They allow access to land for the urban poor without infringing the private-property concept; while the interests, legal or not, of landowners, developers, speculators and others can be maintained (McAuslan, 1985: 51). Given the difficulties of organizing them, and the nature of the opposition that would be created in the process, it seems likely that mass squatter invasions of private land would tend in most societies to be a last resort for poor urban residents contemplating feasible means of access to housing. Where land is available without competing claims, especially where the authorities are considered somewhat tolerant, pirate subdivision or infiltration would seemingly allow easier access to housing than would mass invasion of private land. Lower levels of proletarianization and urbanization, of land commoditization and accumulation, of state control over land and of organization among the urban poor have been characteristic of many African societies as compared with much of Latin America. To date these lower levels have tended to produce less pressure on peri-urban land, and to encourage squatter access to land in and around African cities without resort to mass invasions of private land.

Attitudes to Squatter Settlements

Government authorities are highly reluctant as a rule to recognize squatters' legal rights to the land they occupy and thereby end their squatter status, even where the land is not claimed as property by an aggrieved private landowner or earmarked for specific use by the authorities. There are exceptions in Africa, notably in Lusaka (Hansen, 1982) and Nairobi (Kayongo-Male, 1980), where squatter settlements have been legalized and upgraded by the provision of public amenities. But most of those that have not been demolished remain in an ambiguous situation, still standing yet illegal and under threat of demolition at any time. And even in those cities where squatter neighbourhoods have at times been upgraded and legalized by the authorities, at other times the same authorities have demolished and blocked the provision of amenities to squatter housing. Examination of policies towards squatters in cities around Africa shows contradictions between different levels of government, inconsistencies between policy and implementation, and reversals through time of both policy and implementation (Norwood, 1975: 119–27; Peattie, 1979: 1,020–1). It all adds up to a notable ambivalence in authorities' attitudes towards squatters. This ambivalence, like the squatter settlements it nurtures, must somehow be functional within peripheral capitalist societies under certain development conditions.

Changes in attitudes to squatter settlements can be detected among social scientists and urban planners as well as government officials during recent decades. The hostile view that circulated widely twenty or thirty years ago, with little contradiction, was that squatter settlements were 'perfect havens for the criminal element . . . terrible areas' containing residents who were 'sponging from a community to which they are contributing nothing' (*Zambia News*, 1970; quoted by Van Velsen, 1975: 295). That view has long been rejected by most social scientists and many planners, but is still propagated by the media in many countries and accepted implicitly if not explicitly by many individuals in government. Though it flies in the face of a mountain of evidence to the contrary, such a view persists because it is useful:

> To view the urban poor as helpless, indolent, steeped in rural mores helped maintain the hegemony of the middle classes: indeed it even shaped the self-image of the poor who came to believe themselves helpless and dependent. . . . Furthermore it justified a continuance of low-cost housing project schemes in

which the interests of the powerful construction industry were heavily invested; it also provided them with a rationale for the eradication of 'unsanitary' uncontrolled settlements. (Ward, 1982: 6)

By the 1960s, however, this strongly negative view of squatting in Third World cities was being superseded in many circles by a liberal explanation concerning difficulties of access to legal housing for many Third World urban residents. Rapid population growth in general had been compounded in the cities by high rates of net rural–urban migration; economic growth in contrast had been generally slow or even, at times, negative. Many of the urban poor had been caught in the middle, unable to afford the cost of legal housing, and had therefore had to provide their own low-cost shelter outside the legal sector. Squatter housing was thus a rational response to the inability of some Third World societies to provide sufficient cheap legal urban housing. Moreover, many squatters were sufficiently motivated to put considerable energy into improving their housing conditions, especially if their tenure was legalized. In this light squatters were no longer 'the problem', but a solution through their own efforts to the real problem of urban housing (Mangin, 1967; Turner, 1976).

Though sympathetic to the plight of Third World squatters, and a welcome illumination in the darkness of implacable hostility to squatters, the liberal analysis is unconvincing in some respects. The work of Mangin, Turner and most of those who followed their analytical lead was set in Latin America, and referred mainly to squatter communities created by invasion of private land. Their assumptions concerning squatters' motivation to improve their dwellings and communities appear optimistic in some other Third World regions where squatter settlements are the product of processes other than invasion (Lloyd, 1979: 32). A broader misgiving raises the question why, in situations where market forces are supposedly paramount, legal housing is too expensive for 40 or 50 per cent or more of city populations. Adequate consideration of this problem, surely the nub of the matter, must place housing needs in the context of societies undergoing incorporation into the global economy (Burgess, 1982).

The Function of Squatter Settlements in Peripheral Capitalist Societies

Capitalist development requires cheap labour in Third World cities, and labour costs are depressed by the presence of surplus labour ready to take the jobs of employed workers who are unwilling to accept whatever wages they are offered. Many members of the formal-sector workforce and most of those who 'get by' in the informal sector are unable to get access to adequate accommodation in the formal or legal housing market because costs there are beyond their means, especially when they are endeavouring to provide for their families as well as for themselves. If they wish to remain in town – and economic conditions are usually worse in the rural sources from which many have migrated – the informal or illegal housing market is the only alternative. Thus squatter settlements are functional for capitalist development as locations for the continuing reproduction of the urban labour supply. They provide cheap accommodation that reduces pressure for wage rises: through housing employees more cheaply than would otherwise be possible, and through housing people without formal employment many of whom would otherwise be unable to reside in the cities. Besides, a buoyancy is imparted to prices in the legal land and housing markets by excluding a sizeable proportion of the urban poor from them, thereby encouraging profitable speculation and accumulation by the budding bourgeoisie. These are the main reasons why squatter settlements are so widespread in the Third World. Such neighbourhoods also provide:

(a) additional profit opportunities for building and building-supply companies, the more so if they are demolished from time to time;
(b) a sump, being typically land of little speculation value, in which to drop poorer residents who have been evicted from higher-value urban land; and
(c) a potential electoral advantage for politicians, or a client advantage for other patrons, who are cast in a favourable light merely by seeing that squatters are not evicted. (Gilbert and Gugler, 1982: 113–14)

Far from being a symptom of the breakdown of the urban order in Third World societies, then, squatter settlements are

a stable component of the structure of peripheral urban economies. Not only has the phenomenon existed for decades without posing any visible challenge to the dominant classes, but these classes have been known to promote land invasions and organize clandestine settlements in many occasions. (Portes and Walton, 1981: 96–7)

It is no coincidence that squatter settlements exist in cities in all Third World regions, wherever processes of incorporation into the global economy are sufficiently developed.

Thus squatting is a solution not only for the urban poor who are squeezed out of, or otherwise denied access to, legal housing. It is also a solution for class interests which require the urban residence of cheap labour in employment and surplus labour out of employment, so long as subsequent urban poverty does not act as a brake on profit-making opportunities in the urban land and housing markets.

Capital's need for squatters means that government authorities cannot consistently implement policies to abolish squatter settlements through eviction and bulldozing, or even through 'enlightened' schemes such as public housing (which in most cases would cost far too much anyway) or cheaper self-help projects. In order to maintain them in their precarious situation, government action regarding squatters has therefore to be ambivalent. Changes in government action reflect the changing needs of capital for surplus urban labour, higher urban land prices, more high-value urban land, a lower inflation rate, or for popular support, depending on which needs are dominant at a given time (Collier, 1976: 37): 'much of the zigging and zagging of government policies towards such settlements is explicable in terms of the irreconcilable competition between the policies suggested by [conflicting] pressures' (Peattie, 1979: 1,021).

Planned Urban Development and Changes in Land Tenure in Kano: The Creation of Squatters

Metropolitan Kano is a northern Nigerian city of probably between a million and one and a half million inhabitants in the late 1980s, which has for most of the past five hundred years been the major urban centre in Hausaland. Housing is clearly a big problem for many of Kano's residents, who pay a sizeable proportion of their income to obtain accommodation. Many of Kano's squatters are long-established urban and peri-urban residents who have been evicted from land which they previously held securely under customary tenure; they have therefore been turned into squatters by government action. Squatting may provide a housing solution for some of them, but it also leaves them open to the threat of eviction, besides encouraging the ongoing expropriation of surplus value from them and from other urban workers. This section demonstrates how planned urban development and changes in land tenure have squeezed many of the urban poor out of legal land occupation in metropolitan Kano.

State powers of land expropriation have been exercised on occasion for hundreds of years in and around Kano (Last, 1983: 77 and 84). Prior to the establishment of colonial rule in 1903, urban expansion around Hausaland's major cities took place according to the principle of *gida ya kore gona* (Hausa; 'the house drives away the farm'), which permitted the emir to confiscate farmland for urban use; the displaced user was given access to equivalent land not required for urban purposes (Frishman, 1977). Peri-urban pressure on land around Kano City at least since the nineteenth century contributed, along with state controls over land, to the development of a complex land-tenure system. Land rights could be transferred by a variety of means including not only inheritance and gift but also sale, officially forbidden but the existence of which in practice is a significant element of transformation in a communal society; and by other means including pledge and loan, which might be the preliminaries to sale (Hill, 1972: 205–81; Mortimore, 1972: 64). Farmers displaced from their land were not necessarily satisfied with the replacement land allocated, but there was little they could do about it. During the colonial period, when most urban expansion for the first time took place outside the walled city (*birni*), this problem was acknowledged in the payment of a disturbance fee, popularly considered as, in effect, a payment for land. For some of those affected by extensive low-density colonial residential and military land takeovers to the east of the *birni* in the early decades of the twentieth century, resettlement village layouts were provided at Dakata, Giginyu and Tarauni and elsewhere around the urban periphery (see Figure 2.1). The replacement by low-density (ten to twenty people per hectare) elite residential suburbs for colonial officers and business-men, laid out on garden-city principles, of long-established, mainly dispersed, settlements occupied under customary tenure, and the relocation of the latter in peripheral high-density resettlement villages of up to several hundred people per hectare set the tone for subsequent government involvement in providing for residential urban development (Mortimore, 1966; Mohammed, 1980).

Incorporation into the global economy entered a new phase after 1945, with industrialization in Kano and increasing land commoditization, and Kano's urban and peri-urban land values began to rise steeply (Mortimore, 1972: 64). The 1962 Land Tenure Law further entrenched the practice of transferring peri-urban farming land to urban use through, in effect, 'taxing poorer farmers and subsidising richer urban residents' (Frishman, 1977: 308): desirable occupiers were allocated plots in the new 'settlement areas' under statutory rights of occupancy, and they paid compensation fees through the government to those who were evicted. Compensation was paid not for the land itself, which was considered a gift of God, but for improvements to the land including buildings and wells, unexhausted crops and economic trees. This amount bore little relation to the land's market value: by 1973–4, for example, compensation of 120 naira per acre was being paid for land in metropolitan Kano valued by the market at between 200 and 600 naira per acre (Frishman, 1977). This discrepancy encouraged businessmen and civil servants and the old aristocracy to seek plot allocations by whatever means possible – while at the same time many of them were speculating through the land market on farmland in areas where public-sector land development was least likely, notably to the west of *birnin* Kano (Main and Cline-Cole, 1987: 164).

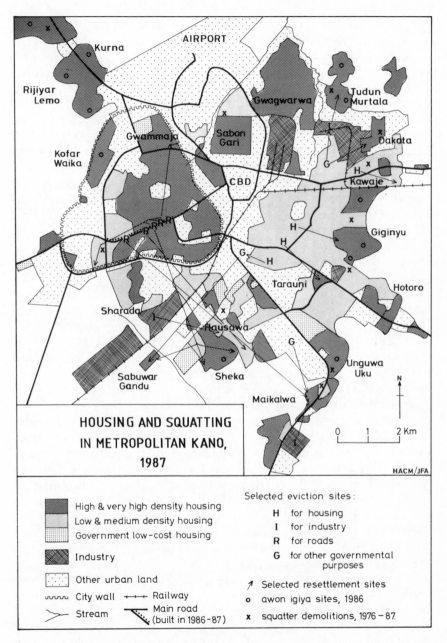

Figure 2.1. Housing and squatting in metropolitan Kano, 1987.

As Nigeria's oil-dependent economy boomed during the 1970s, soaring land prices and endless litigations associated with compulsory acquisition of communal and private land were increasingly perceived as constraints to development, especially in areas of rapid urban growth and agricultural commercialization. The 1978 Land Use Decree, a major advance in the extension of capitalist land relations in Nigeria, was designed to remove such constraints by making public-land acquisition and allocation, and thereby private-land acquisition, quicker and cheaper; it also provided for title in a legally identifiable document. The Decree was heralded as a protector of small landholders and a curb to land speculation, limiting urban landholdings to a maximum of half a hectare per person, but the spirit of this provision is easily subverted through legal or illegal loopholes. The overall effect of the Decree has inevitably been the opposite of these ostensible aims: 'the Decree itself has not performed so well since it was introduced. Indeed, it appears to be ignored even by those who are supposed to enforce and implement its provisions' (Nwaka, 1980: 74). Although its powers of expropriation and reallocation might in theory be used for equitable ends, they have in fact been used quite consistently to benefit those with sufficient wealth or political power, or with the right contacts (Francis, 1984; Famoriyo, 1987: 108).

Land market prices had soared so high by the early 1980s that peri-urban expansion would have been severely constrained had realistic compensation been payable for land compulsorily acquired. In fact, compensation had fallen far behind even the low levels of a few years before (Main and Cline-Cole, 1987: 175). Many of those evicted from land held under customary tenure preferred by this time to be compensated through the allocation of an alternative plot, if this option were available, rather than by a paltry sum of money. But this too gives scope for unfair discrimination by the authorities, given the Land Use Decree's ambiguity on questions of compulsory land acquisition and compensation, 'so that those who are evicted from land required for state purposes may be compensated richly or meanly depending on who they are, how many they are, and the size of the available budget' (Main and Cline-Cole, 1987: 163). The construction of a new road inside birnin Kano during 1986–7 entailed the eviction of people from five neighbourhoods (see Figure 2.1). A few fortunate Daneji householders were relocated on plots in Gwammaja, inside the walls of the birni and quite close to the CBD, each of which was a few months later worth a reported 30,000 naira on the market. A much larger number of Mandawari householders were allocated plots at Sabuwar Mandawari, out on the southern urban periphery, which by the end of 1987 were selling for 800–1,000 naira each. There was little difference between Daneji and Mandawari in compound or household size or composition prior to evacuation (Kurawa, forthcoming). Sabuwar Mandawari's unpopularity as a neighbourhood, largely but not only because of its peripheral location, has meant that few have actually occupied the plots allocated to them there. Many have remained in Mandawari, making the most of what small spaces are still available. Others have moved to squatter neighbourhoods such as Kofar Waika. Like Sabuwar Mandawari, this is on the urban periphery in the sense that it is adjacent to peri-urban farmland; but, more important culturally, it is sited within the *birni* walls and is relatively close to their neighbourhood with all its ties.

The Land Use Decree represented a marriage between legislative control of land and easier access to previously communal land for capitalist investment. It attempted to consolidate the land-related procedures operating in northern Nigeria and extend them to the remainder of the country, though in the latter it has not succeeded partly because pre-existing tenurial arrangements were so different in many areas (Mortimore, 1987: 17). In acknowledging the diversity of land-access systems extant in different Nigerian societies, the Decree recognized that most landholders had obtained their land rights according to customary tenurial practice, which in Hausaland would usually entail witness by the village head or other local individual but would not furnish any documentation. This was true of many landholders at the rural edge of cities like Kano. Under the provisions of the 1978 Land Use Decree, however, land transactions had to be formalized according to the following procedure (Kano Municipal Local Government, 1987):

(i) *mai unguwa* (village head or neighbourhood head) provides a letter confirming that he has witnessed the land transaction, in the case of inheritance, or where land has been purchased he endorses the papers used for the transaction;
(ii) *dagaci* (ward head) endorses this letter or papers;
(iii) the office of *hakimi* (district head) provides a covering letter;
(iv) all documentation is exchanged by the local government Land Registry for a customary right of occupancy (*takardar mallaka*).

The procedure for converting customary to statutory right of occupancy is as follows (Kano State Lands and Survey Division, 1987):

(i) five documents and 100 naira are presented to the Lands and Survey Division in order to open a file;
(ii) the application is processed, the land is surveyed and improvements are valued;
(iii) survey fees are paid, along with ground rents accruing since the date when the file was opened;
(iv) a Certificate of Occupancy granting statutory tenure is issued.

Application is then made to Kano State Urban Development Board for planning permission, to ensure that the user's intentions for the plot correspond to the Board's plans, and that required specifications are met.

Few have taken recourse to a route of land tenure 'formalization' involving so many hurdles, along with the attendant encouragements to bureaucrats that under many circumstances are necessary: 'the process can be tortuous, exasperating, long drawn out, and costly' (Igbozurike, 1987: 117), even for educated professionals with experience of the system, let alone bewildered peasants. Recent surveys in Kano have indicated that, almost a decade after the Land Use Decree was implemented, few squatters or potential squatters know of the pertinent provisions. None of those surveyed in one major high-density neighbourhood, Tudun Murtala, had made any attempt at legalizing their tenure, and only 50 per cent of landlords said they even knew of the necessary procedures (Omusi, 1987: 111); and a similar situation prevailed in Kofar Waika, a recently built high-density neighbourhood on the other side of the city (Abdu, 1986: 80).

The colonial principle of government responsibility for housing its senior officers has remained to the present. Some plots on residential layouts are reserved for those in the higher grade levels of government service, and many educational, medical, military and other institutional compounds have low- and/or medium-density residential quarters. Since the mid-1960s, government has extended its provision of public housing outside institutional compounds to 'low-cost' housing estates for middle-ranking civil servants. Through maladministration or informal arrangement, however, many of the people resident in public 'low-cost' housing are not those for whom they were designed. A sample in one such housing estate in Kano in 1986 found that 30 per cent of residents were not entitled to reside there, and that their income averaged 20 per cent higher than the legal residents' income (Bonah, 1986). This was one of the reasons cited by President Babangida in 1987 for a government review of its direct involvement in the construction of dwelling houses. He also said that

> the direct construction of dwelling houses by government in the past had resulted in little or no impact on the nation's economy and was therefore being reconsidered. The measure, he noted, was in line with . . . aspects of the Structural Adjustment Programme [which] included relying on market forces rather than administrative controls in reordering the economy. (*New Nigerian*, 1987: 1)

Government takeover of land through compulsory acquisition has been a more or less ongoing process. Between 1976 and 1979, the Urban Development Board reportedly displaced 6,672 people in claiming land for future development, and federal government displaced thousands more in 1980 to build low-cost housing units for civil servants. On each occasion stark insufficiencies of compensation or alternative land reallocation turned many of those displaced, through no fault of their own, into squatters (Frishman, 1988: 114–16).

Urban expansion outside the walled city of Kano during the twentieth century, especially in recent decades, has therefore had several recognizable effects on urban housing, among which (see Figure 2.1) are:

(a) the removal of existing urban and peri-urban neighbourhoods for commercial, industrial, transport, administrative and other governmental as well as residential purposes;

(b) the creation of extensive low-density elite residential areas, and of smaller pockets of somewhat similar housing in many government institutional compounds (which appear in Figure 2.1 among 'other urban land');

(c) the creation of public 'low-cost' housing, designed for middle-ranking civil servants and used in many instances by those under the patronage of wealthy businessmen and others;

(d) tremendous demand for accommodation in those high-density residential areas of legal status (inside *birnin* Kano, and in Sabon Gari, Tudun Wada, Dakata and other layouts) where rental costs for often cramped conditions are beyond the pockets of many of the urban poor; and

(e) the presentation of highly effective legal and logistic obstacles to land-tenure regularization for those (typically but not exclusively) peri-urban residents who have obtained their land access under customary tenure.

The consequent housing plight of the urban poor in metropolitan Kano today is clearly a product not just of rapid population growth and rural–urban migration, but arguably more of government policies. It is hardly surprising that squatters exist under such conditions – indeed, were government to acknowledge that its land and housing policies were designed to create squatters, it could be congratulated on its success in achieving that goal.

Squatter Settlements in Contemporary Metropolitan Kano: The Residence of Squatters

Legal land development in metropolitan Kano may be constituted by any of four means (Kano State Urban Development Board, 1987):

(i) developments marked on official maps up to 1976 that are registered with local government;

(ii) developments covered by customary tenure and registered with local government, which have been informed to the Urban Development Board prior to any building or alteration of existing buildings after 1976 – i.e. which have cleared the nine hurdles outlined in the previous section;

(iii) developments in formal layouts with either (a) a Certificate of Occupancy or (b) a letter of grant and a survey plan, and built according to an approved building plan;

(iv) developments in resettlement layouts that have allocation papers and have obtained Urban Development Board building permission, in which case no building plan is required.

Anything else is illegal. Four categories of illegal urban development are identified by Kano State Urban Development Board (1987):

(i) 'outright squatters', i.e. buildings on public land;

(ii) *awon igiya* ('measured with rope'), i.e. informal buildings constructed after the owners of peri-urban farmland partition their land into plots and sell it without the necessary regularization as outlined above;

(iii) buildings in formal layouts (a) without building permission – even with a statutory right of occupancy; (b) with building permission and an approved building plan, but where the plan has been altered; or (c) with building permission and an approved building plan, but encroaching on public land or reservations;

(iv) buildings on resettlement layouts, where building plans are not necessary, but of which the Urban Development Board has not been properly informed.

It is noteworthy that Kano has not yet experienced any mass squatter invasions of private land. Most of the squatters in the metropolis in 1987 fell into the *awon igiya* category, of which about a dozen major settlements are readily identifiable and appear in Figure 2.1 (Abdu, 1986: 53 and 109; Omusi, 1987: 121; Kurawa, forthcoming). By McAuslan's classification, *awon igiya* neighbourhoods are pirate subdivisions; they are poorly served by municipal amenities but make their own piecemeal arrangements to acquire roads, drainage, electricity and other infrastructure. A slightly different case is presented by the one example of 'outright squatters' on public land reported by Kano State Urban Development Board: farmers in Hausawa were compensated and resettled in the late 1970s, but – because the land was not subsequently built on by government – the farmers then partitioned the land and sold it for housing. This is also pirate subdivision, and from the new residents' viewpoint no different from other *awon igiya* neighbourhoods. A sizeable number of Kano squatters are resident in illegal developments on resettlement layouts, utilizing land between and adjacent to legal housing where others have previously been resettled. Infiltration is evident in many sites scattered around the metropolis: where buildings have encroached on public land in formal layouts, especially inside the *birni*, and where residential buildings have been constructed on land approved for other purposes.

The speculative purchaser of an *awon igiya* plot in effect gambles on future government action (demolition or legalization), or on potential buyers' perceptions of that action. Land in Kofar Waika was changing hands at about 2,000 naira per 50 × 50-foot (15 × 15 m) plot in 1986, while land in a government-approved layout on the other side of the main road cost about 10,000 naira for the same area (Abdu, 1986: 77). Speculators here may lose their investment on eviction or quintuple it when selling their plots, but in the meantime they are doing well enough from the rents paid by their tenants. At about ten naira per month for a room in Kofar Waika – typical in 1987 of recently settled *awon igiya* neighbourhoods in Kano – the cost of a plot plus construction of a compound may be recouped in about five years; or sooner if neighbourhood residents perceive that their tenure is becoming more secure and rents rise accordingly along with amenity provision. Monthly rents for a room are about ten to twenty-five naira in most parts of the *birni*, and higher in many other parts of metropolitan Kano. A two-bedroomed flat in Sabon Gari, where many southerners live, costs about 150 naira per month. These rents compare with the official minimum monthly wage of 125 naira, which is more than most of the urban poor get in 1987. Any incremental improvements to *awon igiya* neighbourhood amenities, despite the strong disincentives associated with illegal tenure, tend to be made more difficult and costly by the fact that these neighbourhoods are mainly on land which is undesirable for development in the legal land market: on awkward terrain (as at Rimin Kebbe), along airport flight paths (e.g. Rijiyar Lemo), or in polluted zones adjacent to industry (e.g. Tudun Murtala).

The tremendous difficulties of tenure legalization, and the widespread lack of knowledge of what is needed, encourage corruption. Impersonators claiming to represent the Urban Development Board who issue bogus papers for a fee; administrative officials who connive in the illegal sale of plots in return for sufficient inducement, or who dupe buyers into thinking that their plots are legal and then take 'land taxes' for their own pockets; these and many other forms of sponging off the residents of *awon igiya* and other squatter neighbourhoods have been reported in Kano in recent years.

Government Action Concerning Squatter Settlements in Metropolitan Kano: The Maintenance of Squatters

This section seeks to demonstrate the ambivalence of government actions concerning squatter settlements in metropolitan Kano, to relate aggressive and *laissez-faire* periods of government attitudes to squatting to the changing needs of dominant capitalist interests in the context of the Nigerian economy, and to identify variables other than the evident needs of capital that are pertinent at different times in explaining Kano squatters' relative security or insecurity of occupation.

Kano has a long history of forcible action by government authorities against squatters, including those who have held their land securely and legally until decisions concerning urban expansion have turned them overnight into 'squatters'. One incident of forcible eviction soon after colonial rule was established in 1903, which has had repercussions down to present-day Kano, was when the colonial authorities wanted land for a military camp in Bompai. Some of the inhabitants who were unwilling to move were forcibly removed while their compounds were set ablaze. In the belief that they had been unfairly treated, they named their new site Tudun Allah Ya Isa ('May God Judge' Upland). Subsequently their children were evicted when their new site was needed for an industrial estate in the 1950s. Their third site was renamed Tudun Murtala in 1976, after the assassination of Nigeria's head of state, General Murtala Muhammed, when residents' representatives felt that the bitterness of the past should be put behind them. During the next two years, a period of rapid growth in Tudun Murtala, extensive demolitions were conducted among newly constructed buildings. Force was also used in Kawaje in 1978 to evict farmers and cattle-rearers, some of whose families had lived there for generations; they had refused to move to a new layout nearby where they had been allocated plots that were far too small for their needs. Some of the Kawaje families had been evicted from peri-urban land around Kano three or four times since early in the colonial era, being pushed on each occasion further from the *birni* where they had strong ties (Ringim, 1988).

Cases like these of forcible eviction leading to physical conflict are not in themselves proof of bad or unjust municipal administration. Urban growth inevitably consumes rural land, and transfers residential into non-residential land uses. Indeed there are many other cases of compulsory resettlement, some of them shown in Figure 2.1, in which evicted residents have more or less complied with the authorities' demands. But residents like those in Bompai and Kawaje have not resisted eviction through a disregard for real municipal needs; their resistance has stemmed from what they consider is the authorities' failure to make fair provision for their needs in alternative sites. Their case is strengthened, however, when they see the land from which they have been evicted entering the land market through administrative allocation and subsequent sale of low-density residential plots, or not developed at all.

But there have been years in Kano when squatters have felt reasonably secure in their accommodation, during periods when little or no organized action has been taken against squatters by the authorities. The decade and a half after Nigeria's independence in 1960 was one such period, when municipal government by and large overlooked widespread infiltration by unauthorized occupiers. This included encroachment into building-free zones, lands a quarter of a mile wide designed to separate urban residential sectors from each other and from the central commercial district, which were used instead in the mid-1960s for storage and retail as well as residential purposes (Frishman, 1988: 112). Considerable administrative in-fighting went on during this period, mainly between the traditional authority of the emir, by which many housing plots were allocated, and the Urban Planning Department, which disapproved of the allocations; as a result, squatting thrived in many parts of the metropolis. But in 1975 the military government backed the warnings of the Planning Department, previously considered toothless by the squatters, and almost 1,000 houses were demolished, leaving approximately 5,000 people homeless (Hamma, 1975: 47–53).

Between 1975 and 1979, many squatter neighbourhoods were demolished in metropolitan Kano. Still, this by no means implied tight co-ordination of policy implementation between different arms of government. One authority was demolishing in Tudun Murtala, for example, while land on the other side of the stream was being allocated by another authority along lines that ignored the first authority's plan. In the confusion, illegal construction began again in Tudun Murtala (Omusi, 1987: 124 and 141).

It is evident that much less demolition of illegal buildings occurred during the Shagari civilian administration of 1979–83, and that it increased markedly again in 1984 with a return to military government. But the simple equation of hardline military administrations and liberal civilian administrations does not always hold. Direct actions against squatters in Kano were muted from about 1985, when the state military governor 'warned against the indiscriminate demolition of buildings without the approval of the state government by Kano Municipal Local Government officials' (New Nigerian, 1985: 9). The Urban Development Board even unveiled upgrading plans for Tudun Murtala and several other squatter neighbourhoods (Sunday Triumph, 1986: 1). The Babangida military administration has apparently been softer on squatters than was the Buhari military administration from which it took power in 1985. But again, in late 1987, the Kano State Task Force is 'to demolish all unauthorised buildings suspected to harbour criminals' (Sunday Concord, 1987: 7).

Municipal anti-squatter measures can be used as a pretext for all sorts of apparently unrelated policies or *ad hoc* purposes.

The need for cheap urban labour is likely to be felt most at times of rapid industrialization, and the lack of concerted action against Kano's squatters during the first half of the 1970s may be explained as a result of Nigeria's petroleum-fed boom after 1970 and rapid industrialization in Kano and elsewhere. High rates of rural–urban migration by the middle of the decade were providing sufficient labour for the factories, and surplus labour to keep wages down. It may be that the spate of squatter demolitions after 1975 was released by changing perceptions of the labour situation, and also related to shortages of accessible urban land felt by those with capital to invest in land for industry or other purposes; such shortages on a national scale led to the 1978 Land Use Decree. Later, as the Nigerian economy underwent deep recession during the early 1980s, and heavy retrenchment in most employment sectors along with inflation bit further into the pockets of the urban poor, the need for more surplus labour again receded whereas land continued to attract investment. Indeed, by 1984 urban migrants were being exhorted by government to go 'back to the land'. Few of them did so, but demolition in some squatter settlements in 1984–5 may have been part of a strategy to encourage them to do so, or at least was not in conflict with that aim.

But Kano's social and political reality is too complex for the identification of associations between dominant bourgeois interests on the one hand, and periods of squatter demolition and squatter *laissez-faire* on the other, to be altogether convincing; conflicting interests among fractions of the Kano bourgeoisie have been so interwoven that a wide range of considerations may influence any given government action. The lull in squatter demolitions during 1979–83 is related not only to the civilian nature of President Shagari's national government, for example, but also to the fact that Kano State was administered during those years by a populist government for which squatters in general were an important political constituency. Kano State was in ideological and political conflict with national government, and when it did exceptionally order the bulldozing of a squatter neighbourhood in 1981 it was in the elite residential suburb of Gadon Kaya where political allegiances were mainly hostile to it.

Conclusion

Kano's long history of urbanism, the high rural population densities around the city, and the developed system of customary land tenure which preceded statutory provisions and still today underlies them distinguish Kano from many Third World urban societies in ways that are potentially important for squatting. Comparative data on squatting are unreliable, but it may be that these factors have combined to produce fewer squatters as a proportion of Kano's population than of the populations of many other Third World cities of similar size and in societies with comparable levels of proletarianization and urbanization.

This chapter has focused mainly on the ways in which existing urban and peri-urban Kano residents with rights of land access have been turned into squatters through government action. Urban migrants tend to be even more vulnerable, having less access to urban residential alternatives and weaker social or political support systems. Having been born locally, many of Kano's residents have been able to retain the right to reside in their family homes without the threat of eviction. Yet even here, as the above account demonstrates, government policies associated with urban development have created certainly tens and probably hundreds of thousands of squatters.

The transition in land tenure during recent decades from customary towards increasingly widespread statutory access has been used as a vehicle by which to deny many their existing rights to legally recognized housing. The urban poor with only customary rights previously posed no immediate threat to the functioning of land and housing markets, and could as a rule reside in and around the city without harassment unless their land was required for urban expansion. But as land has become a major potential source of capitalist profit, and customary rights have necessarily been replaced by statutory rights, the latter must be denied to the urban masses. Besides proletarianizing the masses, this is in order to prevent them from demanding market prices for their land or housing, and thereby denying cheap and easy access for those who wish to use the land to make monetary profit.

REFERENCES

Abdu, S. A. (1986) 'Squatter settlement control in Metropolitan Kano'. Unpublished M. Sc. thesis, Department of Geography, Bayero University, Kano.

Bonah, L. (1986) 'Intra-urban residential mobility in Kano Metropolitan'. Unpublished B. Sc. thesis, Department of Geography, Bayero University, Kano.

Burgess, R. (1982) 'Self-help housing advocacy: a curious form of radicalism. A critique of the work of John F. C. Turner', in: Ward, P. M. (ed.) *Self-Help Housing: A Critique*. London: Mansell, 56–97.

Collier, D. (1976) *Squatters and Oligarchs*. Baltimore, Maryland: Johns Hopkins University Press.

Famoriyo, O. A. (1987) 'Acquisition of land and compensation in Nigeria', in: Mortimore, M. J., Olofin, E. A., Cline-Cole, R. A. and Abdulkadir, A. (eds) *Perspectives on Land Administration and Development in Northern Nigeria*. Kano: Bayero University, 101–13.

Francis, P. (1984) '"For the use and common benefit of all Nigerians": consequences of the 1978 land nationalisation'. *Africa*, 54(3), 5–28.

Frishman, A. (1977) 'The spatial growth and residential location pattern of Kano, Nigeria'. Unpublished Ph.D. thesis, Northwestern University.

Frishman, A. (1988) 'The rise of squatting in Kano, Nigeria', in: Obudho, R.A. and Mhlanga, C.C. (eds) *Slum and Squatter Settlements in Sub-Saharan Africa*. New York: Praeger, 105–19.

Gilbert, A. and Gugler, J. (1982) *Cities, Poverty and Development: Urbanization in the Third World*. Oxford: Oxford University Press.

Hamma, S.Y. (1975) 'Government policy and development opportunities in metropolitan Kano'. Unpublished M.P.A. thesis, Institute of Administration, Ahmadu Bello University, Zaria.

Hansen, K.T. (1982) 'Lusaka's squatters: past and present'. *African Studies Review*, 25(2/3), 117–36.

Hill, P. (1972) *Rural Hausa: A Village and a Setting*. Cambridge: Cambridge University Press.

Igbozurike, U.M. (1987) 'The Nigerian Land Use Act as a mechanism for urban land acquisition', in: Mortimore, M.J., Olofin, E.A., Cline-Cole, R.A. and Abdulkadir, A. (eds) *Perspectives on Land Administration and Development in Northern Nigeria*. Kano: Bayero University, 114–19.

Kano Municipal Local Government (1987) Interview reported in Omusi (1987) 133–4.

Kano State Lands and Survey Division (1987) Interview reported in Omusi (1987) 133.

Kano State Urban Development Board (1987) Interview reported in Omusi (1987) 121–3.

Kayongo-Male, D. (1980) 'Community development in urban squatter areas in Kenya'. *African Urban Studies*, 8, 21–36.

Kurawa, S.A. (forthcoming) 'Land acquisition for public project and the issue of compensation and resettlement: a case study of Sani Mai Nagge Road, Kano Municipality'. Unpublished M.Sc. thesis, Department of Geography, Bayero University, Kano.

Last, M. (1983) 'From sultanate to caliphate: Kano *circa* 1450–1800', in: Barkindo, B.M. (ed.) *Studies in the History of Kano*. Ibadan: Heinemann (Nigeria), 67–92.

Lloyd, P. (1979) *Slums of Hope? Shanty Towns of the Third World*. Harmondsworth: Pelican.

McAuslan, P. (1985) *Urban Land and Shelter for the Poor*. London: IIED/Earthscan.

Main, H.A.C. and Cline-Cole, R.A. (1987) 'Land-related processes in peripheral capitalist societies: metropolitan Kano's western peri-urban fringe', in: Mortimore, M.J., Olofin, E.A., Cline-Cole, R.A. and Abdulkadir, A. (eds) *Perspectives on Land Administration and Development in Northern Nigeria*. Kano: Bayero University, 161–80.

Mangin, W. (1967) 'Latin American squatter settlements: a problem and a solution'. *Latin American Research Review*, 2(3), 65–98.

Mohammed, H.E. (1980) 'The morphology of urban Kano 1903–1960: a study of colonial urban planning policy'. Unpublished M.A. thesis, Department of Geography, Ahmadu Bello University, Zaria.

Mortimore, M.J. (1966) 'Land use in Kano City and township'. Occasional paper, Department of Geography, Ahmadu Bello University, Zaria.

Mortimore, M.J. (1972) 'Land and population pressure in the Kano close-settled zone, northern Nigeria', in: Prothero, R.M. (ed.) *People and Land in Africa South of the Sahara*. Oxford: Oxford University Press, 60–70.

Mortimore, M.J. (1987) 'The lands of northern Nigeria: some urgent issues', in: Mortimore, M.J., Olofin, E.A., Cline-Cole, R.A. and Abdulkadir, A. (eds) *Perspectives on Land Administration and Development in Northern Nigeria*. Kano: Bayero University, 13–23.

New Nigerian (1985) 'Governor Daku warns against indiscriminate demolition of buildings'. *New Nigerian*, 16 October, 9.

New Nigerian (1987) 'Housing: government may withdraw'. *New Nigerian*, 3 December, 1–3.

Norwood, H.C. (1975) 'Squatters compared'. *African Urban Notes*, **B2**, 119–32.

Nwaka, G.I. (1980) 'Land administration and urban development: a Nigerian case study'. *Civilisations*, **30**(1/2), 73–82.

Obudho, R.A. and Mhlanga, C.C. (eds) (1988) *Slum and Squatter Settlements in Sub-Saharan Africa*. New York: Praeger.

Omusi, M.C. (1987) 'Spontaneous settlement in Tudun Murtala, Metropolitan Kano: need for change in government attitude'. Unpublished M.Sc. thesis, Department of Geography, Bayero University, Kano.

Peattie, L. (1979) 'Housing policies in developing countries: two puzzles'. *World Development*, **7**, 1,017–22.

Peil, M. (1976) 'African squatter settlements: a comparative study'. *Urban Studies*, **13**, 155–66.

Portes, A. and Walton, J. (1981) *Labor, Class, and the International System*. New York: Academic Press.

Ringim, M.I. (1988) 'Urban expansion and its effects on rural settlements in the rural fringe: a case study of Kawaji residential development in Kano'. Unpublished B.Sc. thesis, Department of Geography, Bayero University, Kano.

Sunday Concord (1987) 'Kano State task force to pull down illegal structures'. *Sunday Concord*, 1 November, 7.

Sunday Triumph (1986) 'Upgrading plans for Tudun Murtala'. *Sunday Triumph*, 3 August, 1.

Turner, J.F.C. (1976) *Housing by People: Towards Autonomy in Building Environments*. London: Marian Boyars.

Van Velsen, J. (1975) 'Urban squatters: problem or solution', in: Parkin, D. (ed.) *Town and country in Central and Eastern Africa*. London: Oxford University Press for the International African Institute.

Ward, P.M. (ed.) (1982) *Self-Help Housing: A Critique*. London: Mansell.

Zambia News (1970) *Zambia News*, 31 May.

[3]
Post-Colonial Urban Residential Change in Zimbabwe: A Case Study

Sioux D. Cumming

Introduction

The process of urban change in Third World cities has received a great deal of attention since McGee's 'growing disillusionment with the application of the theories that have emerged from the study of the urbanization process in the West' (McGee, 1971: 9). It has become necessary for geographers and other social scientists in the Third World to study their own environments in order to provide the detailed information necessary for an understanding of the specific processes affecting Third World cities.

Zimbabwe is an example of a previously colonial country (Rhodesia) which has recently become independent and is undergoing rapid and dramatic urban changes. Its cities are a palimpsest of colonial tenure systems (Drakakis-Smith, 1987) which spatially separated urban land uses and, in particular, separated the residential areas occupied by the major racial groups. For the purposes of this study, the population is divided into two major groups: blacks and whites. The term 'blacks' is used to describe the group formerly known as the 'African' population while the term 'whites' is used to describe all non-African population groups. Legislation in the country prior to independence used the terms Africans, Europeans, Coloureds and Asians but these are no longer acceptable. However, when early legislation is referred to these terms will be used.

Figure 3.1 illustrates the separation of the high-density suburbs which housed the blacks, and the low-density suburbs which housed the whites in the capital of Harare. Although the physical differences between these areas still remain after independence, the racial division no longer has legal backing and thus the population structure of the residential areas is changing. This is particularly true of the low-density suburbs, formerly European areas, which are the focus of this study.

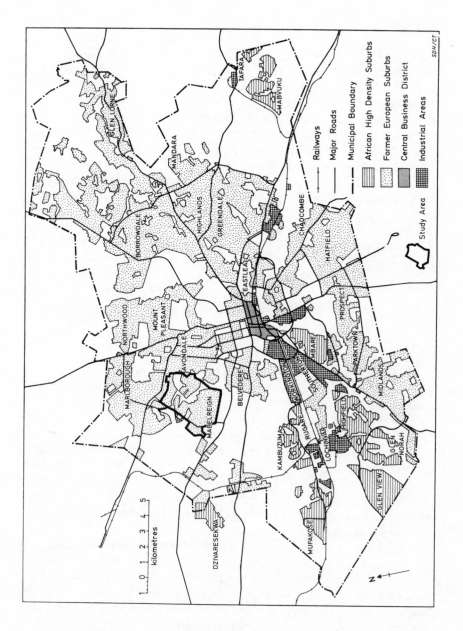

Figure 3.1. The residential areas of Harare, Zimbabwe.

Pre-Independence Background

The spatial separation of the two major population groups was the result of a number of legislative measures which have been comprehensively reviewed by a number of authors (Floyd, 1962; Kay, 1970; Christopher, 1971; Bannerman, 1982; Zinyama and Whitlow, 1986). As long ago as 1906, the Native Locations Ordinance initiated the concept of spatially separate housing for those blacks employed within the urban areas, and the enactment of the Land Apportionment Act in 1930 prevented blacks from owning land within the urban areas which were classified as 'European' land. The Native (Urban Areas) Accommodation and Registration Act of 1946 restricted blacks to the areas designated for them and restricted access to housing to those formally employed in the towns. At this stage, the local authorities were also committed to the provision of housing for the blacks and thus, through employment and restricted access to housing, the migration of blacks to the towns could be effectively controlled. The local authorities further manipulated the migration levels of blacks by providing predominantly 'single' men's hostels and thus preventing the migration of families from the rural areas.

During the years of the Federation of Rhodesia and Nyasaland (1953–63), a more liberal political climate prevailed and conditions for the urban blacks improved slightly. Provision of family housing increased and an amendment to the Land Apportionment Act in 1963 allowed blacks access to freehold tenure of urban land.

However, after the Unilateral Declaration of Independence (UDI) in 1965, the early restrictions on black occupation within urban areas were further tightened in the form of the Land Tenure Act of 1969. The act divided the country into European, African and National Land, with all the urban centres falling within the European areas (Harvey, 1987). The African townships within the urban areas had to be specially designated as African enclaves within the European areas and Africans were not permitted to occupy any other land within the towns unless living in residential occupation at their place of employment (i.e. as domestic workers). Thus, occupation by blacks beyond the boundaries of the African townships was strictly controlled.

Immediately prior to independence, while the two races were still strictly segregated, two different processes were occurring within their respective housing areas within Harare. The high-density areas (and the squatter camps) were the reception areas for increasing numbers of migrants and refugees from the rural areas as the liberation war intensified. Because the amount of housing was limited, extreme overcrowding inevitably resulted as relatives and friends provided shelter for the migrants or charged rents to increasing numbers of lodgers. In contrast, more and more houses became vacant in the low-density suburbs as increasing numbers of whites left the country, and houses often remained empty as the size of the white population declined. Demand for housing by whites in the low-density areas was very low, while in the high-density areas there was a 'ponding-up' of demand which far outstripped the accessible supply (Harvey, 1987; Wills, Haswell and Davies, 1987).

In February 1979, the Land Tenure Act was repealed and, as a result, access to housing and freehold tenure was made available to all, within the usual economic constraints of the housing market. Thus while the morphology of the towns still mirrors the legislative restrictions of the colonial past, many social changes are occurring within that overall physical framework.

Within Harare, a filtering process began from the high- to low-density suburbs in what had become a single housing market. Some of the pressure in the high-density suburbs was relieved by the movement of the higher-income blacks to the low-density suburbs within the restraints of their financial ability and the availability of housing stock. This process occurred at differing rates in different parts of the city, and Harvey (1987) identifies several areas which received relatively large numbers of blacks immediately after the legislative changes. Parktown, Prospect and Midlands in the south, the Avenues near the city centre and Mabelreign in the west received many of the early migrants (Figure 3.1). They are located close to the high-density suburbs and the major industrial and commercial areas which form the centres of employment.

Mabelreign: A Case Study

The City of Harare municipal electricity accounts provided a comprehensive source from which to monitor intra-urban residential change (Harvey, 1987). The names and addresses of the consumers are recorded for each month and it is a simple task to divide the consumers into blacks and whites on the basis of their names. It was not possible, however, to identify the difference between renters and owners from this source; it merely shows occupation as it is usually the occupier who pays the electricity bill. Further information concerning the change in property values and plot sizes was obtained from the Deeds Registry, where a sample of transfers was examined for each year between 1980 and 1986.

The focus of this chapter is on the pattern of changing residential mix in Mabelreign, one of these early 'target' areas. The building of this suburb was started in 1951 by the National Housing Board in order to provide housing for the post-Second World War white immigrants who were attracted to the country by its need for skilled artisans (Wilson, 1980). The suburb is based on the 'garden city' concept with many avenues and greenways and small properties, while the other northern suburbs tend to have large properties, subdivided less systematically from the original farms. While there are a large number of small properties in Mabelreign, the area still retains a feeling of openness and greenery because of the greenways and large undeveloped tracts of land.

In this study, Mabelreign is divided into six sub-areas which vary in property size and value and are identified as Ashdown Park, Mabelreign, Greencroft, Sentosa, Meyrick Park and Haig Park (Figure 3.2A). The criteria used for this division of the study area are the average size of the stands in each sub-area (Table 3.1) and their physical separation from each other. Figure 3.2A shows that the density of stands also varies considerably between the sub-areas from the very high-density small stands in Ashdown Park to the low-density large plots in Meyrick Park. Sentosa is the only sub-area which combines both high and low densities of stands.

Table 3.1. Average size of stands in each sub-area of Mabelreign*

Sub-area	Size (sqm)
Ashdown Park	877
Greencroft	1,032
Haig Park	1,061
Sentosa	1,639
Mabelreign	1,774
Meyrick Park	6,031

* Based on the average size of a sample of properties sold in June, July and August of each year 1980–6.

The case study presented here examines the changing residential mix in Mabelreign between 1980 and 1986, thus covering the first seven years of independence in Zimbabwe. Figure 3.2A shows all the stands as white-occupied, which means, in terms of the twofold division in this study, that they were either occupied by whites, or the property was vacant. Legally this was the position under the Land Tenure Act of 1969, when blacks were not permitted to own, lease or occupy land in European areas, although, as the repeal of this act became inevitable, a small number of properties were illegally occupied by blacks immediately prior to 1979.

Figure 3.2.   Residential occupation in Mabelreign, Harare: A. Prior to 1979; B. 1980.

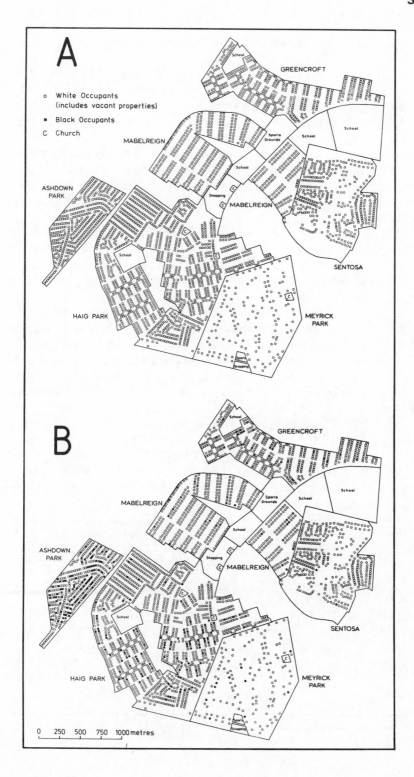

Changes in Residential Occupation

The change of residential occupation in Mabelreign is examined by recording the occupational mix in July of each of the seven years included in the study. This illustrates the cumulative change through time. Figure 3.2B shows the pattern of occupation in July 1980 the first year of independence, and eighteen months after the repeal of the Land Tenure Act. By this stage, very little change had occurred in this historically white preserve, with black in-movement being very low in all areas except Ashdown Park where concentrations were already apparent. A weak concentration was also evident in the centre of Haig Park. The change in Sentosa was negligible.

Figure 3.3A shows the position in July 1981 and it is quite clear that a significant occupational change took place between 1980 and 1981. The most notable increases occurred in Ashdown Park, where black occupation increased from 26 per cent in 1980 to 55 per cent in 1981, and in Haig Park, where black occupation increased from 9 per cent in 1980 to 27 per cent in 1981, a threefold increase. The concentration in the centre of Haig Park was intensified while in all other areas there was a mixing of blacks and whites. Although Ashdown Park had almost equal proportions of blacks and whites, micro-scale clustering was evident along streets. The other areas also experienced increases in the proportion of black-occupied properties, but none as great as for the two areas mentioned above.

By July 1982, the initial trends were being consolidated as Ashdown Park achieved 71 per cent black occupancy and Haig Park experienced a less rapid increase to 39 per cent (Figure 3.3B). The remaining white (or vacant) properties in Ashdown Park were scattered randomly throughout the area, while in Haig Park the central cluster of black-occupied properties was more apparent as several avenues became entirely black-occupied. To the north of the central cluster in Haig Park, a conspicuous area of predominantly white occupation remained. A weak grouping of black-occupied properties was also becoming apparent in the western part of Haig Park. Mabelreign and Greencroft experienced a doubling of their 1981 levels to 31 per cent black occupancy and Sentosa and Meyrick Park also experienced significant increases over their 1981 levels, but they were still predominantly white-occupied, while Ashdown Park was still the main receiving area for black migrants.

By July 1983, 81 per cent of the properties in Ashdown Park were occupied by black families (Figure 3.4A), which is a dramatic change

---

Figure 3.3.   Residential occupation in Mabelreign, Harare: A. 1981; B. 1982.

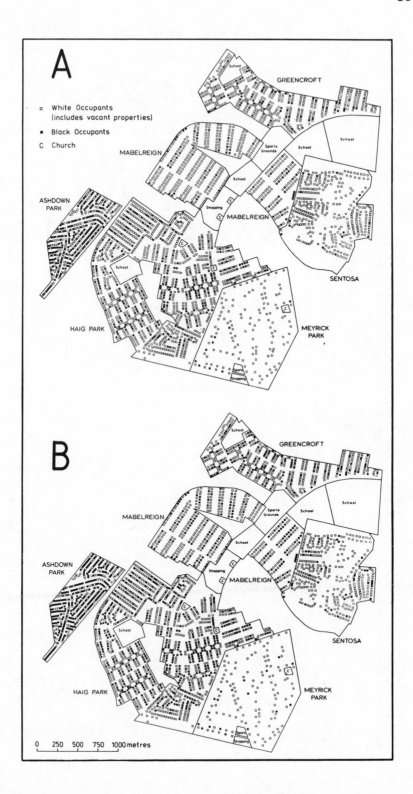

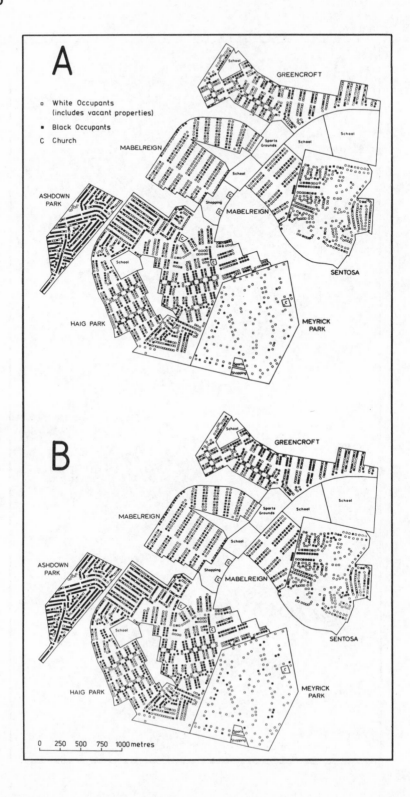

from the 26 per cent of only three years before and the negligible amount prior to 1979. This change was very much more rapid than in any other area. In Haig Park the central and western concentrations intensified and the north-west also emerged as an area of concentration. The white predominance to the north of the central cluster still remained. The change in Sentosa between 1982 and 1983, from 12 to 23 per cent, was also significant and was due to the occupation of the smaller stands in the west and east of the area while the larger stands in the centre remained under white occupation.

Figure 3.4B indicates that, by 1984, Ashdown Park seemed to have stabilized around a residential occupation mix of 80 per cent black and 20 per cent white/vacant while all other areas experienced further consolidation of existing patterns. Greencroft, which had previously exhibited a random mix when blacks were in the minority, now achieved a 56 per cent black occupation with distinctive groupings along streets. The same sort of pattern emerged in Mabelreign where black occupation increased from 38 to 51 per cent between 1983 and 1984. The eastern and western concentrations in Sentosa were still noticeable.

Occupational levels in 1985 and 1986 (Figure 3.5) show a significant slowing down in the rate of black occupation in all areas. Clustering in Haig Park could no longer be clearly identified in any specific region. All the other sub-areas exhibit increases but these were not confined to particular locations. In Sentosa and Meyrick Park, black occupation remained low (42 and 23 per cent respectively in 1986) with large areas still predominantly white. By July 1986, the whole of Mabelreign had an overall black occupation of 63 per cent, but in the individual areas this ranged from a maximum of 83 per cent in Ashdown Park to a minimum of 23 per cent in Meyrick Park.

These changes in residential occupation are summarized in Figure 3.6, where the very rapid initial change in Ashdown Park and its subsequent levelling off are clearly shown. The largest changes occurred before 1982 in most areas, although Greencroft and Mabelreign show a later increase between 1983 and 1984. All the graphs begin to level off after 1985, which suggests that the very dynamic situation of the first six years of independence was beginning to stabilize. This observation is supported by the change in the volume of monthly property sales in Mabelreign as a whole between 1980 and 1986. Three months were sampled in each year (except 1982 where the ledgers have been mislaid by the Deeds Office) and it was found that the average monthly sales in the whole area, irrespective

Figure 3.4.   Residential occupation in Mabelreign, Harare: A. 1983; B. 1984.

of race, increased from 40 in 1980 to 54 in 1983 and then dropped quite rapidly to 26 in 1985. If the figures for 1987 are also considered, the number of sales drops still further to 12 (Table 3.2).

Table 3.2. Average number of properties sold per month*

Year	Average monthly property sales
1980	40
1981	49
1982	data missing
1983	54
1984	35
1985	26
1986	28
1987	12

* Based on the months of June, July and August from each year, 1980–7.

Discussion

The trends in the occupation of residential properties by blacks in Mabelreign between 1980 and 1986 have been described and it is necessary to examine some of the possible explanations for these patterns.

First, it is important to explain why the study area experienced some of the most rapid initial changes in population composition. During the years of UDI there had been a gradual loss of whites from the city and this intensified in the years immediately prior to independence. Even when blacks began to move into the 'white' parts of the city there was a considerable surplus of white out-movement over black in-movement (Harvey, 1987). White movement from Mabelreign to other parts of the city was also occurring as a response to a perceived change in the suburb and was possible because property values were depressed in even the traditionally higher-income suburbs. Intra-urban moves were frequent and affordable because of the excess of housing supply in the low-density suburbs. Mabelreign was thus in a position to absorb, fairly quickly, some of the backlog of housing demand which had been building up in the high-density areas.

Figure 3.5.   Residential occupation in Mabelreign, Harare: A. 1985; B. 1986.

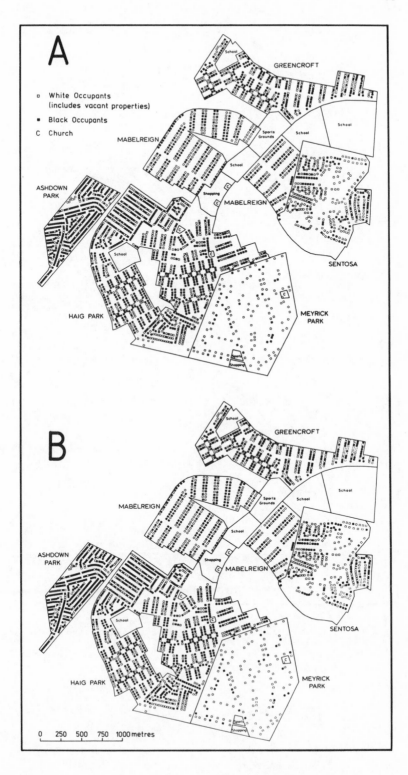

A

□ White Occupants
  (includes vacant properties)
■ Black Occupants
C Church

GREENCROFT

School

MABELREIGN

Sports
Grounds

School

School

Shopping

MABELREIGN

ASHDOWN
PARK

School

SENTOSA

HAIG PARK

MEYRICK
PARK

Sports
Shopping

B

GREENCROFT

School

MABELREIGN

Sports
Grounds

School

School

Shopping

MABELREIGN

ASHDOWN
PARK

School

SENTOSA

HAIG PARK

MEYRICK
PARK

Sports
Shopping

0   250   500   750   1000 metres

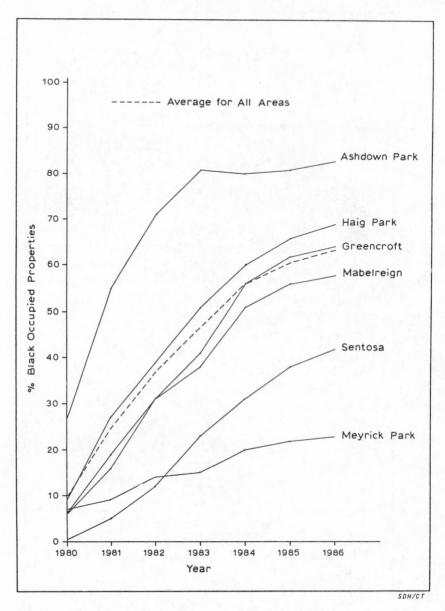

SDH/CT

Figure 3.6.　Percentage of black occupation by sub-area in Mabelreign, Harare, 1980–6.

Figures 3.2B and 3.3 show that there was a delayed reaction to the removal of restrictions on residential occupation caused, in part, by the time required for knowledge to diffuse through to the potential movers, most of whom lived in the high-density suburbs. Further time was required for the potential movers to make the decision to move. A destination had then to be chosen, which may have taken considerable time as many of the potential movers were not familiar with large parts of the former European suburbs. Although the choice of location was large, it was constrained by financial limitations, especially in the first few years, when the number of blacks with high incomes was still low.

It was then necessary for the movers to become familiar with the mechanisms of the housing market in the form of estate agents and the mortgage system because neither of these had operated in the high-density areas where most of the housing was owned by the city or by private companies. It is not possible at this stage, however, to assess the impact of such 'gatekeepers' in these early stages. There was probably an element of caution in that the potential mover might have perceived a hostile reception from the existing white residents when their 'white stronghold' was breached. As a result, it is suggested that many potential movers held back until the nature of the reception to the early movers was established.

It has been suggested elsewhere (Harvey, 1987; Wills, Haswell and Davies, 1987) that the initial black occupation of the former white suburbs would be influenced by stand size and property value. Within Harare there is a very strong relationship between the size of the stand and the value of the property (stand and improvements), as the largest and most expensive houses were built on large stands (more than 4,047 sq m) while small stands tend to be associated with middle- and low-income housing; hence the euphemisms 'high' and 'low' density to describe the different housing areas. Mabelreign consists mainly of relatively small, inexpensive properties and therefore became one of the first reception areas after the removal of restrictions on black residential occupation.

Within Mabelreign itself, this relationship can be further examined to explain partially the variations in black occupation between the sub-areas (see Figure 3.7). It is immediately apparent from all the graphs that a negative relationship does exist between proportion of black occupation and value of property. In 1980 the relationship was weak, largely because the occupation levels were low and there was little price differential between the sub-areas. As the percentage black occupation increased in subsequent years, so the visual relationship becomes stronger. Greencroft is the anomaly on virtually every graph, because although its average property values were relatively low its occupation levels were not as high as other sub-areas of a similar value. No obvious explanation for this is available, but by 1986 this anomaly seems to have disappeared. Sentosa also deserves comment because in 1980 its black occupation level was

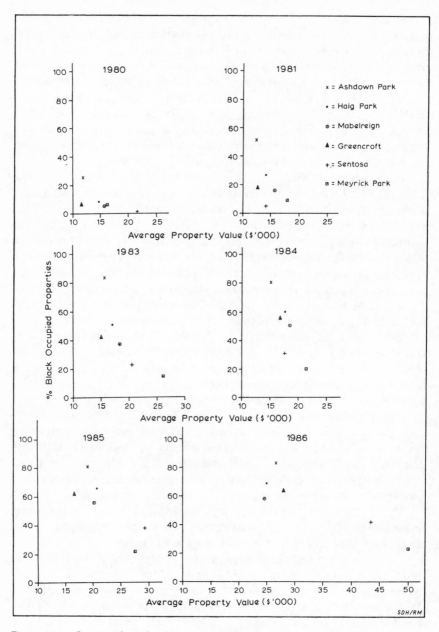

Figure 3.7. Scatter plot of percentage black occupation against market value of properties by sub-areas for Mabelreign.

the lowest, while its average property values were the highest, but in 1981 its occupation level was still the lowest, but its property values had become low. This can be explained by the variation of property values within the suburb related to the different property sizes (Figure 3.2A) which therefore cause the average value of property sold to fluctuate markedly (Figure 3.8).

At the time of the repeal of the Land Tenure Act, property values in the low-density suburbs were very low by international and even by African standards. This was due to the country's isolation during the years of UDI and to the gradual white exodus, which caused a surplus of housing for the dwindling number of white buyers, thus depressing prices. In Mabelreign, in 1980 the prices were uniformly low and from 1980 to 1984 the increase in property values was steady but unremarkable for all areas (Figures 3.7 and 3.8), indicating a balance between supply and demand. However, in 1985 there was a more dramatic rise in property values in Sentosa and Meyrick Park, and by 1986 this increase was also apparent in the other four areas. By 1987 property values had increased dramatically to three or even four times their 1980 levels, particularly in Ashdown Park and Greencroft (Figure 3.8).

The reasons for these changes are complex and relate to developments in the rest of the city at the time. The post-independence exodus of whites gradually began to slow down as peaceful conditions prevailed, while the demand for housing from the rapidly expanding middle-income black sector continued. In Mabelreign, the effects of these two processes began to be felt from 1985 onwards when the remaining whites, often elderly, found they could not afford to move to other areas where similar or even larger price increases were occurring. The volume of sales therefore declined and the asking price for properties began to rise because of the large number of willing purchasers. Figure 3.6 indicates a levelling off of the rate of black occupation in all the sub-areas after 1985 and this was largely caused by the conditions described above, where demand exceeded supply throughout the city and the normal processes of intra-urban mobility became constrained by spiralling prices within a limited housing supply.

Concluding Remarks

It is clear then that during the first few years of independence the low-priced, small properties such as those in Ashdown Park and Haig Park were the most attractive for occupation in large numbers. The larger, more expensive properties such as those in Sentosa and Meyrick Park were not as attractive, nor were they as freely available, and so these areas have experienced low levels of black occupation.

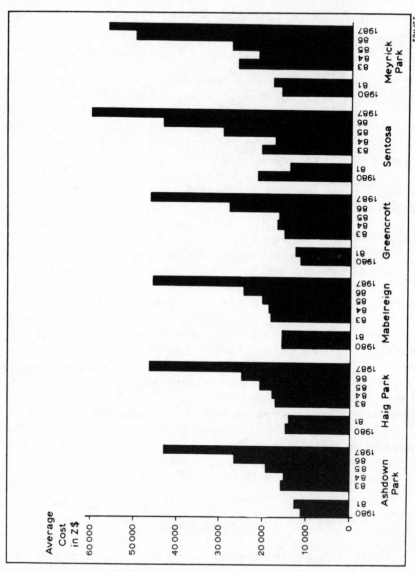

Figure 3.8. Average market value of properties by sub-area in Mabelreign, Harare, 1980–7 (1982 data missing).

The focus of attention on the problems of low-income housing in Harare (Butcher, 1986; Ministry of Public Construction and National Housing, 1986; Mutizwa-Mangiza, 1986; Teedon and Drakakis-Smith, 1986) has tended to mask a very real and growing problem of housing shortage among the middle- and high-income brackets. The sudden escalation of property values in areas such as Mabelreign which have traditionally been 'affordable' to the middle-income groups and the declining rate of increase in black occupation in this area indicate that the problem is becoming serious and requires closer attention. Some solutions have already been offered in the form of new middle-income house-building schemes such as those in Bluff Hill and Emerald Hill (Figure 3.1) but, while they have relieved the pressure on areas like Mabelreign, they are limited in extent.

While this study has provided information concerning the trends of occupational change within Mabelreign, it has also suggested a number of questions which must be addressed in order to understand fully the process of adjustment to new social and political goals. For example, what proportion of Mabelreign is under black ownership as opposed to rented accommodation? Have other middle-income areas experienced similar trends? How do the high-income areas differ? These and other questions will form the basis of further analyses.

REFERENCES

Bannerman, J. H. (1982) 'The Land Apportionment Act: a paper tiger?'. *Zimbabwe Agricultural Journal*, **79**, 101–6.

Butcher, C. (1986) *Low Income Housing in Zimbabwe: A Case Study of the Epworth Squatter Upgrading Programme*, Regional and Urban Planning Occasional Paper No. 6. Harare: University of Zimbabwe.

Christopher, A. J. (1971) 'Land tenure in Rhodesia'. *South African Geographical Journal*, **53**, 39–52.

Drakakis-Smith, D. W. (1987) 'Housing', in: Pacione, M. (ed.) *Progress in Third World Studies*. Beckenham: Croom Helm.

Floyd, B. N. (1962) 'Land apportionment in Southern Rhodesia'. *Geographical Review*, **52**, 566–82.

Harvey, S. D. (1987) 'Black residential mobility in a post-independence Zimbabwean city', in: Williams, G. J. and Wood, A. P. (eds) *Geographical Perspectives on Development in Southern Africa*. Papers from the Regional Conference of the Commonwealth Geographical Bureau, Lusaka, 1982.

Kay, G. (1970) *Rhodesia: A Human Geography*. London: University of London Press.

McGee, T. G. (1971) *The Urbanization Process in the Third World: Explorations in Search of a Theory*. London: Bell & Hyman.

Ministry of Public Construction and National Housing (1986) 'Public and private partnership in housing'. *Zimbabwe Science News*, **20**(3/4), 31–9.

Mutizwa-Mangiza, N.D. (1986) 'Post-independent urban low-income shelter policies in Zimbabwe: a preliminary appraisal of affordability', in: Romaya, S.D. and Franklin, G.H. (eds) *Shelter, Services and the Urban Poor* Cardiff: University of Wales Institute of Science and Technology, 81–98.

Teedon, P. and Drakakis-Smith, D.W. (1986) 'Urbanization and socialism in Zimbabwe: the case of low cost housing'. *Geoforum*, **17**(2), 309–24.

Wills, T.M., Haswell, R.F. and Davies, D.H. (1987) Pietermaritzburg 2000: The Probable Consequences of the Repeal of the Group Areas Act for Pietermaritzburg, Report No. 16. Pietermaritzburg: City of Pietermaritzburg, RSA.

Wilson, D.C.K. (1980) 'The development of a residential neighbourhood: American principles applied in Mabelreign, Salisbury'. *Zimbabwe Science News*, **14**(9), 214–18.

Zinyama, L.M. and Whitlow, J.R. (1986) 'Changing patterns of population distribution in Zimbabwe'. *Geojournal*, **13**(4), 365–84.

[4]

Urbanization, Housing and Social Services in Nigeria: The Challenge of Meeting Basic Needs

Ademola T. Salau

Introduction

The last two decades have witnessed an unprecedented rate of urbanization in the history of Nigeria. This overall period witnessed the outbreak and the end of the thirty-month civil war, and the subsequent reconstruction efforts, as well as the advent of the so-called 'oil boom' brought about by the increased exploitation of, and revenue from, petroleum.

Undoubtedly, judging by the conventional yardsticks employed to measure economic performance, the country experienced a high rate of economic growth during this period. However, it is now obvious that the benefits of this growth were not equitably distributed nor totally cost-free. The increasingly acute shortages of housing, overcrowding and inadequate social services offer testimony to this fact. The substantial revenue received from the export of petroleum enabled the government to devote more resources to the provision of some basic social services. The question addressed in this chapter is whether this has improved the situation fundamentally, referring specifically to the housing situation.

The chapter follows four broad avenues. The first section examines the nature of the recent urbanization process in Nigeria and the factors which may be held responsible. In the second part, the 'livability' of Nigerian cities is examined, especially in relation to the housing problem and the provision of adequate social services. A third approach presents the results of an empirical study based on a sample survey of 1,352 residents of government housing estates in six Nigerian cities. The purpose is to assess the impact of the planning programme which led to their development. In other words, the question is to what extent has the massive amount of money devoted to social services gone to fulfil the basic need for shelter? The fourth and final section is an attempt to suggest a framework for the effective provision of shelter as a *basic need* in Nigerian cities.

Urbanization in Nigeria

Nigeria is the most populous African country and its urban population amounts to more than the combined total urban population of the other West African countries put together. The urbanization process in Nigeria predates the arrival of the Europeans. This is a different situation from that of most parts of Africa, where urban development was initiated during the colonial period. Nevertheless, the contemporary urban system of Nigeria is an outcome of a multitude of forces of which colonialism is a key part. Before the coming of the British, a well-developed system of cities had existed in Nigeria. The system of cities, however, was not integrated but was composed of various isolated sets of cities which related to existing socio-political groups. Colonialism brought a superimposition of another system on these indigenous sub-systems. Thus, the contemporary national urban system of Nigeria represents an amalgam of these different components.

The proportion of the total population living in cities with 20,000 or more population was estimated to be 4.8 per cent in 1921 and 6.7 per cent in 1931 (Table 4.1). This had risen to 10.2 per cent by the 1952/3 census, and 19.2 per cent in 1963. However, if we adopt 5,000 as the minimum population size of an urban centre, then, according to the 1952 census, the urban population of Nigeria at that time was 9.3 million (about 30 per cent of the total population). If the same 5,000 threshold is used for 1963, the urban population would have reached 30.6 million (about 55 per cent of the total population).

Table 4.1.   Urban population in Nigeria 1921 – 63

Year	Total population (000s)	Total urban population (000s)	Urban population as a percentage of total population	No. of cities with populations of 20,000 and above	Number of cities with populations of 100,000 and above
1921	18,720	890	4.8	16	—
1931	20,056	1,343	6.7	24	2
1952/53	30,402	3,101	10.2	54	7
1963	55,670	10,702	19.2	183	24

Source: Ekanem (1972: 59).

It can be concluded that the 20,000 figure is the most appropriate one for defining settlements as urban in Nigeria. In 1921, there were twenty cities with populations of 20,000 and above. By 1931, the number of such cities had risen to twenty-four, and of these only Lagos and Ibadan had populations exceeding 100,000. By 1953, there were seven cities with populations of 100,000 and above, and eleven others had 50,000 and above.

In 1963, the number of cities with 100,000 and above had risen to twenty, and thirty-one others had 50,000 and above. According to many estimates, urban population has been growing very rapidly over the past two decades, in fact at an annual rate exceeding 5 per cent.

However, the rate of growth of cities has not been uniform. Major cities have recorded the most phenomenal growth and the number of cities with 500,000 inhabitants and above has risen from only two in 1963 (Table 4.2) to about fourteen in 1984. As there are no officially accepted census figures after those of 1963, a projection of the population of some cities is presented in Table 4.3. First, it must be kept in mind that the projections are based on the 1963 census figures which by all indications remain

Table 4.2. The rank-size of cities in Nigeria and their rate of growth

City	1952 population	Rank	1963 population	Rank	Percentage growth p.a. 1952 – 63
Ibadan	459,196	1	627,379	2	2.88
Lagos	267,407	2	665,246	1	8.64
Ogbomosho	139,535	3	319,881	3	7.84
Kano	127,205	4	295,432	4	7.96
Oshogbo	122,728	5	208,966	5	4.96
Ile-Ife	110,790	6	130,050	18	1.47
Iwo	100,006	7	158,583	12	4.28
Abeokuta	84,451	8	187,292	7	7.50
Onitsha	76,921	9	163,032	11	7.07
Oyo	72,133	10	112,349	19	4.11
Ilesha	72,029	11	165,822	10	7.88
Port Harcourt	71,634	12	179,563	8	8.72
Enugu	62,764	13	138,457	15	7.45
Aba	57,787	14	131,003	17	7.72
Maiduguri	56,740	15	139,965	14	8.56
Zaria	53,974	16	166,170	9	10.75
Benin City	53,753	17	100,694	20	5.86
Katsina	52,672	18	90,538	22	5.04
Sokoto	51,986	19	89,817	23	5.09
Iseyin	49,683	20	95,220	21	6.09
Calabar	46,705	21	76,418	24	4.47
Ede	44,808	22	134,550	16	10.52
Kaduna	44,540	23	149,910	13	11.67
Ilorin	40,994	24	208,546	6	15.93
Akure	38,857	*	71,106	*	5.60
Jos	38,527	*	90,402	*	8.33
Ikere-Ekiti	35,584	*	107,216	*	10.41
Ila	25,584	*	114,688	*	14.47
Ado-Ekiti	24,166	*	157,519	*	18.25
Minna	12,870	*	59,988	*	14.92

* There were other higher-ranked cities ahead.

Source: Population census of Nigeria, 1952 and 1963.

Table 4.3. Projected population of some Nigerian cities, 1972, 1982 and 1984

City	1972* population	1982* population	1984** population	Rank
Lagos	1,568,650	4,068,578	4,485,607	1
Ibadan	1,479,359	3,836,987	4,230,278	2
Ogbomosho	496,231	808,339	891,194	8
Kano	578,338	1,500,056	1,653,812	3
Oshogbo	324,169	528,057	582,183	11
Ile-Ife	201,747	328,636	362,321	23
Iwo	246,010	400,739	441,815	18
Abeokuta	290,546	623,686	689,819	10
Onitsha	252,912	411,982	454,210	17
Oyo	174,287	283,906	313,006	24
Ilesha	257,240	419,032	461,983	16
Port Harcourt	351,513	911,731	1,005,183	6
Enugu	326,482	846,789	933,585	7
Aba	203,225	331,045	354,977	22
Maiduguri	273,995	710,672	783,201	9
Zaria	257,780	419,912	462,953	15
Benin City	197,119	511,274	563,680	12
Katsina	140,452	228,796	252,241	29
Sokoto	175,826	456,046	502,791	14
Iseyin	147,715	240,621	265,285	27
Calabar	149,596	388,012	427,783	20
Ede	208,727	340,008	374,859	21
Kaduna	353,488	916,835	1,010,811	5
Ilorin	408,250	1,058,892	1,167,428	4
Akure	110,307	237,544	261,892	28
Jos	176,971	459,016	506,065	13
Ikere-Ekiti	166,324	270,935	298,706	26
Ila	177,915	289,817	319,523	25
Ado-Ekiti	244,359	398,051	438,851	19
Minna	93,059	200,402	220,943	30

* Based on a minimum annual growth rate of 5 per cent for all cities except state capitals, for which figures are based on a 10 per cent growth rate.

** Based on a 5 per cent annual growth rate for all cities.

somewhat controversial. Secondly, the projections assume a minimum growth rate of 5 per cent for all cities between 1963 and 1984. However, in the case of state capitals, the assumed rate of growth as from the year they became state capitals is put at 10 per cent. Thus, from 1967 onwards, the populations of Kano, Port Harcourt, Maiduguri, Benin, Sokoto, Ilorin, Jos and Calabar were assumed to have been increasing at an annual rate of 10 per cent, while those of Minna, Akure and Abeokuta were assumed to have been increasing at the same rate from 1976 when they became state capitals (see Table 4.3). From 1982 to 1984, based on the belief that the accelerated tempo of activities had reduced somewhat in most of the state capitals, and also the fact that economic recession had set in, the annual rate of growth in these cities has been placed at the 5 per cent level once again.

Lagos, Ibadan, Kaduna and Enugu have been placed in a special category as they have been federal (Lagos), regional or state capitals (Ibadan, Kaduna and Enugu) from 1963 to 1982. Thus, their population was assumed to have increased at an annual rate of 10 per cent throughout the period. In 1963, Mushin and Agege, which are actually part of metropolitan Lagos, were treated as separate cities and had populations of 145,976 and 45,986 respectively. If these figures are included, the 1963 population of metropolitan Lagos becomes 857,208 and the projected population for 1982 would be 5,242,598 (Table 4.3). Of course, these projections are based on an assumed, albeit unrealistic, uniform rate of growth and thus the figures presented in Table 4.3 may be higher or much lower than reality for some cities. Nevertheless, they do give a plausible picture of the magnitude and rate of growth of some major cities in Nigeria.

The two components of growth of Nigerian cities are natural increase and internal net migration. Some studies have tended to show that the rate of natural increase is higher in the urban areas than in the rural areas (Ekanem and Farooq, 1976). The reason advanced for this is that while there is little difference in the fertility rate of women in the urban and rural areas, the mortality rate is generally lower in the urban areas. Nevertheless, there is overwhelming evidence that the rapid growth of most Nigerian cities is due, to a great extent, to high rates of rural to urban migration. According to Milone and Green (1973: 6), 644,000 people migrated to Lagos within the ten-year period 1953 to 1963, and the World Bank (1972) calculated that migrants accounted for 75 per cent of the total population growth of Lagos between 1952 and 1963. The rural–urban migration stream which had started during the colonial period gained momentum after independence. To a considerable degree, this has resulted from the neglect of the rural areas and the inherent *urban bias* enshrined in national development planning. This bias is manifested in the location of industries, infrastructural facilities and social services. Most government policies and investment programmes have clearly continued to favour the cities as opposed to the rural areas of Nigeria.

The Livability of Nigerian Cities

Livability may be defined as the sum total of the qualities of an urban environment which tend to induce a state of well-being and satisfaction in its citizens (Wilson, 1962). Therefore, the livability of a city must take into consideration not only the objective condition of that particular city,

but also residents' perceptions of the quality of life in the city. There is
a general consensus that the explosive rate of growth of Nigerian cities
has contributed to increasing environmental degradation, as well as to
great strains being placed on existing social services in the cities.

Housing is perhaps the most acute and visible problem facing Nigerian
cities. There is a serious shortage of housing units in most cities. For
example, in 1975 Lagos alone required an additional 10,000 dwelling units
per year (Nigeria, 1975: 308). Another aspect of the urban housing problem
in Nigeria relates to the quality of the existing dwelling units and their
inability to satisfy individual socio-economic and psychological needs.
A large proportion of the houses in most cities are overcrowded, physically
inadequate, substandard or lack basic facilities such as water, electricity,
and the exclusive use of a kitchen and washroom. This is clearly exemplified for Nigeria's major urban places in Table 4.4.

Water, a basic necessity, constitutes a critical problem for most urban
residents. In some cities, clean and adequate water has become a luxury,
because water taps are usually dry and many residents have to rely on
boreholes, wells and rivers. Sewage and refuse disposal presents another
major problem. There is no city in Nigeria with an integrated sewage
system, and the few available flush toilets are found in high-income areas
where they are usually connected to septic tanks and 'soak away'. Many
cities have become incapable of coping with the disposal of their solid
wastes on a regular and continuous basis. Likewise, urban transportation
facilities have not been able to cope with the rising demands of urban
residents. Intra-city movements now constitute an immense problem in
most Nigerian cities, for roads are generally narrow, untarred and tortuous
(Table 4.5).

However, in spite of the numerous problems which tend to detract
from the livability of Nigerian cities, in a study conducted by the present
author (Salau, 1986) it was found that the majority of urban residents
found their cities livable irrespective of size. As can be seen from the data
in Table 4.6, about 68 per cent of all respondents in the study rated their
neighbourhood as 'very good' or 'fairly good'. This perhaps accounts for
the increasing rate of rural–urban migration, for until the cities are perceived
to be less livable than the rural areas the rural dwellers will continue to
flock to the major urban areas.

The Provision of Shelter as a Basic Need in Urban Nigeria

The core of basic human needs includes food, water, health, shelter and
education. The tremendous increase in revenue generated by petroleum
export has enabled the Nigerian government to allocate quite substantial amounts of money to the provision of some of these basic needs.

Table 4.4. The nature of housing problems in some Nigerian cities 1973–4 (sample survey)

Cities	Building type* (%)	Average number of house-holds per house	Average number of persons per room	Owner-occupied** houses (%)	Rented houses	Average rent per room	Water in house (%)	in com-pound (%)	Washroom shared (%)	exclu-sive (%)	Kitchen shared (%)	exclu-sive (%)	Latrine pit (%)	pail (%)
Lagos	74.61(CI)	4.39	2.51	36.09	63.91	10.69	42.25	34.66	74.84	21.68	72.78	22.78	2.69	48.51
Port-Harcourt	100 (CI)	7.64	2.42	9.48	90.52	2.14	3.96	67.17	94.42	5.58	93.04	6.42	0.36	92.02
Onitsha	94.07(CI)	5.44	2.63	37.17	62.83	4.86	8.94	59.20	91.41	7.95	91.64	7.95	2.44	75.28
Enugu	71.51(CI)	6.57	2.97	19.16	80.84	5.40	10.48	55.68	90.72	9.28	90.78	9.22	2.65	60.67
Jos	52.37(CI)	4.34	2.19	43.45	56.55	4.99	2.65	73.72	88.66	8.32	87.90	9.83	34.40	55.76
Makurdi	50.60(CI)	4.03	2.02	39.22	60.78	3.29	0.00	9.06	87.40	6.30	79.92	6.50	7.68	85.83
Benin	64.82(CMI)	3.75	2.36	65.58	34.42	4.62	2.74	19.61	90.19	9.24	88.26	11.29	97.95	0.57
Kaduna	46.72(CMI)	5.08	2.20	22.38	77.62	4.80	0.00	99.63	98.35	1.65	98.53	1.47	73.95	25.92
Ibadan	64.27(CMI)	2.50	2.34	72.30	27.70	3.87	6.06	14.80	81.82	11.77	84.03	10.72	74.48	6.06
Ilorin	67.16(CMI)	1.94	1.55	97.17	2.83	2.06	1.13	56.22	57.83	10.34	71.73	12.76	37.64	0.48
Kano	64.36(O)	2.04	1.81	82.61	17.39	2.82	9.87	51.68	23.53	18.91	39.08	29.20	82.35	16.39
Calabar	39.75(O)	3.22	1.80	45.49	54.51	1.94	0.20	1.38	88.34	9.88	90.32	8.50	70.55	22.53
Sokoto	80.47(O)	1.28	2.30	95.44	4.56	2.61	5.60	9.05	38.79	28.02	36.85	25.43	95.47	0.22
Zaria	65.85(O)	1.71	2.05	98.72	1.28	2.08	83.87	3.55	36.34	55.46	22.13	33.88	96.17	3.28

*CI Cement block/brick walls with corrugated iron or asbestos roofs.
CMI Mud walls rendered with cement and corrugated iron or asbestos roofs.
O Mud, bamboo and other walls.
**Includes people living free in the house or paying nominal rent.
Source: Nigeria (1981: 311–18).

Table 4.5.   The nature of roads by city size in Nigeria

Size of city	Percentage of roads/streets that are classified as:		
	Tarred	Untarred	Footpath
Large city	44.4	45.8	9.8
Medium city	32.8	60.3	6.9
Small city	24.3	59.3	16.3
Mean*	36.6	53.4	10.0

* Mean for all cities irrespective of size.

Source: Salau (1986: 196).

Table 4.6.   The rating of urban neighbourhoods by residents in Nigeria

City size	Percentage of respondents seeing area as:			
	Very good	Fairly good	Average	Poor
Large	19.1	39.4	24.8	16.6
Medium	26.4	43.5	24.4	5.7
Small	28.2	48.7	17.3	5.8
Mean	24.6	43.9	22.2	9.4

Source: Salau (1986: 199).

As Table 4.7 shows, important basic-needs sectors such as education, electricity and water supply received substantial increases in the level of

Table 4.7.   The sectoral distribution of the expenditure in Nigeria's Second and Third Development Plans

Sector	Actual public expenditure 1970 – 4 (millions of naira)	Planned public expenditure 1975 – 80 (millions of naira)
Agriculture, forestry and fishery	218.6	1,300
Mining and quarrying	20.9	1,400
Manufacturing and crafts	88.5	3,800
Electricity and water	241.9	1,000
Building and construction	—	—
Distribution	56.3	100
Transport and communication	570.9	5,500
General government	476.4	3,000
Education	254.6	1,500
Health	112.0	400
Other services	196.5	2,000
Total	2,236.6	20,000

Source: Nigeria (1975: 25, 53).

investment allocated in the period between the Second and Third National Development Plans.

In the Third National Development Plan (1975–80), the sum of 2.5 billion naira was allocated for the housing programme, with over 90 per cent of this being intended for the construction of low-cost housing units for low-income groups. The main objective was 'to achieve a significant increase in supply and bring relief especially to the low income groups' (Nigeria, 1975: 308).

It was envisaged that by 1980 about 202,000 housing units would be provided, comprising 8,000 units in each of the nineteen states and approximately 50,000 in Lagos (Table 4.8). Each state was also expected to build another 4,000 units itself. In October 1979, the civilian administration took office and promptly adopted housing and agriculture as its two main areas of priority. The administration introduced a new housing scheme which provided for the construction of 2,000 housing

Table 4.8. Total number of houses completed and plots allocated as at 30 January 1980

State	No. of housing units completed	Sum total of housing units completed plus plots allocated	Target projected for 1975/80	Percentage achievement
Lagos (FHA) Festac Town and Ipaja	8,616	8,616	46,000	18.7
Anambra	400	400	8,000	5.0
Bauchi	1,819	1,819	8,000	22.77
Bendel	250	250	8,000	3.1
Benue	38	38	8,000	—
Borno	2,480	2,480	8,000	31.0
Cross River	525	1,076	8,000	13.4
Gongola	382	382	8,000	4.8
Imo	488	488	8,000	6.1
Kaduna	1,620	1,620	12,000	13.5
Kano	976	976	8,000	12.2
Kwara	941	941	8,000	11.8
Lagos	848	848	8,000	10.6
Niger	520	520	8,000	6.5
Ogun	512	1,405	8,000	17.6
Ondo	1,370	1,408	8,000	17.6
Oyo	323	1,402	8,000	17.5
Plateau	1,000	1,000	8,000	12.5
Rivers	281	281	8,000	3.5
Sokoto	1,000	1,000	8,000	12.5
Total	24,389	26,950	202,000*	13.3

Source: Federal Housing Authority, Lagos (1980).

units per annum in each of the nineteen states in the country. The objective was to build a total of 200,000 housing units at a cost of 2.45 billion naira between 1981 and 1985. The scheme placed emphasis on the construction of housing units for people in the low-income group, with 80 per cent of the total expended being for this purpose. Under the scheme, occupiers are also the owners and are given twenty-five years in which to repay the cost of the house, at not more than one-fifth of monthly salary. Such low-cost houses are located in three main types of area: state capitals, local government headquarters, and industrial, commercial or large towns, all of which have substantial economic activity. In spite of the massive amount allocated to the housing sector, little has actually been accomplished. As can be seen from the data in Table 4.13, fewer than 15 per cent of the 202,000 housing units envisaged by the 1975–80 plan were actually completed and allocated. Also, of the 200,000 new housing units planned for construction between 1980 and 1985, only 19 per cent were actually built.

However, as indicated elsewhere (Salau, 1984), the number of housing units completed tells only part of the story. The main issue is the extent to which the massive amount of money allocated has actually gone to fulfil the basic needs of the low-income urban residents to whom the housing programmes were targeted. In order to address this issue, a random sample survey of 1,352 residents of government housing estates in six cities was undertaken between June and August 1982. The cities selected were Minna, Kaduna, Jos, Kano, Sokoto and Maiduguri.

As can be seen from Tables 4.9 and 4.10, it seems that in the case of each of these cities a disproportionate number of such houses were allocated to civil servants. These houses were intended for the low-income segment of the population, defined as those earning about 200 naira or less monthly. However, the survey revealed that many of the occupants fell into much higher income categories (Table 4.10). Thus, there was a substantial leakage of such properties to people outside the low-income group.

This circumstance is not surprising. Government-built houses are often too expensive, especially when compared to those built in the private sector by individuals, groups or commercial entities. This is due to the high standard of construction adhered to, and the inclusion of many luxury items which may well not be necessary. Also, the space standards of these houses and even their design tend to be generous, and may often be at variance with the real needs of low-income families. Perhaps more importantly, the fees charged by the contractors of government-built houses in Nigeria are often padded out with hidden costs, particularly those incurred as kickbacks. Thus, the allottees had to pay inordinately high rents or the repayments on a mortgage, which most low-income families could not afford. As can be seen from Table 4.11, if the allottees of the government-built houses in the Festac Village, Lagos, expended only 20 per cent of their monthly salary in mortgage or rent payments,

Table 4.9. The occupation of residents of the government low-cost houses in six Nigerian cities

| Occupation | Percentage of the total population by occupational group in the following cities: | | | | | |
	Minna N = 200	Kaduna N = 450	Jos N = 141	Kano N = 211	Sokoto N = 150	Maiduguri N = 200
Civil service	76.5	54.0	70.9	50.7	56.0	42.7
Self-employed	4.5	15.8	19.9	21.3	16.0	23.6
Technicians	5.0	15.3	6.4	12.3	2.7	5.9
Managerial/executive	3.0	8.0	—	15.2	10.0	16.4
Politicians	4.5	—	—	—	—	—
Others	6.5	6.9	2.8	0.5	15.3	11.4
Total	100.0	100.0	100.0	100.0	100.0	100.0

Source: Salau (1984).

Table 4.10. The income of resident of government low-cost houses in six Nigerian cities

| Income group | Percentage of the total population falling into various income groups in the following cities: | | | | | |
	Minna	Kaduna	Jos	Kano	Sokoto	Maiduguri
No income	5.0	3.0	—	3.3	6.7	3.2
Low income (less than 141.7 naira monthly)	5.0	15.0	7.1	7.6	14.7	17.7
Middle income (141.7 – 331.7 naira monthly)	46.0	56.0	60.9	62.1	58.6	57.7
High income (more than 331.7 naira monthly)	44.0	26.0	31.9	27.0	20.0	26.4
Total	100.0	100.0	100.0	100.0	100.0	100.0

Source: Salau (1984).

these houses could not be paid off in the stipulated twenty-five year period. Inevitably, therefore, these houses were, in fact, allocated to people in far higher income categories than originally intended, and even then many of these would not be able to repay the mortgages in the time stipulated.

The cost of government-built houses as compared to what the same structure would cost if built by individuals in the private sector is very revealing indeed. For example, Wahab (1977) found that while the government was building three-bedroomed housing units costing 6,000–21,000 naira each in 1974, the same type of structures were being constructed

Table 4.11.   Costs of houses constructed by government in Festac Village, Lagos, 1977

Spatial Unit	Cost/unit (in naira)	Grade/level qualification (in naira)	Units to be allocated	Grade level allocated (in naira)
1-bedroom flat	Below 9.00	01 – 723 02 – 807 03 – 903 04 – 1,167 05 – 1,143	1,500	
3-bedroom flat	16,500 plus 30% government subsidy + infrastructure	07 – 2,499 08 – 3,264	1,000	09 – 4,368 10 – 5,460 11 – 6,445 12 – 7,104
3-bedroom house (undetached)	28,000 subsidy + infrastructure			10 – 5,460 11 – 6,445 12 – 7,104
4-bedroom house	121,000	09 – 4,368	450 (50 reserved)	12 – 7,104 and above

Source: Aradeon (1978).

privately at almost the same time in Ile-Ife at 4,470 naira each. The effect of the high cost of the government-built houses has been not only the exclusion of most members of the low-income groups for which ostensibly they were being designed, but also many of these houses being left vacant.

Apart from the fact that a direct construction programme is not the most efficient way of spending the nation's resources, experience has also indicated that government-built houses are not only more costly but are often poorly constructed. The quality of construction is often so poor that such houses deteriorate far more rapidly than privately built homes. Not surprisingly, in the field survey of houses in six cities it was found that many of the residents expressed complaints about the houses in which they were living (Table 4.12). Specifically, these tended to stress the poor design of such houses as well as the poor standard of their construction (Table 4.13). A commission of inquiry which reported in 1975 judged the design and quality of construction of the Kundila housing estate in Kano to be very poor. In fact, a number of houses on the Barnawa government low-cost housing estate in Kaduna collapsed in February 1981, killing the occupants. As a direct result of this, the remaining houses on the estate had to be demolished at great cost.

Table 4.12. The percentage of residents, by city, who had complaints about their house

Response	Minna	Kaduna	Jos	Kano	Sokoto	Maiduguri
Yes	54.0	63.2	74.5	69.7	54.7	60.5
No	40.5	34.1	25.5	28.9	45.3	37.7
No Response	5.5	2.7	—	1.4	—	1.8
Total	100.0	100.0	100.0	100.0	100.0	100.0

Table 4.13. The features that residents specifically disliked about their houses (percentage by city)

Response	Minna	Kaduna	Jos	Kano	Sokoto	Maiduguri
Not spacious enough	18.5	14.0	50.4	29.4	42.0	19.1
Poor ventilation	8.5	20.0	3.6	23.2	28.7	48.6
Poor construction	14.0	35.0	17.0	32.2	22.7	12.7
Others (poor kitchen, drainage system etc.)	52.0	31.0	29.0	4.7	6.7	15.4
No response	7.0	—	—	10.5	—	4.2
Total	100.0	100.0	100.0	100.0	100.0	100.0

The government often fails to address the fact that, for low-income groups, housing is only part of a total demand package for services. These services include space, accessibility to the place of work and amenities such as water, health facilities, education and retail markets. As Chatterjee (1982: 63) has pointed out, these services are vital for they not only improve the physical welfare of the poor but also help in the acquisition of human capital and increasing productivity. It is not enough to provide dwelling units for low-income families without appreciating this wider fact. In the field sample survey there was considerable evidence that most of the government-built houses failed to take the needs of the residents into consideration. As the results listed in Table 4.14 demonstrate, a substantial proportion of residents felt that the houses they occupied were too far from basic life-supporting facilities.

Towards a Framework for Meeting the Basic Needs of Nigerian Urban Residents

Satisfying the basic needs of citizens is perhaps the biggest challenge facing any country. This goal is undoubtedly rendered all the more difficult because we still do not fully appreciate how to go about realizing this

Table 4.14. The percentage of total respondents, by city, who felt that their house is too far from basic urban facilities

Places	Minna (N = 200)	Kaduna (N = 450)	Jos (N = 141)	Kano (N = 211)	Sokoto (N = 150)	Maiduguri (N = 220)
Central market	30.5	47.8	93.6	59.7	65.0	12.7
General hospital	30.5	66.2	92.9	55.9	54.0	75.0
Shopping	60.0	38.7	94.3	46.9	38.0	6.8
Place of work	65.0	59.8	78.0	33.6	33.3	69.5
Railway/bus depot	35.5	69.1	81.6	54.0	44.0	—
Recreation facilities	21.0	60.0	92.9	60.6	26.0	55.4

important objective. Some scholars have contended that it can be achieved by massive increases in public expenditure. Linn (1979: 146) has advanced this line of argument forcefully:

> Public expenditure, and in particular provision of public services is the most important means by which the alleviation of urban poverty must be sought in the short and medium terms, since productivity and employment opportunities for the poor can be increased only slowly. In theory, relatively small shifts in public expenditure would suffice in some countries to raise the absolute poor above the poverty threshold.

Because of the 'oil boom', the Nigerian government has increased public expenditure and a great deal of money has been invested in the provision of certain basic needs. Nevertheless, there is consensus that the basic needs of Nigerians are as far from being met today as they were a decade ago.

As the results of the field survey revealed, government intervention in the housing sector in the form of direct construction and the allocation of more resources is unlikely to solve housing problems, especially those of poor and low-income families. In fact, the bitter truth is that the nation does not have sufficient resources to solve the housing problems of all its citizens. Government expenditure on housing has resulted only in the construction of a few over-expensive dwelling units. The high cost is due to many factors. First, it takes government far too long to complete housing construction schemes. Secondly, the standards of government houses are set too high. The fees charged by professionals are exorbitant and the profit margins of the contractors very high. Thereby so-called 'low-cost' housing units for the poor and low-income families end up being unaffordable by the households which are most in need of them. In another study it was found that, in 1975, the poorest 40 per cent and the top 20 per cent of all Nigerian households could only afford housing valued at US$863 (about 590 naira) and US$5,400 (3,600 naira) respectively (Chatterjee,

Table 4.15.   Affordable housing by income group in Nigeria, 1975 – 90 (base case 1975 US$)

Region	Income Group	Affordable (1975)	1985 House	1990 House
Nigeria	Top 20	5,395	7,100	9,816
	Bottom 40	863	1,260	1,429
Bauchi	Top 20	3,579	5,500	6,279
	Bottom 40	642	787	998
Kano	Top 20	3,746	7,210	10,711
	Bottom 40	667	1,130	1,529
Lagos	Top 20	7,581	10,893	11,463
	Bottom 40	1,454	1,847	2,600
Ondo	Top 20	3,957	5,800	6,467
	Bottom 40	645	838	1,187
Rivers	Top 20	3,682	5,571	6,870
	Bottom 40	479	818	1,177
Benue	Top 20	3,636	4,958	6,023
	Bottom 40	591	792	896

Source: Chatterjee (1982: 71).

1982). Further, as can be seen from Table 4.15, while some households in the upper part of the top quantile may be able to afford housing valued much higher than 5,400 naira, the average household cannot afford the typical house which is being produced by the government at the present time. However, in contrast, some of the houses that are being built privately by individuals themselves are much closer to the affordability level of most households. Thus, it can only be concluded that housing is not the kind of basic need that can be effectively and efficiently provided by the state. However, this is not to call for an entirely *laissez-faire* policy for the provision of shelter. It is still open to debate whether a *laissez-faire* or free-market policy can ration the available supply of housing equitably among the different groups in society. However, there is no doubt that a reappraisal of government's role in housing is necessary. Some governmental interventions have clearly produced unintended and undesired effects. Government initiatives in the field of housing have not been restricted to direct construction but have included the control and regulation of the housing market through various means such as town planning and building regulations, rent controls and land allocation. Part of the housing problems can be attributed to these interventions. Some people have argued that the government must engage in direct housing construction for low-income families because housing for such people is not commercially attractive to the private sector. However, in spite of public housing schemes, more than 90 per cent of low-income families are to be found accommodated in privately built houses. The private sector can contribute more towards solving the present housing problems if some of the obstacles hampering the smooth operation of this sector are removed. For example, private-sector housing has been hindered by the excessive delays which are frequently encountered by individuals in obtaining a certificate of registration for land, and building permits from local governments and planning authorities. Okpala (1978: 251), for example, found that in Ibadan fewer than two-thirds of all building applications submitted annually between 1963 and 1976 were approved, and in Nsukka and Zaria only 47 per cent and 78 per cent respectively of all applications were approved.

The town planning and building regulations of Nigeria are generally regarded as being elitist in nature, and are often predicated on upper- and middle-class values. As a result, it is often suggested that they tend to ignore the daily experiences and needs of most citizens. Because the standards invariably set by the authorities are too high, many building plans are not approved. It is not surprising, therefore, that numerous new buildings are constructed in contravention of the planning and building regulations. In order to secure a reprieve for the low-income earners who, in view of the housing shortage, have been known to pay more than one-third of their income in rents, the government has in the past enacted a system of rent controls. In 1976, the federal government promulgated a rent-control edict in which all states were directed to adopt appropriate rent levels. In Lagos, the highest rent per room in the best high-density locations was stipulated as not exceeding 12 naira. In addition, the rent for an entire house in a low-density area was pegged at 25 per cent less than the market rate prevailing at the time. Rent control cannot but fail, as will any intervention in the market which ignores the forces of supply and demand. Rent controls have proved to be not only ineffective, but counter-productive. It has been argued that rent control discourages investment in rental housing by cutting the prospective profits of potential investors, thereby removing the incentive to invest. Rent controls were implemented in a more comprehensive fashion in the case of rooming housing and other high-density units, while single-family and other low-density housing units were generally subject to less control.

The effect of this was a reduction in the stock of the kinds of high-density units which provide shelter for low-income earners, and a shift towards the construction of low-density units. Some rooming houses were actually converted by landlords into flats. It is also true that, in many cases, the landlords were able to evade and subvert the control system. Prospective tenants were subjected to heavy down payments or rent in advance for one year or more. Some were forced to pay rents at much higher levels than allowed under the rent-control system, with receipts not being given, or otherwise issued for much less than the amount actually paid.

It can be argued that if the basic-needs strategy in housing depends solely on direct construction by governments, solutions to the problems of providing shelter for the majority of the people will remain elusive. The direct construction programmes have succeeded in the provision of public housing for a select few and have resulted in the mismanagement of the nation's resources. The real need is to establish a proper role for government in the housing sector. As Turner (1976: 32) has argued: 'the proper role of government is to ensure that those who are best able to build, either for themselves or for their neighbours, have access to the tools and basic resources for the job'. The present author agrees with this view, for once those capable of building for themselves are helped to do so by various means, those who are unable to provide shelter for themselves can then be appropriately cared for by the government. Full participation and the ability of the individual to influence the decisions affecting his or her life must be part of any basic-needs approach in housing. The direct construction of houses by government seems so frequently to negate this yearning for self-actualization. The proper role of government may be to provide support or assistance in some form to potential homebuilders. This view seems to be borne out by the results of two housing studies which were recently carried out in Nigeria. As can be seen from the results shown in Table 4.16, only 2.4 per cent of all respondents in the rural areas and 2.7 per cent of those in the urban areas wished the government

Table 4.16. The type of aid families feel they should be able to expect from government in respect of housing (percentages)

Type of aids	Rural	Urban
Building materials	7.3	11.8
Completely built houses	2.4	2.7
Loans	55.7	69.5
Loans and materials	18.7	N/A
Land	0.6	28.0
Relax building codes	N/A	2.2
Certificate of occupancy	2.4	N/A
Ease plan approval	N/A	2.2
No assistance	12.7	N/A
Total	100.0	100.0

N/A Not applicable

Sources: NISER (1983), Onibokun (1986).

to build complete houses for them. In contrast, 55.7 per cent of rural residents and 69.5 per cent of urban dwellers required government assistance purely in the form of loans. Saliently, in the urban areas, a number of families would like to see the government relax the existing building codes and ease the approval of plans.

Thus, a critical requirement for potential builders is access to loans. Housing finance institutions are very ineffective in Nigeria and their limited resources often go to the middle- and high-income groups, at interest rates which represent explicit or implicit subsidies. These institutions also sometimes discriminate against the construction of rooming houses or high-density housing areas in favour of expensive single-family and other low-density housing units. Most low-income families are effectively denied loans as a result of the banks' emphasis on creditworthiness, status and security. Thus, a reform of these institutions is of the utmost necessity. The government should also establish the provision of loans in kind, such as the supply of building materials. This would ensure that the money voted for the housing sector is actually utilized for building low-income dwellings.

Perhaps more important is the fact that the basic-needs approach to housing must draw to a great extent on indigenous and individual resources. There is a need to take advantage of indigenous methods and the existing building skills of local artisans and craftsmen. The cost of houses for the majority of the citizens can be lowered if the excessive fixation and reliance on Western standards is overcome, and use is increasingly made of the abundant local building materials which exist. There is also a need to fashion a housing policy which puts emphasis not on direct construction alone, but which also ensures the maintenance, rehabilitation and full utilization of the existing housing stock and services.

Thus, some efforts should be directed toward site and service and aided self-help schemes. The provision of infrastructural elements such as roads, water, electricity, sewerage lines, the costs of which are so high, should be left to the government. In the absence of such help, new urban houses are all too frequently built without any means of access to them, nor with the necessary services. This is also true for the rural areas where land and local building materials are available at cheap rates and thus the primary need here is 'not for complete houses but for the basic infrastructural services of water supply, roads, and electrical energy and technical assistance in housebuilding' (United Nations, 1976, 26). The virtual nationalization of all lands in the country by the Land Use Act has created many problems, especially for low-income housebuilders. Laudable as the objectives of the Act are, its actual implementation has served to aggravate housing problems. It has led to the superimposition of one bureaucracy upon another with all the attendant difficulties and delays that this implies in securing land for development. There seems little doubt that there is urgent need for a comprehensive review of the Land Use Act.

REFERENCES

Aradeon, D. (1978) 'Regional assessment of human settlement policies in Nigeria'. *Habitat*, **3**(4), 311-39.

Chatterjee, L. (1982) 'Effective targeting for basic shelter provision'. *Economic Geography*, **58**(1), 62-74.

Ekanem, I.I. (1972) *The 1963 Nigerian Census*. Benin City: Ethiope Press.

Ekanem, I.I. and Farooq, G.M. (1976) *The Dynamics of Population Change in Southern Nigeria*, mimeograph. Department of Demography and Social Statistics, University of Ife.

Linn, J.F. (1979) *Policies for Efficient and Equitable Growth of Cities in Developing Countries*, World Bank Staff Working Paper No. 342. Washington, DC: World Bank.

Milone, V. and Green, L. (1973) *Urbanization in Nigeria – A Planning Commentary*. New York: Ford Foundation.

Nigeria (1975) *Third National Development Plan 1975-80*. Lagos: Federal Ministry of Economic Development.

Nigeria (1979) *Social Statistics in Nigeria*. Lagos: Federal Ministry of Economic Development.

Nigeria (1980) *The National Accounts of Nigeria 1973-75*. Lagos: Federal Ministry of Economic Development.

NISER (1983) *Rural Housing in Southern States of Nigeria*. Ibadan: NISER, p. 191.

Onibokun, P. (1986) *Urban Housing in Nigeria*. Ibadan: NISER, p. 330.

Salau, A.T. (1984) 'Public policy and housing problems in Nigeria: an appraisal of the government role in the provision of shelter as basic needs'. *Journal of Issue in Development*, **1**(2), 26-39.

Salau, A.T. (1986) 'Quality of life and city size: an exploratory study of Nigeria'. *Social Indicators Research*, **18**, 193-203.

Salau, A.T. (1987) *Nigerian Cities: The Evolution and Dynamics of an Urban System*. Oguta, Nigeria: Zim's Pan African Press.

Turner, J.F.C. (1976) 'A new universe of squatter builders'. *UNESCO Courier*, 12-33.

United Nations (1976) *World Housing Survey 1974*. New York: Department of Economic Affairs.

Wahab, K.A. (1976) 'Value judgements and housing policies', *African Environment*, **2**, 87-93.

Wilson, R.L. (1962) 'Livability of the city: attitudes and urban development', in: Chapin, F.S. and Weiss, S.F. (eds) *Urban Growth Dynamics in a Regional Cluster of Cities*. New York: John Wiley.

World Bank (1972) *Urbanization*, Sector Policy Working Paper. New York: World Bank.

[5]

Shelter in Urban Barbados, West Indies: Vernacular Architecture, Land Tenure and Self-Help

Robert B. Potter

Introduction

Barbados has an indigenous quasi-self-help housing system, the origins of which go right back to the days immediately after colonization by the British in the first quarter of the seventeenth century. But in a seemingly aberrant manner, this has not led to a genuine form of progressive upgrading in the sense implied by J. F. C. Turner (1967; 1968; 1976; 1982). The majority of houses are still constructed primarily of wood, and therefore require a great deal of upkeep. Further, many houses are located on a temporary loose-rock pile foundation. This is despite the fact that Barbados is a nation of proud home owners, with 70.2 per cent of households being owner-occupied in 1980. Indeed, state housing and squatting are of minor importance, providing only 4.9 and 0.03 per cent respectively of the total housing stock.

After a short overview of changing perspectives on the provision of low-income housing in Third World countries as a whole, the salient features of the Barbadian housing system are initially considered in this chapter. First, it is shown how the present-day vernacular housing style found in Barbados represents a combination of the shared characteristics of southern English and West African folk dwellings of the seventeenth century. It is also demonstrated how the quality of such housing is explained by the history of slave emancipation and the located labour system which operated on sugar plantations. Together these gave rise to a body of homeless and landless labour, and led to a very insecure system of residential land tenure. These forces have all meant that full housing upgrading has not occurred, despite a long history of spontaneous self-help in the country.

The latter part of the chapter presents some preliminary findings of research which, using enumeration-district data derived from the 1980 Population Census of the Commonwealth Caribbean, sought to provide the first-ever comprehensive socio-geographical analysis of housing conditions in Barbados. Finally, the urban scene of Barbados is examined. This research, focusing on variables such as age of dwellings, material of construction, house type, tenure, water provision, toilet type, provision of electricity and use of gas for cooking has demonstrated that housing conditions in Barbados leave little room for complacency, especially when quality rather than quantity is the criterion. This is illustrated by a multivariate analysis of enumeration-district housing data, which affords a composite picture of variations in housing disamenity in metropolitan Bridgetown. In conclusion, it is stressed that owing to the historical influences of the tenantry system, housing quality has lagged behind general economic development in Barbados to a degree which is quite surprising.

The Context: Changing Views on Third World Housing Policy

As chronicled recently by Conway (1985), perspectives on Third World low-income housing have altered dramatically during the past twenty years. In overall terms, the negative and basically pejorative views which were widely expressed concerning indigenous self-help and squatter housing in the 1960s as propounded by Oscar Lewis (1959; 1966) have now given way to the view that governments are best advised – and indeed in many instances have no option but – to assist people in their efforts to help themselves. As with most intellectual and pragmatic transformations, there were several principal agents of this change. One of these was Stokes (1962) who, in discussing housing in both the developed and developing realms, differentiated between what he regarded as 'slums of despair' and 'slums of hope'. Another very important voice was undoubtedly that of Charles Abrams, and his book *Housing in the Modern World* (1964) was highly influential. Abrams remonstrated that in situations where a housing shortage prevails, razing homes to the ground, however inadequate they may appear, amounts to a monumental folly. This line of argument was strongly taken up by John Turner (1967) and William Mangin (1967). Mangin propagated the view that squatter settlements and shanty towns are to be seen both as a problem and as a potential solution to the desperate housing situations that are faced by so many countries. But it was John Turner, a British architect who, working in Peru for over eight years, promoted what amounted to a radically different perspective on the issue of Third World housing. He maintained that spontaneous self-help represented a situation where, to paraphrase his original remarks, 'never before had so many done so much with so little' (see Turner 1982: 102). On the basis of his own involvement with low-income groups, he argued that they are invariably hard-working and diligent in their efforts to improve their situations. The main outcome of this 'let the people build for themselves' philosophy is, of course, that Third World governments are best advised to help the poor to help themselves by facilitating processes of self-help. This has given rise to the strong advocacy of programmes of aided self-help, generally involving squatter upgrading, core housing and site-and-service schemes. Thereby, the provision of regular, complete and frequently 'high-tech' housing delivery systems has generally been put to one side as a solution to the housing problems of poor countries. On the macro-scale, such an approach has been strongly endorsed by the World Bank, United Nations and United States Agency for International Development. The change in approach has had a sweeping effect, despite the fact that many radical commentators have taken the view that the advocacy of aided self-help principles represents at best an abdication of responsibility on the part of governments, and at worse an imperialist plot on behalf of the international aid agencies (see, for instance, the critique of Burgess, 1982).

The Evolution of the Self-Built Vernacular Architectural System of Barbados

Barbados has a self-help, self-build housing system, the origins of which go back to the colonization of the island by the British from 1627 onwards. The wider aspects of the land-tenure system of Barbados will be discussed in the next section, but, briefly, we now concentrate on the evolution of the principal house type that is found throughout the country.

With regard to the detailed features of such houses, we can turn to an account of the evolution of the vernacular architecture of the Western Caribbean which has been provided by Jay D. Edwards (1980). In this, the author argues that 'the folk-architectural traditions of the Caribbean remain, perhaps, the least-studied major institution of the culture of these islands' (Edwards, 1980: 91). Certainly, it is surprising that relatively little has been written from an academic standpoint on the nature of Caribbean architecture, with only a few exceptions (see Potter and Dann, 1987: 235–41 for a bibliographical listing). However, a marked and very recent upsurge in popular interest is clearly apparent (Berthelot and Gaume, 1982; Fraser and Hughes, 1982; Slesin et al., 1986).

Edwards considers the development of Caribbean popular housing as falling into five broad stages, the first four of which apply to the entire West Indies, with only the final one being unique to the islands of the western portion of the region (Table 5.1). The author distinguishes between 'folk' and 'vernacular' architecture, the former referring to houses that are designed and constructed primarily by the people who live in them, and the latter to houses constructed for the people under the direction of a master builder or carpenter. In the words of Edwards (1980: 297), both 'folk and vernacular traditions are transmitted orally'.

Table 5.1. Five stage sequence in the development of vernacular architecture in the Caribbean according to Edwards (1980)

Stage	Description	Approximate time period
0	Antecedents	c. 1627 – 75
1	Preadaptation and the grounding of separate folk/vernacular traditions	1628 – c. 1660
2	Simplification: reduction of Old World variability	1642 – c. 1800
3	Initial amalgamation and reinterpretation	c. 1650 – 1700
4	Elaboration: innovation and borrowing	c. 1670 – present

The first stage, broadly from 1627 to 1675, was the period of original English settlement of islands such as Barbados, St Christopher and Nevis. During this period, labelled 'Antecedents', the planter-pioneers constructed what amounted to crude temporary huts. These were often wattled, and followed quite closely the design of indigenous Arawak dwellings. The second stage, 1628 to c. 1660, is described as the period of 'Preadaptation and the grounding of separate folk/vernacular traditions'. As soon as sawn timber became available to English planters, they began to build English-style cottages. These were constructed in a similar manner to the types of folk houses prevalent in the south of England at that time. Interestingly, these dwellings shared many basic structural characteristics with the folk houses found in the areas of West Africa from which slave labourers had been transported. In both traditions, the unit was a two-room module which acted as the basis for future expansion. The main door was placed asymmetrically on the long wall of the house, and the roof was generally a thatched gable. Edwards suggests that at this juncture there were many British and African cottages, but little or no synthesis of their forms. It was only as a third and distinct stage that a move toward a new synthesis occurred between 1642 and c. 1800 depending on the locality. Edwards describes this as a period of 'Simplification and reduction of Old World variability', during which a process of evolutionary change occurred, whereby the commonalities of the two formerly separate systems were combined to give a new regional form. The destruction of houses in the region by hurricanes and fires played a vital role in this process of syncretism. Thus it was as a fourth stage, from 1650 onwards locally, that the process of 'Initial amalgamation and reinterpretation' of house forms occurred. Edwards attributes a key role in this process to the characteristics shared between European and African houses, in particular the fact that they were both based on two-roomed-cottage modules of rectangular proportions with the length generally being twice the width. This effectively became the norm for houses in the region and a process of local reinterpretation and development then occurred. In this respect, the raising of cottages off the ground was significant, this being done partly to reduce the destructive effects of ants, termites and vermin. A further series of local adaptations reflected climatic influences, these including the use of wooden shingles, large windows with three-batten shutters and a careful orientation with respect to the prevailing wind.

The result of this gradual evolutionary process was that, by 1700, true indigenous Caribbean dwellings were to be found throughout the region. In his paper Edwards looks at the fifth stage, 'Elaboration: innovation and borrowing', specifically in relation to the western Caribbean. But, in Barbados, as in other parts of the region, a strong Georgian influence can be recognized, including the incorporation of verandahs and terraces and a strong tendency toward symmetry of the front facade.

Land Tenure and the Nature of Self-Help in Barbados

The end product of this evolutionary process in Barbados is what is referred to locally as the 'chattel house' (Figure 5.1). As will be explained, the significance of the chattel housing system is that it has come to dominate not only the rural but also the urban scene in Barbados.

This distinctive dwelling form cannot be explained in architectural terms alone. In the post-emancipation period, freedmen had available little or no land on which to set up their smallholdings. Virtually all the productive land was owned and already cultivated by the sugar plantations. Former slaves thereby had no option but to sell their labour to these large agricultural concerns, and in return were provided with small plots of land on which to build houses. Such house spots were invariably located on infertile, inaccessible and difficult sites at the edge of the plantation, on what is commonly referred to as marginal or 'rab' land. The workers had virtually no security of tenure and remained on such sites at the pleasure of the landlord. If dismissed, it was necessary for workers to dismantle and move such houses to a new locality. Thus evolved a movable housing system, involving building in wood and on a loose-rock foundation. Inevitably, the *ad hoc* nature of the development of such houses meant that they were normally laid out in a far from thoughtful manner, with little or no attention being given to lot configuration, the provision of adequate roads, water supply, or indeed any other utility (Jones, 1987).

This explains the situation today whereby, although over 70 per cent of all houses are officially designated as being owner-occupied, as many as 33 per cent are chattel houses on rented tenantry spots. It can be argued

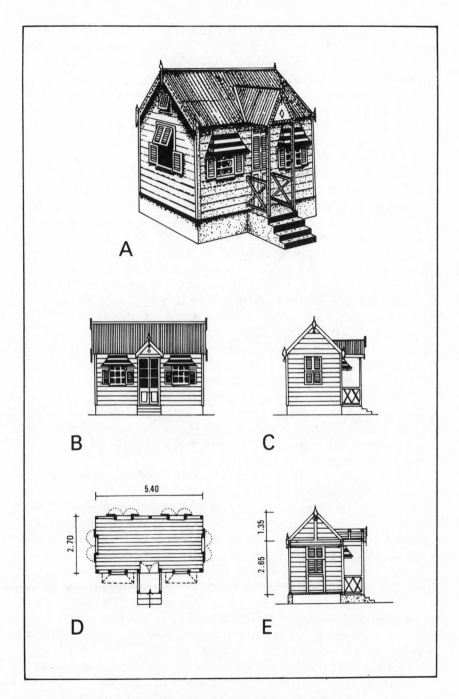

Figure 5.1. Details of the Barbadian chattel house.

that such a situation has had a profound impact on housing quality in Barbados (Potter, 1987). In particular, while it was possible for households to improve and expand their wooden houses, insecurity of tenure meant that they could not build more permanent structures. As Jones (1987) has recently noted, the system also served to perpetuate pit latrines as the means of waste disposal, for landlords were generally not prepared to grant permission for conversion to a water-borne system. Hence, even in 1980, just over 12 per cent of all homes still made use of pit latrines. However, despite these limitations, Barbadians have made every effort to improve and develop their houses. In respect of the resourcefulness and responsiveness of the population, classic Turnerian concepts appear to be well-exemplified. As family and financial circumstances have changed, so households have slowly upgraded such vernacular houses in a manner which connotes a genuine process of self-help.

As Figure 5.1 suggests, the basic chattel house is little more than a wooden unit with dimensions of 9–10 by 18–20 feet (c. 3 m by 6 m). This space might be home for a low-income family of four or more persons. Generally the unit would be divided internally by a wooden partition into two spaces. One of these would be used for sleeping, the other for living, dining and cooking. The pit latrine and bathroom area is generally located outside in the yard. A representative example of a basic timber chattel of this type is shown in Figure 5.2A. The first stage in the process of spontaneous self-help is the addition of a second unit to form what may be referred to as a bipartite chattel (Figure 5.2B). In this manner, a second bedroom and a separate dining area are obtained. Logically, the process can be continued to render a tripartite timber chattel, this structure affording three bedrooms and entirely separate living, dining and kitchen spaces (Figure 5.2C).

Each of these evolutionary units is associated with insecurity of tenure, as indicated by the loose-rock foundations shown in Figure 5.2A–C. In time, if tenure becomes secure, families have endeavoured to add a wall structure at the back of the house in order to provide a toilet, bathroom and kitchen (Figure 5.2D). In 1980, some 10 per cent of the national housing stock was constructed jointly of wood and wall, whereas the equivalent statistic had only been 4 per cent ten years previously. Further, while dwellings constructed entirely of wood amounted to 75 per cent of the housing stock in 1970, a decade later this had fallen to 57 per cent (see Potter, 1987). Ultimately, if the land on which the house is built is owned, then the entire house may be converted to a permanent wall structure, often by building around the outside of the wooden house.

The housing situation can be described as quasi-self-help because insecurity of tenure has placed firm restrictions on what individual households have been able to achieve in the way of upgrading. Further, the wider environment and the provision of adequate infrastructure have

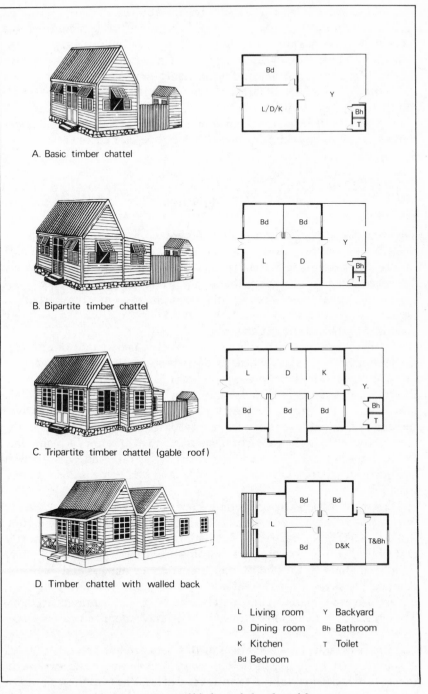

A. Basic timber chattel

B. Bipartite timber chattel

C. Tripartite timber chattel (gable roof)

D. Timber chattel with walled back

L Living room   Y Backyard
D Dining room   Bh Bathroom
K Kitchen   T Toilet
Bd Bedroom

Figure 5.2. Spontaneous self-help and the chattel house.

remained as real problems. The cost in time and money involved in painting such houses and replacing sections of the timber can be very considerable indeed. On the other hand, the slow process of upgrading has meant that households have not had to obtain loans. Rather, they have either been able to afford to pay for such improvements in cash, or have purchased materials on credit from builders' merchants (Jones, 1987). In this regard, the chattel system is an excellent example of an appropriate and afford-able system of self-help, albeit one that has placed a relatively rigid upper limit on the types of improvement that can be carried out.

Present-Day Housing Conditions in the Metropolitan Area of Bridgetown

The vernacular architectural system of low-income housing is ubiquitous in Barbados. Further, the process of urbanization saw the extension of the plantation-dominated tenantry land tenure system into the urban zone. This occurred as Bridgetown, the highly primate capital city, grew and spread into what were formerly plantation lands. Thus the Barbadian housing system of today is essentially a rural-based one which has slowly been transferred to the urban scene.

In the overall context of a wider project which sought to appraise the low-income housing system of Barbados, an attempt was made to provide the first-ever comprehensive analysis of the state of housing in the country as a whole. The first approach in this effort to provide a much-needed informational base for further more detailed studies was the analysis of data provided by the 1980/1 Population Census of the Commonwealth Caribbean. The Census included questions which relate to key housing variables such as water supply, dwelling type, tenure, age of construction, material, toilet type, and fuel used for lighting and for cooking.

Eight key variables reflecting these important aspects of housing quality were selected. These were eventually mapped for the 300-plus enumeration districts making up Barbados. This approach stresses only too clearly that while there are few squatters, housing problems of considerable mag-nitude remain to be tackled by politicians, policy makers and planners. Although, as stressed elsewhere (Potter, 1987), these problems are anything but exclusive to the urban zone, that is the concern of the present account. Thus, the 121 enumeration districts making up Greater Bridgetown repre-sent the focus here.

The full results of the analysis of this data are not presented in this chapter. Only a brief and partial summary is given which relates directly to the present-day outcome of the processes of housing evolution discussed previously. The incidence of houses constructed entirely of wood is obviously an important index, for although some modern houses are still constructed in this manner the variable primarily serves to pinpoint traditional chattel-style houses. It has already been noted that the proportion of houses built entirely of wood has declined quite markedly in the recent past, and is a clear sign of overall housing improvement and upgrading. However, as with any statistic measured at the national scale, that of 57.31 per cent built of wood in 1980 conceals marked variations. The situation for metropolitan Barbados is shown in Figure 5.3. The first point is that very considerable areas of Bridgetown are characterized by levels saliently higher than that pertaining to the nation as a whole. In fact, the upper quartile of enumeration districts have more than three-quarters of their houses constructed entirely of wood (Figure 5.3). One enumeration district located to the north of the central city area had 91.2 per cent of its total housing stock built of wood. The overall spatial patterning revealed in Figure 5.3 demonstrates clear concentrations of enumeration districts with high proportions of wooden dwellings. The first occurs in a broad zone surrounding the city centre. In fact, many of these areas are private urban tenantries, such as that of New Orleans. A second form of concentration is witnessed by small wedges of enumeration districts with high values running out towards the urban periphery. The main one of these extends out toward the central-eastern peripheral boundary of metropolitan Bridgetown. This, in fact, is a former plantation area which now exists as an urban tenantry. Low proportions of the total housing stock having been built of wood are typical of the northern, southern and south-eastern suburbs of the urban zone, where either private or government-sponsored recent residential development has predominated.

One further variable is considered here, that of the dependence of dwellings on pit latrines. Although once again there is a tendency for those concerned with housing policy and planning in Barbados to consider this toilet type to be a thing of the past, the 1980 Census does not substantiate this. As shown in the historical account presented in the first half of this chapter, wherever land tenure is still insecure pit latrines dominate the residential scene. Thus, if the incidence of pit latrines is mapped at the enumeration district level for Bridgetown (Figure 5.4), a pattern broadly similar to that shown for wooden buildings is revealed, although it is somewhat more sharply polarized. The overall national figure of 52.22 per cent is exceeded in approximately half the enumeration districts, while levels in excess of 63 per cent pertain in a quarter of them (Figure 5.4). With respect to high incidences of this key variable, virtually the entire central urban area is highlighted, as is much of the eastern periphery of the urban zone. Once more, the northern and southern peripheral suburban areas stand in sharp contrast to the remainder of the urban area.

There is so much overlap between the eight diagnostic housing variables examined in the full analysis that clearly there was need to summarize

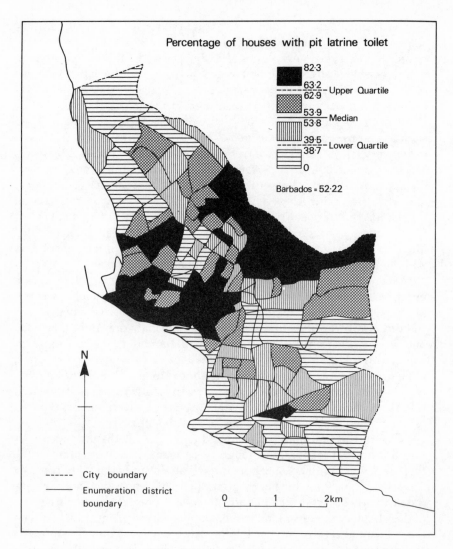

Figure 5.3. The proportion of housing constructed of wood in Bridgetown.

the complex associations existing among them. Accordingly, the summary method of principal components analysis was applied to these data. The results derived are summarized in Tables 5.2 and 5.3. Turning first to Table 5.2, the highest correlation, significantly, was recorded between the percentage of houses constructed of wood in enumeration districts

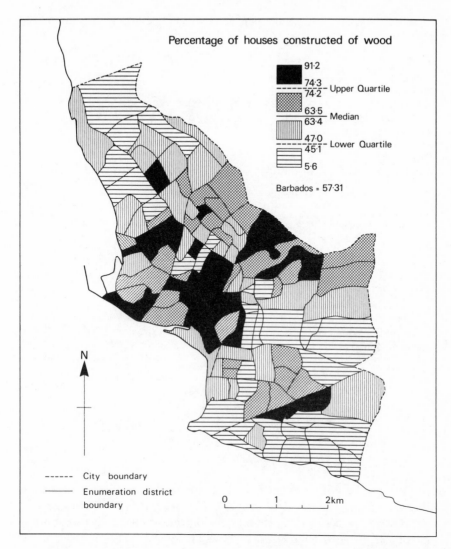

Percentage of houses constructed of wood

91·2

74·3
——
74·2 Upper Quartile

63·5
——
63·4 Median

47·0
——
45·1 Lower Quartile

5·6

Barbados = 57·31

N

- - - - - - City boundary

———— Enumeration district boundary

0   1   2km

Figure 5.4.   The proportion of houses with pit latrines in Bridgetown.

and the proportion making use of a pit latrine (+0.91). Other high correlations were recorded between gas as a cooking fuel and electricity for lighting (+0.84), the percentage of houses using electricity for lighting and the proportion dependent upon public standpipes for the provision of water (−0.73), and the percentage of houses owned and separate houses (0.72).

Table 5.2. Matrix of correlations between the eight housing variables for the 121 enumeration districts making up Greater Bridgetown

Variable	SP	SH	O	X	W	PL	EL	GC
Public standpipe (SP)	1.00							
Separate houses (SH)	0.16	1.00						
Owned (O)	−0.25	0.72	1.00					
Built before 1960 (X)	0.37	−0.08	−0.25	1.00				
Constructed of wood (W)	0.52	0.69	0.31	0.13	1.00			
Pit latrine (PL)	0.48	0.69	0.36	0.07	0.91	1.00		
Electric lighting (EL)	−0.73	−0.20	0.21	−0.29	−0.59	−0.56	1.00	
Gas for cooking (GC)	−0.65	−0.26	0.10	−0.22	−0.67	−0.68	0.84	1.00

Table 5.3. The loadings of the original housing variables on the three components derived

Component 1: Chattel housing 50.3%		Component 2: Ownership/amenity 26.9%	
Constructed of Wood	0.91	Owned	0.90
Pit latrine	0.90	Separate houses	0.69
Gas for cooking	−0.85	Built before 1960	−0.51
Electric lighting	−0.81	Public standpipe	−0.46
Public standpipe	0.73	Electric lighting	0.42

Components 3: Age of housing
10.1%

Built before 1960   0.81

We can now look at the actual results of the principal components analysis, as summarized in Table 5.3. The original variables loading on the first component summarizing housing conditions in Barbados are of particular interest. High levels of housing constructed of wood, the use of pit latrines and public standpipes are all strongly positively correlated with the first component extracted. On the other hand, the proportion of houses making use of gas for cooking and electricity for lighting are strongly negatively associated with it. In other words, the first major component of residential variability is a clear reflection of the chattel-housing system, and thereby summarizes most effectively areas suffering from poor housing conditions. In contrast, component 2 emerges as a composite index of house ownership and amenity, whilst component 3 is an index of housing age.

Mapping the scores of the enumeration districts on component 1

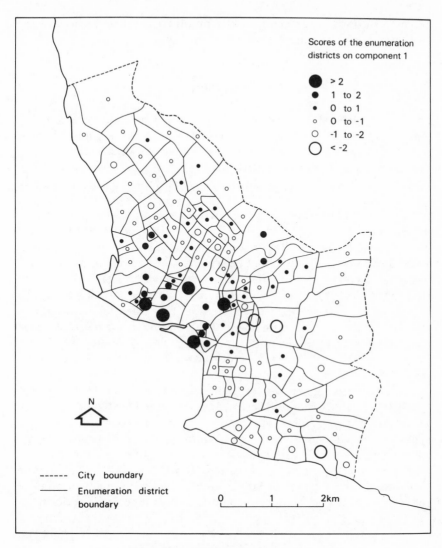

Figure 5.5.   Scores on component 1.

provides an excellent summary measure of present-day housing quality
in the metropolitan zone (Figure 5.5). Component 1 as a measure of chattle-
style housing not only picks out all of the enumeration districts which
face problems of housing disamenity relating to the historical housing
processes described in the first half of the chapter, it also serves to suggest
their relative order of seriousness. Once more, the former plantation
tenantries and present-day urban tenantry zones of the northern, western

and eastern portions of the inner city and the extreme periphery of the eastern urban zone are highlighted by the analysis.

Conclusion

This chapter has set out to show how poor housing conditions today in the urban zones of Barbados – as indeed in the rural districts – largely reflect the interplay of the land tenure system, the vernacular architectural form and the constraints that these institutional forces have served to place on a low-income population which has long since been generally convinced of the virtues of spontaneous self-help. It is possible to suggest that this has led to a real mismatch between housing quality and economic development in contemporary Barbados. Postwar developments in the invited industrial sector (Potter, 1981) and in the field of tourism (Potter, 1983), however much they may be seen by some as representing mixed blessings, have resulted in Barbados's emergence as an MDC (More Developed Country), along with Trinidad, Jamaica and Guyana in the region during the post-independence era. On the other hand, as a direct result of the factors elaborated here, it is tempting to suggest that, overall, Barbados currently exhibits a relatively poor standard of housing, especially when judged in relation to Less Developed Countries of the Eastern Caribbean.

Finally, thinking in wider terms, the case of Barbados illustrates only too well something that all those concerned with Third World housing would do well to remember. Specifically, housing problems are not entirely synonymous with squatter settlements and shanty towns (Potter, 1985). Rather, present-day housing conditions are only to be fully understood with reference to the history of varnacular architecture, the land tenure system and other aspects of the socio-legal and economic evolution of societies as a whole during the colonial and post-colonial periods.

REFERENCES

Abrams, C. (1964) *Housing in the Modern World: Man's Struggle for Shelter in an Urbanizing World*. London: Faber and Faber.

Berthelot, J. and Gaume, M. (1982) *Kaz Antiye (Caribbean Popular Dwelling)*. Pointe-à-Pitre, Guadeloupe: Éditions Perspectives Créoles.

Burgess, R. (1982) 'Self-help housing advocacy a curious form of radicalism: a critique of the work of J. F. C. Turner', in: Ward, P. M. (ed.) *Self-Help Housing: A Critique*. London: Mansell.

Conway, D. (1985) 'Changing perspectives on squatter settlements, intraurban mobility, and constraints on housing choice of the Third World urban poor'. *Urban Geography*, 6, 170–92.

Edwards, J.D. (1980) 'The evolution of vernacular architecture in the western Caribbean', in: Wilkersen, S.J.K. (ed.) *Cultural Traditions and Caribbean Identity: the Question of Patrimony*, Gainesville, Florida: Center for Latin American Studies.

Fraser, H.S. and Hughes R. (1982) *Historic Houses of Barbados: A Collection of Drawings, with Historical and Architectural Notes*, St Michael, Barbados: Barbados National Trust.

Jones, A. (1987): 'The housing experience of Barbados'. *Cities*, 4, 52-7.

Lewis, O. (1959) *Five Families: Mexican Case Studies in the Culture of Poverty*. New York: Basic Books.

Lewis, O. (1966) 'The culture of poverty'. *Scientific American*, 215, 19-25.

Mangin, W. (1967) 'Latin American squatter settlements: a problem and a solution'. *Latin American Research Review*, 2, 65-98.

Potter, R.B. (1981) 'Industrial development and urban planning in Barbados'. *Geography*, 66, 225-8.

Potter, R.B. (1983a): 'Urban development, planning and demographic change 1970-80 in Barbados'. *Caribbean Geography*, 1, 3-12.

Potter, R.B. (1983b) 'Tourism and development: the case of Barbados, West Indies'. *Geography*, 68, 48-50.

Potter, R.B. (1984) 'Spatial perceptions and public involvement in Third World urban planning: the example of Barbados'. *Singapore Journal of Tropical Geography*, 5, 30-44.

Potter, R.B. (1985) *Urbanisation and Planning in the Third World: Spatial Perceptions and Public Participation*, London and New York: Croom Helm and St Martin's Press.

Potter, R.B. (1986a): 'Housing upgrading in Barbados: the tenantries programme', *Geography*, 71, 255-7.

Potter, R.B. (1986b) 'Spatial inequalities in Barbados, West Indies'. *Transactions of the Institute of British Geographers*, new series, 11, 183-98.

Potter, R.B. (1987) 'Housing in Barbados: good, bad or beautiful?', *The New Bajan*, 1, 26-34.

Potter, R.B. and Dann, G.M.S. (1987) *Barbados, World Bibliographical Series*, No. 76. Oxford: Clio Press.

Potter, R.B. and Potter, V. (1988) *Barbados, Let's Visit Series*. Basingstoke: Macmillan.

Stokes, C. (1962) 'A theory of slums'. *Land Economics*, 38, 187-97.

Slesin, S., Cliff, S., Berthelot, J., Gaume, M. and Rozensztroch, D. (1986) *Caribbean Style*. London: Thames and Hudson.

Turner, J.F.C. (1967) 'Barriers and channels for housing development in modernizing countries'. *Journal of the American Institute of Planners*, 33, 167-81.

Turner, J.F.C. (1968) 'Housing priorities, settlements patterns and urban development in modernizing countries'. *Journal of the American Institute of Planners*, 34, 354-63.

Turner, J.F.C. (1976) *Housing by People: Towards Autonomy in Building Environments*. London: Marian Boyers.

Turner, J.F.C. (1982) 'Issues in self-help and self-managed housing', ch. 4 in: Ward, P.M. (ed.) *Self-Help Housing: A Critique*. London: Mansell.

[6]

Self-Help in Fiji: Squatter Housing and Informal Employment as Responses to Poverty

Jenny J. Bryant

Introduction

The urbanization experiences of Fiji in the past decade have been little different from those of other developing countries. An urban housing shortage is reflected not only in the increasing number of squatter settlements and pirate subdivisions, but also in their intensification (Bryant, 1989). Households are becoming increasingly overcrowded as families let and sublet rooms to others in an attempt to obtain further income. In addition, with more difficult economic circumstances, high unemployment and a decline in real incomes, people are increasingly searching for alternative sources of income and thus the informal employment sector is expanding.

This chapter examines the presence of urban poverty in Fiji and two responses to it: the phenomenon of squatter renting (in particular, the subletting of rooms within squatter households), and the increasing diversification of the household economy into both formal and informal activities in order to provide people with a reasonable standard of living. The account is based partly on a survey carried out in 1986, the detailed results of which have already been published (Bryant, 1989), and partly on a further survey carried out in mid-1989 for which the analysis is still preliminary. The chapter does not include all the statistics gathered to date; nor will it attempt to provide a definitive history of Fiji or lengthy theoretical 'explanations' for poverty and possible responses. Instead it provides a preliminary discussion of the changing nature of the urban employment scene in Fiji. A detailed and lengthy analysis will be presented at a later date.

Housing Demand, Supply and Quality

As in other Third World countries, housing demand in Fiji far outstrips supply. By 1977, 8,702 urban households, or 21 per cent of urban households, were on the waiting list of the Fiji Housing Authority, the statutory body which provides housing for low-income workers. By 1982 the size of the waiting list was almost halved, largely because people had tired of waiting and found alternatives. But by 1988 the waiting list had again reached around 8,000 (Fiji Housing Authority, 1988, pers. comm.).

As the population of Fiji has become increasingly urbanized, there has been a tendency towards the establishment of more and smaller households. In 1976 there were 97,509 households in Fiji, and by 1986 124,323, an increase of 27.5 per cent. Average household size fell from 6.0 to 5.8 in the same period. One of the impacts of declining household size and the increase in numbers has been an increase in the demand for housing.

The 1977 Household Income and Expenditure Survey summarized the housing conditions of the Fiji population at the time as:

> 60% of urban households . . . in single-unit dwellings, 30% in flats and 10% in shacks, bures,[1] or temporary structures. Half of the homes were constructed primarily of concrete, a third wood, 13% corrugated iron and the remaining 7% less substantial bures or shacks. (Fiji Central Planning Office, 1980: 230)

By 1986 the census showed that 30.4 per cent of homes were constructed of tin or corrugated iron, and although there is some doubt over the accuracy of the housing statistics in that census it appears that housing conditions for the population of Fiji are worsening. The squatter settlements of the major towns are no exception.

Housing for the Poor

The term 'squatter' is used loosely in Fiji to include all spontaneous or informal settlements which have substandard and unauthorized structures and which lack basic services. It does not apply only to those households occupying land illegally. Using this broad definition, it is estimated that somewhere between 12 and 20 per cent of the population of Suva, the capital city, were squatters in the late 1970s (Walsh, 1984: 185; Suva City Council, 1983: 2). Other cities such as Lautoka, Ba and Labasa also have sizeable squatter populations. The exact figures are difficult to measure accurately, but, most importantly, the squatter population has been estimated as increasing at more than 500 households a year in Suva alone (Fiji Central Planning Office, 1980: 232).

By 1986 a Suva City Council survey showed that one out of every eight people living in Suva was a squatter. Of these, 5,349 (56.7 per cent) were Indian, 3,733 (39.6 per cent) Fijian and the remaining 348 of other races. These figures demonstrate a slight increase in the proportion of Fijian squatters since 1983 and a corresponding decline in the Indian proportion. Squatters in Suva live in twenty-six locations, largely sited 3–5 km away from central Suva. Some of the areas, such as Jittu Estate, the Muslim League and Deo Dutt, are well settled, having been in existence for more than fifteen years, and have the air of established suburbs with gardens, backyard industries and sometimes service connections. Not all have such amenities, however, and both the new and the old settlements are showing increasing overcrowding, demonstrated in the expansion of subletting of rooms within the dwellings (Bryant, 1989).

With more difficult economic circumstances, high unemployment and a decline in real incomes, it is likely that squatting will increase and perhaps demonstrate conditions which are more marginal than at present, with increased pressure on basic services and on living space. The response of the urban dwellers to the economic pressures of the 1980s has largely been in the informal sector – not only in housing, but also in informal employment. The increasing number of fresh food stalls, yaqona sellers, grass cutters, bottle collectors and so on has been obvious in the main towns, particularly in Suva, in the past two to three years.

While Fiji had been considered a relatively fortunate country, both economically and socially, it is clear that even before the military coups and consequent economic disturbances of 1987 there were many aspects of daily life and basic needs which required greater attention. What to do about housing the low-income groups is of major concern. The key provider of housing for the low-income groups is the Fiji Housing Authority, although there are also church-based organizations such as the Housing and Relief Trust (HART) and the Bayly Foundation which attempt to house and assist destitutes. The Fiji Housing Authority is having considerable difficulty meeting the demand, partly because of its limited budget, its detachment from the real concerns of tenants, land shortage, and the inability of people to pay for the housing which they have been allocated. From 1980 to 1985, for instance, the Housing Authority achieved only 28 per cent of its rental scheme target, 49.3 per cent of its home purchase plan/loan scheme and 35 per cent of its rural housing scheme (Fiji Central Planning Office, 1985: 128). Recent discussions between the Fiji Housing Authority and the World Bank about self-help building schemes for people earning less than F$75 per week may result in major housing schemes beginning in Fiji, but it remains to be seen whether or not those most in need will be the ones who benefit from these schemes.

Subletting as a Response to Poverty

An earlier paper examined the increasing incidence of letting and subletting in urban squatter settlements in Fiji and in particular one area known as the Muslim League settlement in Suva (Bryant, 1989). In that study the extent of the practice of subletting was evaluated, as well as its importance in terms of rental income. Such an evaluation was timely since a great deal of ill-informed prominence is often given by the media to people living in squatter settlements. Publicity given to squatting in Fiji sometimes focuses upon the fact that certain groups of squatters are exploiting even poorer groups in order to pay off their assets of a house and land elsewhere.

In the earlier survey an attempt was made to discover how rental income was spent and what proportion of the weekly income of landlords and tenants was constituted by received rent. Whether or not the money involved was significant, and could be regarded as exploitative, was an important aspect of the survey. The results demonstrated, in fact, that while there was little evidence of exploitation by 'landlords' of subtenants, the money earned was certainly assisting squatter landlords to live a slightly more comfortable life than would otherwise have been possible (Bryant, 1989).

In a more recent survey of the household economy in urban Suva and Labasa, it was found that involvement in alternative methods of earning income (including letting out rooms to other families) was such a normal practice and involved people from all sections of the community, in the full range of housing conditions and occupational status and income earned, that it is virtually impossible to state whether or not people are exploiting one another for gain. It seemed, from the recent survey, that an apparent decline in living standards has prompted a widespread response from the entire population and that subletting and informal-sector employment are to be found in most households, whether 'poor' or not.

The expansion of squatter settlements has been characteristic of Fijian towns since the 1950s, but it is too simplistic to equate squatting with absolute poverty. Poverty is to be found everywhere, and probably more commonly in rural areas than in urban ones. In rural society Bayliss-Smith et al. (1988: 112–13) cited examples of inequality in land distribution, poverty caused by age and sickness, the lack of material goods, and households below the 'poverty line' in many more incidences than might be expected in a society where social networks are theoretically intended to ensure that such things do not occur. Such differences in Fijian society have complex historical roots as well as the obvious and modern causes such as colonialism, capitalism and the like. A number of writers have commented on these inequalities (Durutalo, 1986; Overton, 1989; Sutherland, 1984). But Fiji as a nation, at the same time as it undergoes an economic transition which includes a 12 per cent economic growth rate in the past few months, associated with a boom in tax-free manufacturing zones, is also facing worsening overall poverty as the effects of declining world sugar prices and a major increase in the cost of living are felt.

There has been no systematic survey of poverty in Fiji, although 15 per cent of the population is thought to be suffering acute deprivation (Cameron, 1983: 488). One of the aims of this chapter is to demonstrate whether or not it is poverty which is forcing urban people to turn to alternative (often informal) employment, and to squat in increasing numbers and to sublet rooms in a variety of housing types, including squatter settlements. The suggestion is made that the subletting of rooms in both squatter and other households, as well as increasing participation in multiple-employment activities, are the inevitable attempts at survival by landlords and tenants alike in the face of increasing social inequalities.

The Muslim League Survey

The earlier paper referred to (Bryant, 1989) examined the phenomenon of subletting in the 22-hectare Muslim League settlement off Ratu Mara Road in Samabula, Suva. At the time of the survey there remained 178 squatter structures on the Muslim League site as counted by the Suva City Council in 1983, with a population of 1,162, and a household density of 6.5 persons per structure. Although the people are not strictly squatters in the sense that they have the permission of the Muslim League to be there, the term is used to indicate that the settlement is informal, and that a number of the structures do not have adequate facilities, although all had access to cooking facilities, water and sewerage.

A number of the Muslim League households are supplementing their incomes by letting and subletting rooms, but those interviewed claimed that the money received was for day-to-day survival. It was demonstrated that the average weekly income from subletting in 1986 (when the survey was carried out) was around F$7.50 per week, which represents a significant addition to the average per capita weekly wage in Fiji ($34.60 in 1986) (Bryant, 1989). It would certainly appear from the amount of upgrading carried out on the homes, as well as the number of additional homes owned elsewhere and the proportion of weekly income which rent contributes, that subletting is important in enabling people to improve their lifestyles, something which might not otherwise be possible in an urban, squatting situation.

A high degree of letting and subletting in squatter housing is one response to poverty, but there are many others, particularly in the nature of employment and in the multiple sources of income found in many urban homes.

Household Income and Employment

In July 1989 a survey was carried out in two urban centres of Fiji, Suva and Labasa. Instead of looking at only one means of avoiding poverty, that of taking in subtenants (lodgers) as reported in Bryant (1989), it was decided to look at the situation of low-income earners in all forms of housing. Using involvement in informal-sector employment as the means of finding respondents, 120 households were interviewed in depth about their overall economic situation, including income, expenditure and employment patterns.

It was known that per capita income in Fiji had fallen by 13 per cent since 1987 (the time of the military coups), that the cost of living had increased, and that the Fiji dollar had been devalued by 30 per cent, (although it has subsequently strengthened). With these factors in mind, it was assumed that the standard of living in Fiji had deteriorated, and that increased pressures may have caused a change in the nature of the informal sector as well as forcing more people to participate, since there had been an increase in unemployment since the military coups.

The changing nature of the informal sector in urban Fiji is obvious. The typical roadside fruit and vegetable vendors and women doing domestic work continue, but there is an increase in other, less 'traditional' urban informal activities. Sales of drugs (largely marijuana) have increased, illegal black marketing of beer has become more widespread, and there is evidence of increasing numbers of both male and female prostitutes throughout the urban areas. Backyard garages, carrying out skilled motor vehicle and other home repairs, have always existed in a small way, but their numbers appear to have expanded, as have sales of grocery and other items directly from home, for example cigarettes, yaqona (*Piper methysticum*)[2] and canned food, with associated pirate video rentals. The number of children out of school and working on the streets begging, collecting newspapers, bottles and food from rubbish cans and dumps, as well as more common occupations such as selling cooked peas and peanuts, has also increased.

Bearing in mind the changed nature of the informal sector, a hundred households in the capital of Fiji, Suva, and twenty in the capital of the northern division, Labasa, were interviewed concerning their total household economy. In Suva, households were selected from a range of housing types, from public Housing Authority rental homes (for low-income earners), from housing for the destitute operated by HART, squatter settlements (including the Muslim League estate studied earlier in the survey of subletting), as well as people in poor-quality, low-cost private rental housing in the inner city. In Labasa the interviewees were either in Housing Authority homes or on small nearby subsistence farms. Those living in their own homes were people who had purchased from the Housing Authority and are thus underrepresented compared with the 1986 census (Table 6.1).

Table 6.1.   The housing status of the respondents

| Status | 1989 survey respondents | | 1986 census |
	No.	%	%
Rent	22	18.3	17.5
Housing Authority	35	29.2	5.5
Own home	22	18.3	56.7
Squatting	37	30.8	2.7
Village	2	1.7	—
Other	2	1.7	—

The overall results of the survey were unexpected, given that the aim was to discover how poorer households were coping with the economic downturn. Although households were not particularly well off, they were generally not very poor either, indicating that those with opportunities to work in both the formal and informal sectors in urban areas generally survive very well. More particularly, it would seem that those *already* working in informal employment have access to opportunities in the Suva urban centre. Table 6.2 summarizes some of the wider characteristics of the households included in the sample.

Findings on Poverty

First, although the majority of households have people in casual employment (103 out of 120, or 85.8 per cent), they also have people in formal employment (85 out of 120, or 70.8 per cent) and are therefore not entirely dependent upon the vagaries and uncertainties of non-formal employment. The average annual total income of these households was F$6,674.20,[3] and the average household weekly income F$128.35 (Table 6.3). This is below the purported average income of US$1,800 for Fiji as a whole in 1986 (Cole and Hughes, 1988: 141), but, given that the survey was dealing with the apparently poorest group and not the entire population, that figure has little meaning. In this survey, forty-four of the households (37 per cent) were earning above the average wage.

Table 6.2. Household characteristics

N = 120 households

74 Indo-Fijian households (61.7%) = 406 people (5.7 per house)
(5.1 in 1986 census = in urban dwellings)

45 Fijian households (37.5%) = 267 people (5.4 per house)
(6.2 in census = in urban dwellings)

1 other household (0.8%) = 8 people

Range of household size = 1 – 12
Average house size (mean) = 5.7
Population variation = 4.68
Standard deviation = 2.17
Average length of residence = 10 years

1986 census: Indo-Fijian = 48.7% (note that they represent 51.4% of housing authority tenants and squatters).

Fijian = 46.0% (Fijians represent 41.5% of Housing Authority tenants and squatters in 1986)

Other = 5.3% (Rotuman 1.2%)

Table 6.3. Household income, Suva household survey, July 1989

	F$
Average weekly household income	128.35
Average annual household income	6,674.20
Average per capita weekly income	22.62
Average per capita annual income	1,356.08

Average weekly income for a Fijian household is F$133, and for an Indo-Fijian is F$113.

Instead of dealing with average incomes, it was decided to attempt to define a poverty line for urban households in Fiji. A poverty line based on cash income alone is obviously not relevant in a society where the majority of households have gardens. In fact, the majority – 87 out of 120, or 72.5 per cent – have a garden at home or not far away, and a proportion of weekly income is in the form of food or clothing remittances from relatives in villages or overseas. Nevertheless, there have been some attempts in Fiji to define a 'poverty line', generally including an assessment of nutrition and access to non-cash items.

Cameron's (1983) report to the Fiji Employment Mission, based on the 1977 Household Income and Expenditure Survey, which defined three poverty lines based on adequate nutrition and cash requirements for non-food items, noted that 7,800 households in Fiji were living below 'poverty line' levels (1983: 3). (Forty per cent, or 3,100, of these households were in villages, where they comprised 13 per cent of total of village households.) Using the Fiji Household Income and Expenditure Survey income levels, Cameron found that a larger group of households were found to be 'vulnerable' or at risk of poverty. These are households 'which in 1977 had insufficient cash incomes to sustain cash-equivalent consumption at the poverty line' (Cameron, 1983: 4). Fifteen per cent of Fiji households fell into this group, widely spread among ethnic and social groups as well as geographically. For 1982, Cameron assumed the poverty line to be F$45 per week for a family of six (F$10 per week for an adult). More households in poverty are in rural areas, and more in villages than elsewhere. In urban areas, households in poverty were on average 23 per cent below their poverty line (1983: 10). Indians and Fijians are in a similar position in urban areas. This contrasts with the rural areas, where more Fijians are in poverty, but not as deeply because of redistributive mechanisms. Cameron noted also that the redistributive mechanisms of Fijian villages do not bring equality, but rather a 'floor of hardship' (1983: 11, quoted by Bayliss-Smith et al., 1988: 113).

In the present author's survey, conducted in July 1989, fourteen households were found to be below a cash poverty line (11.7 per cent of the total), which is F$63.10 per week for an average of six people per household.[4] Ten households were considered to be vulnerable. There was a difference in the level of poverty between the two major races in Fiji. Although 20 per cent of all households were found to be below that defined poverty line, 21.3 per cent of Indians and 17.8 per cent of Fijians are in poverty or in a vulnerable situation (Table 6.4). Seventy of the 120 households received 'in-kind' contributions of cash or food from other relatives, but six households living in poverty did not receive anything. Of those in poverty or vulnerable who did receive additional income, all except two were not receiving enough to carry them over the 'poverty line'.

Table 6.4. Number of respondents falling below the poverty line

	Poverty*	Vulnerable*	Total
Indo-Fijian	9	7	16
Fijian	5	3	8
Total	14	10	24

Income and Expenditure

A significant proportion of income earned by these households was from informal-sector activities (Table 6.5), averaging 40.9 per cent of weekly

Table 6.5.   Income sources of the residents

A. Weekly

	No. of cases	Av. p.w. (F$)
Selling goods	84	56.80
Performing services	26	56.90
Other casual activities	17	42.12
Wage/salary	81	92.80
Business	3	90.80
Rent from property	3	17.50
Government (welfare) allowance	4	11.90
Other	4	145.00

B. Annual

	No. of cases	Av. p.w. (F$)
Bank or credit union interest	17	21.00
Insurance	1	00.21
Timber royalties	1	00.83
Lease payments	2	01.40
Education scholarships	11	10.60
Remittances	16	39.00
Other	7	64.80

income. There is a difference between the races: Indians earn (on average) 46.1 per cent of their income from informal activities, and Fijians 31.8 per cent.

In exposure to unemployment since 1987, in fifty-nine of the 120 households someone had lost his or her job in the previous two years (49.2 per cent), and only five of those are not now involved in the informal sector (three Indian and two Fijian). Jobs lost were largely in the unskilled-labour group (eleven or 18.6 per cent), in the building industry, transport and communications, and skilled trades (ten each, or 17 per cent). Of the fifty-nine who lost employment, forty (67.8 per cent) were Indian (but 54 per cent of those surveyed), and nineteen (32.2 per cent) were Fijian (42 per cent of the total surveyed), indicating a higher likelihood of unemployment for Indo-Fijians.

It is clear from these preliminary findings that people are finding life difficult, but they have also found ways of coping. More than 50 per cent of those interviewed had other sources of income, and the majority claimed to make only minimal contributions to traditional obligations such as the temple, church, funerals, etc. in order to avoid going into debt.[5] An unexpected eighty-six of the 120 households (71.7 per cent) claim to save money. Fifty of these were Indo-Fijian (67.6 per cent of

Indo-Fijians surveyed, and thirty-six were Fijian (80 per cent). The higher proportion of ethnic Fijians saving money is contrary to the popular expectations of the ability of Fijians to succeed and is particularly interesting given that those interviewed for this survey were chosen because they were likely to be poor, living in informal and low-cost housing and at least partially dependent upon informal employment.

Expenditure patterns give further support to the ethnic differential in poverty, income, and employment (see Notes, Table 6.6). Mean weekly household expenditure is F$71.90, with most being spent on food (F$40.18, or 56.1 per cent) (Table 6.6). Bayliss-Smith *et al.* (1988: 109–10), support this finding. They discuss a survey of retail prices (1974/6 and 1982/3), where it was found that 25 per cent of expenditure went on carbohydrates (rice, flour, biscuit), and 10 per cent went on each of the categories tinned fish, cigarettes, sugar and beverages. More than 60 per cent of expenditure went on these basic items.

Findings

Although it was not intended that this research would focus on ethnic differentials in poverty, some very clear differences were noted. Ethnic Fijians do not appear to be so clearly in poverty in urban areas, but there are obvious differences between and within households which will be examined in more detail elsewhere at a later stage. Life is harder for all, but is more unstable for some Indo-Fijians, particularly when the incidence of unemployment and participation in formal employment are considered (Table 6.7). To regard all Indo-Fijians as poor, or vulnerable, is a mis-

Table 6.6.   Weekly household expenditure

	F$	%
Food	40.18	50.4
Services	14.79	18.6
Entertainment	9.39	11.8
Rent	4.30	5.4
School fees	2.89	3.6
Traditional obligations	2.63	3.3
Other (clothes, building, etc.)	5.50	6.9
Total	79.68	100.0

Notes:
1. Average weekly Indo-Fijian expenditure is F$88.81 (58.5% on food).
2. Average weekly Fijian expenditure is F$46.62 (52.4% on food).

Table 6.7. Employment of household heads

	Total %	Indo-Fijian No. (%)	Fijian No. (%)
Informal	34.2	28 (37.8)	13 (28.9)
Formal empl. (govt)	23.3	13 (17.6)	15 (33.3)
Formal empl. (private)	21.7	13 (17.6)	13 (28.9)
Own business	0.9	1 (1.3)	—
Casual worker	8.3	6 (8.1)	3 (6.7)
Unemployed	8.3	9 (12.2)	1 (2.2)
Retired	3.3	4 (5.4)	
Total	100	74 (100)	45 (100)

conception. As everywhere else in the world, there are obvious variations in lifestyle, income and expectations which could be attributed to 'class'. I have avoided the use of this term because there is no single (or simple) explanation for variations within society.

What is happening in Fiji today is partly a continuation of recent trends (including global economic trends), but is also inextricably bound up with historical events, laws and practices. Fiji in the late 1980s is not wholly a product of recent political events (which undoubtedly developed out of processes started generations ago), although these have certainly accelerated the processes. The ethnic differentials cannot of course be explained by global economic trends, and while it is true that more Indo-Fijians have lost their jobs recently, they are also to be found more prominently in the wealthier group. Fijians are not so clearly well-off, or badly-off, in urban areas.

It is suggested that this work on poverty indicates the need for a comparative study of rural and urban fringe settlements before any real conclusions can be drawn. In urban areas people have more opportunities for alternative income sources and can readily become involved in petty trading, repair or service activities to supplement household incomes which frequently derive, at least partly, from formal employment for one or two family members. Such opportunities are not so easy to find in rural areas.

Poverty certainly exists in the urban areas of Fiji but it seems not to be of the grinding nature commonly found in other developing nations. Close examination of urban villages and rural areas will surely show that quite severe poverty exists; and this will be the focus of the continuation of this research project.

NOTES

1. *Bure* is the Fijian word for a house, although not one used by a private family. It is more commonly used to denote accommodation for single men or strangers, and often as living quarters for domestic workers.
2. *Yaqona (Piper methysticum)* is the non-alcoholic root of the pepper plant. It is drunk on ceremonial occasions and commonly presented by Fijians in times of obligations, visits or requests. In addition it is widely drunk by both Indo-Fijians and ethnic Fijians as a social beverage.
3. One Fiji dollar was worth US$0.68 in mid-1989.
4. A cash-only poverty line for 1989 was devised by adding annual inflation for the years 1983–1988 to the 1982 poverty line of F$45 per week.
5. This claim needs to be tested further, however, since the degree of participation in traditional activities appears not to have declined generally. It is likely that it is simply difficult to assess, as requests arise at unexpected times.

REFERENCES

Bayliss-Smith, T., Bedford, R., Brookfield, H. and Latham, M., with Brookfield, M. (1988) *Islands, Islanders and the World: The Colonial and Post-Colonial Experience of Eastern Fiji*. Cambridge: Cambridge University Press.

Bryant, J.J. (1989) 'The acceptable face of self-help housing: subletting in Fiji squatter settlements – exploitation or survival strategy?' in: Drakakis-Smith, D.W. (ed.) *Economic Growth and Urbanisation in Developing Areas*. London: Routledge, 171–95.

Cameron, J. (1983) *The Extent and Structure of Poverty in Fiji and Possible Elements of a Government Anti-Poverty Strategy in the 1980s*, Working Paper No. 19, Suva: Fiji Employment and Development Mission.

Cole, R. and Hughes, H. (1988) *The Fiji Economy, May 1987: Problems and Prospects*, Pacific Policy Papers No. 4, Canberra: National Centre for Development Studies, Australian National University.

Durutalo, S. (1986) *The Paramountcy of Fijian Interest and the Politicization of Ethnicity*, South Pacific Forum Working Paper No. 6. Suva: University of the South Pacific Sociological Society.

Fiji Bureau of Statistics (1986) *Census of Population*, Bulletin No. 27. Suva: Census Office.

Fiji Central Planning Office (1980) *Eighth Development Plan 1981–1985*, Vol. 1: *Policies and Programmes for Social and Economic Development*. Suva: Central Planning Office.

Fiji Central Planning Office (1985) *Fiji's Ninth Development Plan, 1986–1990. Policies, Strategies and Programmes for National Development*. Suva: Central Planning Office.

Overton, J. (1989) *Land and Differentiation in Rural Fiji*, Pacific Research Monograph No. 19. Canberra: National Centre for Development Studies, Australian National University.

Sutherland, W.M. (1984). 'The state and capitalist development in Fiji'. Unpublished Ph.D. thesis, University of Canterbury, Christchurch.

Suva City Council (1983) *Report of a Survey of Unauthorised Structures ('Squatter Settlements') within the City of Suva.* Suva: Suva City Council.

Walsh, A. C. (1984) 'The search for an appropriate housing policy in Fiji'. *Third World Planning Review,* 6(2): 185–200.

[7]

Food for Thought or Thought about Food: Urban Food Distribution Systems in the Third World

David Drakakis-Smith

Introduction

Until relatively recently Charles Abrams (1964) spoke for many social scientists in describing food, shelter and clothing as the three most basic of human needs. With the emergence of the oil and fuelwood crises of the 1970s, however, it became clear that this was a Eurocentric interpretation. In most Third World countries clothing received a much lower priority within poor households than the need to find fuel for lighting, heating and cooking (Soussan, 1988). In some ways this justifiable concern with energy issues has masked the fact that food is still the most fundaental requirement of individuals and that most activities of the household unit are structured around its acquisition, preparation and consumption. Indeed, personal and societal mores are often closely connected with dietary patterns.

In any examination of the systems which make available this basic need, the household must constitute a major investigative focus. While the international and national production and distribution of food are undoubtedly important, their full impact on the poor can only be studied at the household level: this is the key decision-making unit with regard to the accumulation and allocation of resources; this is the most appropriate unit for assessing the social issues involved (such as differing gender roles and rewards); this is the point at which surplus value is extracted (via household incomes, expenditure, etc.); and, above all, this is the level at which food (and shelter or energy) problems become most apparent and immediate.

It is the broad objective of this chapter to review some aspects of the food distribution systems that affect the urban poor in the Third World and how these have changed in recent years. However, this is not an easy or straightforward task as material on urban food distribution systems is limited. Despite the pre-eminence of food as the most basic household need, it has received far less attention than housing in the literature on development, particularly from the radical school of analysts. Although there have been studies (discussed below) which have emphasized the commodification of the food system, few have extended their discussion to the household level.

One of the more readily identifiable measures of the importance of food to the low-income household lies in expenditure patterns. Much of the material available in this context comes indirectly from research which has other objectives, but most estimates put the average proportion of the household budget spent on food at somewhere between 50 and 60 per cent of the total. Clearly there will be large variations around this figure but even in affluent Singapore, for example, some 45 per cent of the household budget goes on food (Cheng, 1982). In poorer countries the proportion is much higher; in urban Bangladesh it reaches almost two-thirds of household expenditure where debts permit. Within cities there is an even wider range and it is not unusual to find the poorest families being forced to devote more than three-quarters of their income to food purchases (Drakakis-Smith and Kivell, 1989).

However, these data reveal only part of the picture, for even in urban areas many households still provide at least a proportion of their own food needs through cultivation. Such urban subsistence will be discussed in more detail below, but it must be noted at this point that in general it is of diminishing importance (although this varies substantially within the urban hierarchy and between countries). As other pressures on land remove the space available for cultivation, so the poor are forced into the commercial sector for food. Here there are two contrasting supply systems. The first comprises the petty-commodity sector which, as with all such activities, is organized not only to supply food to low-income households, but also to meet the demands of the urban market for a range of low-cost items, such as staples or fresh fruit and vegetables. Second, there is the capitalist sector which usually comprises a combination of domestic and (increasingly) international interests involved in all aspects of the supply system, viz. production, processing, distribution and retailing. Finally, it must be noted that urban food systems not only encompass the supply of fresh or processed foods but also include cooked foods, an area in which international capitalism is becoming increasingly involved, particularly through fast-food outlets.

The various components constitute a complex system (Figure 7.1) and this chapter presents an overview of its major constituents, using some of the limited illustrative material available. As will be evident, much more work needs to be done to build up a better picture of this important aspect of urban life.

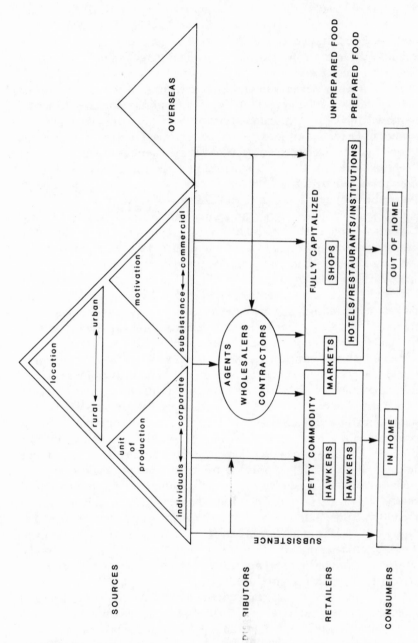

Figure 7.1. The components of urban food systems.

Subsistence Production

There can be no doubt that in recent years interest has expanded rapidly among urban geographers in what might be termed the basic elements of urban survival. As one discussion document reveals, however, most research into food systems has focused upon rural production, exchange and consumption (Dwyer and Williams, 1983). Parallel investigations into the urban components of this system have been few and have tended to focus spatially on large cities, and functionally on urban markets, although there has been increasing attention paid to petty-commodity production and distribution, a point which is discussed below. In little of this work, however, has the importance of urban subsistence production been recognized. Where such production has been uncovered, it is usually merged with petty-commodity production into a rather loosely defined 'informal sector'.

Contrary to popular opinion, there remains considerable evidence of food production in Third World cities, particularly in terms of vegetables, fruit and small livestock. Most urban agriculture is small-scale and intensive and yet can be very successful in meeting the needs of urban residents. W. Skinner (1981, in Yeung, 1988; 81) reports that in several large Chinese cities over 85 per cent of the vegetables consumed are grown within the municipal boundary. However, Chinese cities are notoriously extensive in their administrative areas and encompass what in other countries would be thought of as peri-urban and even outright rural areas. Even so, intensive production can still provide Singapore with 25 per cent of its vegetable needs and almost all of its pork, egg and poultry requirements (Yeung, 1988: 80).

There are, however, several problems with this type of positive analysis, the most important being that not all urban agriculture comprises subsistence production. Indeed, in the Asian cities previously cited, much of the output would be for the commercial market, either through petty- or fully capitalized production systems, and would receive substantial state support. The implication here is that 'subsistence' relates to production and consumption which occurs outside the market economy, a direct production-to-consumption linkage within the household which was considered to be more typical of rural areas, particularly of pre-capitalist systems.

Evers (1983) is one of the few authors to address urban subsistence economies in any great depth. He distinguishes between 'subsistence production for the reproduction of households' (household subsistence reproduction) and the production of living space (habitat subsistence reproduction). The latter is, however, problematic since only habitat reproduction, i.e. cleaning, maintenance, etc., can be properly described as subsistence in nature, since the production of housing is often suffused with petty commodity elements and subsequently acquires exchange value in the process of consumption.

Urban food production which falls into Evers' category of household subsistence reproduction is also difficult to isolate conceptually. Urban households do not survive on subsistence food production. Quite the contrary: subsistence food production is essentially a supplement to food acquired in the market economy. Not surprisingly, it appears to be more important for the poorer households, those located primarily in the petty-commodity sector. Thus Evers (1983) in his studies in Jakarta noted that although the mean contribution to household consumption was just under 18 per cent, this proportion varied inversely with household income as well as relating to the type of employment of the household head.

Accounting for the comparative importance of subsistence food to the household is also complicated by the fact that the household members engaged in its production may undertake several other roles in relation both to production and reproduction. Thus, the growing of crops may be an evening task for schoolchildren, and an after-work activity for adults in the capitalist or petty-capitalist sector of the urban economy. Similarly, although much of the genuinely subsistence food production – that which is directly consumed by the producer household – comes from urban gardens, these may not be owned either in *de jure* or *de facto* terms by the producer. Indeed, most of the evidence available indicates that illegal cultivation is an equally important source of food. Here again, definitions are difficult to produce since all food production within a squatter settlement may be illegal in *de jure* terms, even that within a domestic garden. In other cities communal land may be gardened.

But, above all, it is on the urban periphery where much of the non-household garden food originates. The urban periphery is in itself a complex, changing area (see Drakakis-Smith, 1986; Hill, 1986; Swindell and Sutherland, 1986) which overlaps both municipal and non-municipal land (land which is in the strict legal sense urban and land which is not), and which also contains a full range of food production systems. In general, where population pressures on land resources are greatest there is a tendency for food production, where it exists in the face of speculative activities, to be more market-oriented in nature. But where pressures are less, and traditional values more persistent, subsistence production may well be considerable.

A good illustration of the varied nature of urban subsistence production occurs in Harare, the capital of Zimbabwe (for a lengthier account see Drakakis-Smith and Kivell, 1990). Surveys in three different socio-economic areas of the city (Mabelreign, an ethnically mixed middle-class suburb; Glen View, a government sites-and-service area; Epworth, a squatter settlement) revealed that urban gardens were still very important in the food system. In both Glen View and Mabelreign some four-fifths of those interviewed grew food crops in their gardens, and in Epworth as well, almost all (*de facto*) gardens were used for food production (although only two-thirds had any garden space). In almost all cases the food was consumed by the household itself, rather than sold.

Although only a relatively small proportion of interviewees admitted to cultivating another plot of land (largely because it is illegal), aerial-photographic investigations by Mazambani (1978) have revealed an extensive spread of agriculture in the shallow valleys that characterize the peripheral areas of the city. Ironically agriculture has followed in the wake of the denudation of fuelwood sources, and together these have produced extensive gulley erosion.

The Harare surveys also indicated that the subsistence food consumed in the urban area does not necessarily have urban origins. One-third of the households claimed that they held rights to land outside the city from which they received food crops. Potts (1987) argues that this is a decreasingly important link because of declining numbers (labour) resident on the land. However, in addition to food from their own land, another one-fifth indicated that they received gifts of food (usually maize or vegatables) from family and friends in rural areas in return for periodic labour, processed food or cash gifts.

These latter sources of subsistence food are extremely important, notably for low-income households in the city, and reveal clearly the complex interlinkages that persist even within the subsistence sector alone. Such linkages exist in many cities of the developing world, although increasing commercialization of agriculture in both urban and rural areas has induced rapid change and further complexities as economies develop. It is, therefore, in the relative backwaters of development that urban subsistence can be seen at its most intense, but it is in these areas that research has been thinnest, with the notable exception of Randy Thaman's extensive studies in the Pacific in general, and Fiji in particular. These will be discussed further in the concluding section of this chapter, following a review of the petty-commodity and capitalist sectors of production.

Commercial Supply Systems

The urban food supply systems which can be categorized as commercialized – that is, operating in response to market forces – cover a very wide range of activities and are often interlinked in complex ways. It is not enough simply to identify a formal and informal sector, with all the exclusivity implied by these terms, nor, indeed, to introduce an 'intermediate' category, such as Chinese shophouses in South-East Asia (Guy, 1986).

Most diversity in the commercialized food-supply systems occurs in terms of the original sources of supply and in the retail sales outlet. Both can vary in scale, legality, degree of capitalization and organization from subsistence-surplus/mobile street traders on the one hand, to imported multinational corporation products/chain restaurants/hypermarkets on the other. In contrast, the distribution systems which link sources of supply and retail outlets together are usually highly organized and fully capitalized, irrespective of scale.

Although there has been more work undertaken on the commercial sector of urban food systems (compared to the subsistence), there have been very few fully comprehensive investigations, a deficiency noted by Guy (1986) and Paddison, Findlay and Dawson (1989). One such cluster occurred in the South Pacific in the late 1970s (see Chandra, 1980; Baxter, 1980; Hau'ofa, 1979; McGee, Ward and Drakakis-Smith, 1980), but most studies have tended to focus on segments of the overall picture, often as part of other research objectives. This has been particularly true of research on hawkers (see, for example, McGee and Yeung, 1977), in which the commodity sold is usually less important to the researcher than the operations of the seller.

Only rarely have researchers chosen specifically to investigate the petty-commodity retailing of food, but when they have the results have been very revealing. For example, research in Harare (Drakakis-Smith and Kivell, 1989) has indicated that illegal petty-commodity retailing is not necessarily expressed only through hawking or street trading but can give rise to a plethora of unconventional retail outlets constructed on a more or less permanent basis – in this instance known as 'tuckshops'.

An even more detailed investigation of cooked-food hawkers in Singapore by Grice (1989) has produced an extremely comprehensive picture of an extensive retail system and its complex articulation with other sectors of the economy, with the planning process and even with the development philosophy of the city-state as a whole. Unfortunately intensive studies such as this have been rare.

One relatively popular and related area of research concentration has been that of urban markets. Here the most informative surveys have usually traced the flow of marketed food from its source to the market itself, which may only be an intermediary, if concentrated, point in the process of exchange. Most of the studies undertaken of urban food markets have emphasized the spatial linkages between the rural food sources and urban consumption (for example, see Mahoney, 1979, for Papua New Guinea). Few, however, have investigated the detailed processes which link source and sales so comprehensively as Jim Jackson (1978; 1979), who revealed the intricate network of intermediaries involved in the marketing process and the different organizational structures for various types of produce.

Detailed investigations of the marketing process, such as Jackson's, raise many issues for further research, but for geographers two spatial aspects are of prime interest. First, there is the nature of the articulation of rural and urban space in the production and retailing processes. In this context not enough attention has been paid to the role of the urban periphery as a source of food products. Although Hill (1986) and McGee (1989) have drawn attention to the nature of the changes which occur on the urban periphery, all too often the principal focus of investigation has been the switch from agricultural to non-agricultural land uses (including idle land held in speculation); far less attention has been paid to the intensification of agricultural land use, the switch from staple to vegetable crops and the rise of the producer-entrepreneur.

In this context, recent research undertaken in Hong Kong has been instructive (see, for example, Hill, 1986; Yeung, 1988). Figure 7.2 illustrates clearly the rapid change and intensification in agricultural land use in Hong Kong as the urban population has expanded. Sit (1987: 3–8) has also investigated urban fairs in China and noted that since 1979 the revival of 'a significant privately [sic] and largely unplanned economy' has had a substantial impact on the urban food supply system.

Urban fairs are essentially supervised hawker bazaars which operate separately and quite differently from the state-collective markets, the enterprises being much smaller in nature but with less regulation of business transactions. Although Sit does not specifically address the spatial dimensions of commodity supply, there is clearly an important role for production within the urban periphery or 'suburbs'. For example, in Jin Hua fair in Guangzhou all of the sellers are urban residents and yet 39 per cent are farmers, presumably selling their own produce, much of which comes from the suburban districts of the city.

A second and related spatial factor to emerge from the study of urban markets is the diverse source of many of the commodities marketed. Jackson (1978), for example, indicates that fruit sold in the Pasar Barong wholesale market in Kuala Lumpur comes not only from all over Malaysia but also from international sources. Indeed, almost half is imported from overseas. The national and international dimensions are equally important in reverse flows (i.e. the supply of fresh and processed commodities from a single source). Figure 7.3 indicates the marketing network for fresh and processed fish from Kuala Besut, also in Malaysia (see bin Rahim, 1989).

It is this international dimension which has begun to attract renewed research attention to urban food supply systems in recent years. In these investigations the food supply system has been reorganized as yet another avenue through which international capital has penetrated the economic structure of developing countries. This is not to say that the tendency towards imported food has not been noted previously; this would indeed be strange given its rapid expansion during colonial times. What is attracting attention and concern now is the extent to which imported food

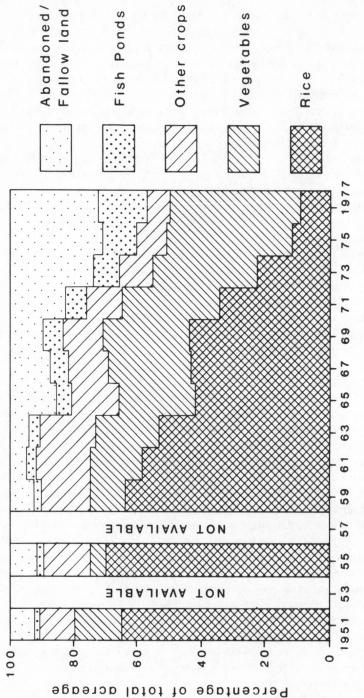

Figure 7.2. Changing agricultural land use in Hong Kong.

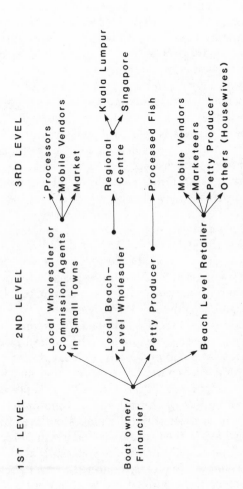

Figure 7.3. The marketing network of fresh and processed fish in Kuala Besut, Malaysia. Source: bin Rahim (1989).

is replacing local food in the diet of indigenous populations.

This tendency towards imported foodstuffs has, of course, paralleled the urbanization process itself. It began with the rapid rise in population of the colonial entrepôts, the majority of the low-income populations of which were fed on imported tea, flour and sugar – staples often grown in other colonial territories and processed in metropolitan Europe. Their subsequent resale in colonial cities thus gave a double profit at the expense of indigenous colonial populations (through production and consumption).

MacLeod and McGee (1989) claim that intensification of the industrialization of urban food supply systems is the result of two processes. The first of these is the 'indirect' changing of consumption patterns; the restructuring of diets usually along Western lines. This is the consequence of a wide range of social changes linked to colonialism, neo-colonialism and urbanization itself, the consequences of which will be discussed below. The second, or direct, process is related to the structural dynamics of food marketing *per se* and the ways in which the domestic and international spheres articulate. One example, given by MacLeod and McGee (1989: 361) is that of refrigeration which has facilitated the transportation of food over long distances. This permits a longer shelf-life and is linked closely to changes in household technologies.

In both of these processes there is clearly an influential role for international capital, largely through the medium of the MNC. This is not a new role. In many small states in the South Pacific, for example, the principal companies involved in food importing, distribution and retailing are still Burns Philp and Carpenters, which have dominated regional food trade since the last century (Chandra, 1980). Moreover, the internationalization of urban food supplies is not confined to commodification and importation; it has also strongly influenced the pattern of retailing. It is still difficult, because of patchy research coverage, to appreciate fully the precise relationship between changes in retailing and importation patterns, particularly in causal terms. The shift to supermarkets, for example, or the growing tide of franchised fast-food outlets, may well be symptomatic of the broader societal changes outlined by MacLeod and McGee, but they have in their turn provided incentives for amended shopping and dietary practices. Guy (1986) suggests that, as far as food is concerned, such changes are largely confined to capital cities and to the more affluent sectors of the population, but this has been challenged by work in a variety of urban settings.

In Hong Kong, for example, MacLeod and McGee (1989) note that between the mid-1970s and mid-1980s the number of supermarkets in the colony increased from 62 to 655, increasing their share of the food retail market to 55 per cent. Clearly, as MacLeod and McGee (1989: 318) observe, much of this success is due to the manipulation of shopping habits by large-scale chains of supermarkets to induce a shift to this form of food outlet. The consequence has been to tap an extensive share of the market, not merely an elitist portion of it. The consequence has been spectacular for some firms. The Wellcome chain, for example, more than doubled its outlets (to 104) during the first half of the 1980s alone, in the process almost trebling its sales and increasing its share of food sales in the colony to 14 per cent.

These trends in the advanced capitalism of Hong Kong are mirrored elsewhere in the Third World. Figure 7.4 reveals that in Harare, for example, supermarkets, often those in the central business district, were the preferred retail focus for a wide range of commodities and social groups (Drakakis-Smith and Kivell, 1989). In the case of each of the purchase categories shown in Figure 7.4, the three columns refer to three separate study areas in the city: Mabelreign, a middle-income area; Glenview, a government low-cost housing area; and Epworth, a large peripheral squatter settlement. Even in comparatively underdeveloped parts of the Pacific the same trends are evident, so that over half of all food sales in Port Vila, the small capital of Vanuatu, occur in supermarket-type stores owned primarily by multinational firms.

Of course, as with similar aspects of capitalist penetration of local economies, the internationalization process has been greatly facilitated by assistance from domestic capital and the local state. Nowhere is this more evident than in Singapore, erroneously regarded as a *laissez-faire* society, in which the state controls almost all aspects of economic and social life (see also Grice and Drakakis-Smith, 1985; Rigg, 1988; Mirza, 1986).

Some of the features of the Singaporean food supply system have been noted earlier. Food accounts for one-third of total retail sales and, despite rising affluence, food purchases still comprise the largest item in the household budget (Table 7.1) (Cheng, 1982), partly because of the widespread habit of eating outside the home. However, this tendency towards restaurant patronage is typical of Chinese urban societies, as is the preference for fresh fruit and vegetables (often purchased several times each day).

The Singaporean food-supply system tends to be a complex structure, and recent changes in it have been closely linked to the growing internationalization and affluence of the economy as a whole. Nevertheless, in almost all instances, from production to consumption, change has been facilitated by state action (see Grice, 1989). For example, the local production of pork and poultry, which has always been considerable (Yeung, 1988), has shifted from small family businesses to large 'factory' units, encouraged by government legislation on health and hygiene which in turn was fuelled by pressure on land from an expanding urban area.

Within the estates that have overwhelmed the small farms, the traditional form of wet-market has lost patronage over the years as economic

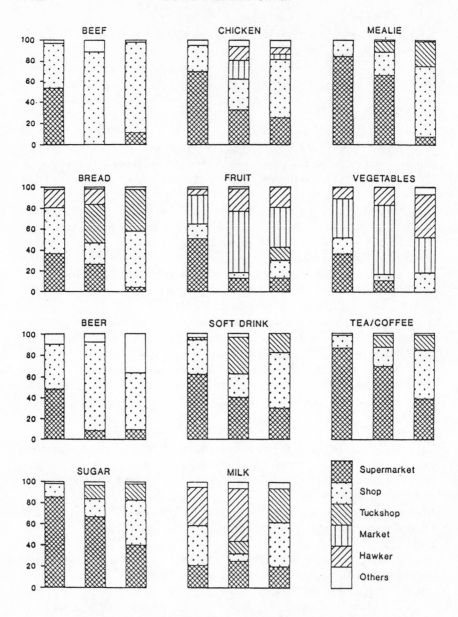

Figure 7.4. Source of selected food purchases in Harare.
The meaning of the three sets of columns is explained in the text.

growth has resulted in more working wives, surplus income for refrigerators
and a once-weekly visit to the supermarket or wholesaler. The government has sought to 'rationalize' such changes in its land-use planning
for its new estates by making larger retail spaces available for food

Table 7.1. Percentage distribution of expenditure by type of foods and monthly expenditure group in Singapore

Type of foods	Total	Households	Monthly expenditure group							
			Below S$300		S$500 – 599		S$1,000 – 1,499		S$2,000 and over	
Rice and other cereals	5.6	12.5	8.9	16.1	7.4	14.4	5.3	11.7	3.0	9.6
Meat and poultry	6.4	14.3	7.6	13.8	7.5	14.6	6.3	13.9	4.4	14.1
Fish	6.4	10.3	6.7	12.2	5.8	11.3	4.5	9.9	2.9	9.3
Dairy products and eggs	2.3	5.1	3.6	6.5	3.0	5.8	2.2	4.8	1.5	4.8
Vegetables and vegetable products	3.3	7.4	5.2	9.4	4.3	8.3	3.2	7.0	1.9	6.1
Fruits	2.2	4.9	1.9	3.4	2.2	4.3	2.4	5.3	1.8	5.8
Cooking oils and fats	1.1	2.5	1.7	3.1	1.4	2.7	1.0	2.2	0.6	1.9
Other food, sugar, sweets, beverages	3.4	7.6	4.2	7.6	3.9	7.6	3.4	7.5	2.4	7.7
Cooked food	15.8	35.3	15.3	27.8	15.8	30.8	17.1	37.7	12.7	40.7

Source: Cheng (1982).

supermarkets in preference to smaller stores or markets, encouraging the latter to convert into cooked-food centres, itself representing a push to formalize the many petty-commodity food hawkers that used to characterize Singapore (see Grice, 1989). Larger-scale activities in food retailing have also been encouraged by the centralization of wholesaling facilities for imported foodstuffs in new centres adjacent to the main west-coast port area.

One result of all this activity is that, since the 1960s, the total number of food hawkers has fallen by almost half to just over 25,000. Perhaps even more important is the fact that over the same period the proportion of total hawkers who are licensed has risen from 17 per cent to over 90 per cent. This also means that the geographical distribution of this activity has become tightly controlled by the authorities.

Consequences

What has been the cumulative impact of the above series of shifts from subsistence into petty-commodity or fully capitalized urban food systems with a growing international dimension? In a nutshell it has meant increasing food dependency across the board from the national level to that of the individual purchaser.

International trade in food has always been extensive (see Tarrant, 1982) but export statistics are far less instructive than import data in reflecting dependency or a lack of it. As Sudarmadji (1979) has shrewdly observed, many of the best food products of South-East Asian countries are exported in order to maximize foreign-exchange earnings. A consequent impact of this is to raise the price of locally produced foods for the local consumer. So as far as most of the urban poor are concerned, the fact that a country has a positive trade balance in food is no indication of surplus or a satisfactory domestic situation.

Of course, in many developing countries the situation is far worse than this with trade figures indicating an extensive reliance on imported foods. This situation not only exists in the more obvious famine-stricken areas of the world but occurs in what might seem to be relatively fortunate regions. For example, in the Pacific Islands, imported foods comprise between 20 per cent and 40 per cent of the total import bill, with starches (usually rice, bread and biscuits), tinned meat and fish being particularly important. Most of this imported food is, of course, consumed in the urban areas. Thus, Harris (1980) reported that Port Moresby consumed one-quarter of Papua New Guinea's total food imports. Put another way, 75 per cent of the capital's 'basic' food consumption was imported.

Clearly this puts the importing countries very much at the mercy of their suppliers. For Pacific Island states which import primarily from

Australia or new Zealand, using foreign intermediaries and foreign ships, the slightest change in exchange rates, labour or shipping costs can present enormous problems. But the difficulties posed for developing countries by dependency on imported food are not only of national economics. There is also the question of nutrition. Sudarmadji (1979: 100) claims that 'hard foreign currencies collected from [food] exports is [sic] indeed more important than local nutritional development'. Where food is in short supply, or is relatively expensive because it is imported, then both the quality and quantity of the food available to the poor will decline. When the opportunity to compensate for this through subsistence cropping is lost, as is increasingly the case in urban areas, the downward spiral of nutrition and health is further compounded.

The growth in imported foodstuffs and the consequent nutritional impacts on the urban poor also give rise to related multiplier effects. One of the most notorious is the effect on infant health caused by the early substitution of a starchy diet for breast milk, caused partly by a decline in lactation by poor women and partly by economic pressures upon them to work to supplement the family budget (see Miles, 1981).

Other knock-on effects are no less disastrous at the national level with the rise in imported foods subverting the demand for local foods, as well as undermining local entrepreneurial initiatives to increase domestic food production for the urban market. Thus over the years imported cereals have displaced root crops from many urban diets in Africa and the Pacific.

It would appear, from the above comments, that there are two basic, interwoven causes for the growing dependency in urban food systems, i.e. the increasing replacement of local by foreign commodities, personnel or enterprises (see Lambert *et al.*, 1979). The first is the penetration of Western capitalism into all aspects of economic life; for many of the companies involved, food is only one part of their overall trading activities. Second is the Westernization of dietary preferences, which is, of course, closely linked to both economic change and to urbanization.

Overall the same model or pattern of evolution can be said to have affected most of the Third World, with local variation in the intensity of change. The origins lay in the colonial period with the widespread substitution of cash-cropping (for both domestic and external markets) for the self-sufficient, subsistence and exchange-based agriculture of the pre-colonial period. Obviously, not all pre-colonial production was non-commercial but the extent of change in the colonial period resulted in a substantial loss of local food production in most colonies, particularly around the urban areas.

Imported foods were first introduced to satisfy the dominant expatriate groups and this itself had a 'demonstration' effect on aspiring local populations – a factor clearly indicated in many former (and current) French colonies where croissants and baguettes are an important element at the breakfast table of most people. However, large-scale labour exploitation, in both urban and rural areas, also encouraged a change in diet through the introduction of imported staples in lieu of, or as a supplement to, basic wages. Where this colonial labour force was imported, massive dietary changes resulted, as in the Pacific where the use of Indian, Vietnamese and Chinese indentured labour was widespread.

Much of this dietary change was, of course, concentrated in the urban areas, where expatriates dominated in influence, if not always in terms of numbers. The trend was continued, even confirmed, on independence as neo-colonial influences expanded and a Westernized way of life became the role model for both rich and poor alike. The very rapid growth of Third World cities accelerated this process not only because of the shift in the balance of urban–rural population ratios but also because of the emergence of a mass consumer market.

For some households the change in diet is a voluntary process as their incomes rise and the amount of discretionary spending increases, encouraging them to be more adventurous in their patterns of food expenditure, thereby introducing an element of elasticity into what for the poor is usually a highly inelastic component of the household budget.

The growth of both the size and elasticity of the urban mass consumer market for food has been accompanied by other changes in the post-colonial period that have combined to affect consumption patterns. First, there have been the technological advances in processing and storing foods which have improved the transport and shelf-life of foods, in both the shop and the home (for example, by canning, refrigeration, dehydration, etc.). Second, there has been a shift in retailing operations towards the supermarket type of operation where less frequent, larger-scale visits have been encouraged. MacLeod and McGee (1989: 321) assert that this shift has been encouraged, even manipulated, by the companies involved since 'consumers need to switch to packaged goods in order for the supermarket to fully exploit its advantages' (over other retail outlets).

These changes have also been paralleled in the retailing of cooked food, which, in some parts of the developing world, notably South-East Asia, constitutes a sizeable part of total household expenditure on food. Once again, particularly in the larger cities, there has been an invasion of international retailing through fast-food outlets. Of course, most of the actual retailing is undertaken by locals through franchises, but the nature of the product and, often, its constituents are imported.

In large and wealthy Third World cities the expansion of fast-food outlets has been phenomenal. In Hong Kong, for example, the growth rate of the fast-food sector between 1977 and 1985 was almost 1,200 per cent (MacLeod and McGee, 1989: 328). In smaller, more vulnerable situations such expansion has brought about nutritional problems as junk food becomes the norm. In the US-dominated Marshall Islands of the Pacific, despite the fact that 'coconut, papaya and banana trees heavy with fruit sway in the afternoon trade winds . . . kitchens are dominated by canned meats and rice, doughnuts and pancakes heavy with sugar. Local foods are valued less than imported goods' (*Pacific Islands Monthly*, August 1988: 44).

It is, perhaps, in the South Pacific more than anywhere else that the sad spectacle of food dependency is most pronounced given the potential for self-sufficiency. The situation has been recorded in detail and depth by Randy Thaman in what is perhaps one of the most continuous and important research programmes of its kind (see Thaman, 1977; 1982; 1984; 1985; 1986; 1988).

Prior to the arrival of the Europeans, most Pacific Island states were not only self-sufficient in food production but were self-contained, too, with no imported fuels or fertilizers. Polyculture was practised and eco-logical balance was maintained without 'plundering the past or mortgaging the future'. Moreover, labour and resources were shared, with social status being linked to generosity in the distribution of food surpluses.

In contrast, the present situation is marked not only by food dependency but even by relative scarcity in certain areas (towns), for certain groups (the poor) and for certain foods (fresh fish, meat and vegetables). The bulk of the imported foods are white flour, milled rice and sugar which are lower in fibre and vitamins than traditional crops, such as taro. Furthermore, the high cost of transport between and across islands means that imported food is often much more expensive away from the main point of arrival.

Of course, not all changes in diets need be detrimental. As Sudarmadji (1979) rightly underlines, education on sound and sensible nutritional practices is an important part of any development programme. However, all of the trends noted above run counter to this and raise important ques-tions as to how Third World governments should respond.

For Thaman (1988) the answer lies in encouraging a revitalization of traditional crops which, as he points out, have particular nutritional merit in the Pacific. For low-income groups in urban areas he recommends a renewed emphasis on urban gardens (Thaman, 1986) which, it is claimed, not only play a positive role in meeting nutritional needs but also have economic, social and ecological advantages. The full impact of domestic gardens is, however, confined primarily to the immediate household. Any attempt to reverse some of the economic and nutritional dependency noted above must be linked to the commercial expansion of traditional crops. In this context the obvious problems relate to the expense involved. Most expansion in production is linked to infrastructural improvements – for example, in transport and marketing facilities – or to subsidies which encourage its consumers to choose traditional, locally produced foods over imported commodities.

However, the economics of food production and marketing comprise only a small proportion of the necessary strategy. As this chapter has been at pains to emphasize, contemporary urban food dependency is but part of a wider process of change. Influencing dietary and consumer preferences will almost certainly involve a re-education process. This can take several forms, from specific educational programmes in schools, to media campaigns or to direct government action, for example by changing the purchasing policies and culinary practices of its own institutions. The canteens and refectories of government offices, schools, colleges, prisons, military establishments and the like are often substantial but uncoordinated and unconsidered in terms of policy potential.

Here we finally arrive at the nub of the full range of issues related to urban food systems in the Third World. If we do not know enough about the ways in which the systems function and why they function in these ways, the formulation of specific policy responses designed to countermand undesirable nutritional, social or economic effects is going to be very difficult, Our knowledge will not improve until there is as much research interest in and debate about urban food systems as there is on urban housing systems – more thought on food in order to promote some food for thought.

REFERENCES

Abrams, C. (1964) *Man's Struggle for Shelter in an Urbanizing World*. Cambridge, Massachusetts: MIT Press.

Baxter, M. (1980) *Food in Fiji: Produce and Processed Foods*, Monograph No. 22. Canberra: Development Studies Centre, Australian National University.

Chandra, R. (1980) *Food Distribution Systems in the South Pacific*. Canberra: Development Studies Centre, Australian National University.

Cheng, L.K. (1982) 'Fresh food suppliers in Singapore'. *Geo Journal*, 4: 61–72.

Drakakis-Smith, D.W. (1986) 'Subsistence urbanization: basic demands on the urban environs', in: Hills, P. (ed.) *State Policy, Urbanization and the Development Process*. Hong Kong: Centre for Urban Studies and Urban Planning, University of Hong Kong, 48–59.

Drakakis-Smith, D.W. and Kivell, P.T. (1990) 'Food production, retailing and consumption patterns in Harare', in: Paddison, R., Findlay, A. and Dawson, J. (eds) *Urban Retailing in the Third World*. London: Routledge.

Dwyer, D.J. and Williams, S.W. (1983) *Progress in Third World Studies*, Occasional Paper No. 6. Keele: Department of Geography, University of Keele.

Evers, H.-D. (1983) 'Households and urban subsistence production'. Paper presented at a seminar on Third World Urbanization and the Household Economy, Universiti Sains Malaysia, Penang.

Grice, K. (1989) 'Institutionalization of informal sector activities: cooked food hawkers in Singapore'. Unpublished Ph.D. thesis, University of Keele.

Grice, K. and Drakakis-Smith, D.W. (1985) 'The role of the state in shaping development in Singapore'. *Transactions of the Institute of British Geographers*, N.S. **10**(3): 347–59.

Guy, C. (1986) 'Retail distribution in Third World cities: some research issues'. Paper presented at the Institute of British Geographers Annual Conference, University of Leeds.

Harris, G.T. (1980) *Replacing Imported Food Supplies in Port Moresby, PNG*, Occasional Paper No. 17. Canberra: Development Studies Centre, Australian National University.

Hau'ofa, E. (1979) *Corned Beef and Tapioca: Food Distribution Systems in Tonga*, Monograph No. 19. Canberra: Development Studies Centre, Australian National University.

Hill, R.D. (1986) 'Land use change on the urban fringe'. *Nature and Resources*, **22**(1–2): 24–33.

Islam, N. (1982) 'Food consumption expenditure patterns of certain households in Bangladesh'. *Geo Journal*, **4**: 7–14.

Jackson, J. (1978) 'Trader hierarchies in Third World distribution systems', in: Rimmer, P.J. *et al.* (eds) *Food, Shelter and Transport in East Asia and the Pacific*, Monograph HG12. Canberra: Research School of Pacific Studies, Australian National University.

Jackson, J. (1979) 'Retail development and Third World cities', in: Jackson, J. and Rudner, M. (eds) *Issues in Malaysian Development*. Singapore: Heinemann.

Lambert, J. *et al.* (1979) 'Food dependency in the Pacific'. *Development News Digest*, **28**: 6–7.

McGee, T.G. (1989) 'Urbanization or Kotadesasi? Evolving patterns of urbanization', in: Costa, F.J. *et al.* (eds) *Urbanization in Asia*. Honolulu: University of Hawaii Press, 93–108.

McGee, T.G. and Yeung, Y.-M. (1977) *Hawkers in Southeast Asian Cities*. Ottawa: International Development Research Centre.

McGee, T.G., Ward, R.G. and Drakakis-Smith, D.W. (1980) *Food Distribution Systems in the New Hebrides*, Monograph No. 25. Canberra: Development Studies Centre, Australian National University.

MacLeod, S. and McGee, T.G. (1989) 'The last frontier: the emergence of the industrial palate in Hong Kong', in: Drakakis-Smith, D. (ed.) *Economic Growth and Urbanization in the Third World*. London: Routledge, 304–35.

Mahoney, C.T. (1979) 'Marketing patterns in Port Moresby and Lae'. Paper presented at the Waigani Seminar, University of Papua New Guinea.

Mazambani, D. (1978) 'Woodfuel trade and consumption patterns in Salisbury's townships'. Unpublished paper, Department of Geography, University of Zimbabwe.

Miles, J.C. (1981) 'Health in the city'. Presidential Address, Fourth Pacific Science Inter-Congress, Singapore.

Mirza, H. (1986) *Multinationals and the Growth of the Singaporean Economy*. London: Croom Helm.

Paddison, R., Findlay, A. and Dawson, J. (eds) (1989) *Urban Retailing in the Third World*. London: Routledge.

Potts, D. (1987) 'Recent rural–urban migrants to Harare, Zimbabwe'. Paper presented at Rural–Urban Links Workshop, School of Oriental and African Studies, University of London.

bin Rahim, A. (1989) 'Production and distribution linkages in a fishing economy: a study of development and underdevelopment in a Malaysia town'. Unpublished Ph.D. thesis, University of Keele.

Rigg, J. (1988) 'Singapore and the recession of 1985'. *Asian Survey*, 28(3): 340–52.

Sit, V. (1987) 'Urban fairs in China'. *Economic Geography*, 53(4): 306–18.

Soussan, J. (1988) *Primary Resources and the Third World*. London: Routledge.

Sudarmadji, S. (1979) 'Food consumption patterns and the ASEAN food dilemma'. *Contemporary Southeast Asia*, 1(1): 92–105.

Swindell, K. and Sutherland, A. (1986) 'Farming on the fringe: African towns and agrarian change'. Paper presented at Institute of British Geographers Developing Areas Research Group, Anglo-Scandinavian Symposium.

Tarrant, J. (1982) 'International food trade'. Paper presented at an SSRC seminar on Food Production and Distribution, University of Keele.

Thaman, R. (1977) 'Urban gardening in Papua New Guinea and Fiji', in: Winslow, J. (ed.) *The Melanesian Environment*. Canberra: Australian National University, 146–68.

Thaman, R. (1982) 'Deterioration of food systems, malnutrition and food dependency in the Pacific Islands'. *Journal of Food and Nutrition*, 39(3): 109–25.

Thaman, R. (1984) 'Urban agriculture and home gardening in Fiji'. *Transactions and Proceedings of the Fiji Society*, 14: 1–28.

Thaman, R. (1985) 'Changing Pacific Island food patterns and nutritional deterioration: implications for child survival and development'. Paper presented at a UNICEF Conference on Child Survival and Development, Suva.

Thaman, R. (1986) 'By the people and for the people: home gardening and national development in the pacific Islands'. Paper presented at the Commonwealth Geographical Bureau Conference on Small-scale Agriculture, Australian National University, Canberra.

Thaman, R. (1988) 'Food, fortune and fatality: economic, social and nutritional challenges of the urbanization of Pacific Island food systems'. Paper presented at a conference on Nutritional Challenges in a Changing World, University of Hawaii, Honolulu.

Yeung, Y.-M. (1988) 'Agricultural land use in Asian cities'. *Land Use Policy*, Jan.: 79–82.

[8]

The New Town as an Urbanization Strategy in Malaysia's Regional Development Planning: The Case of Bandar Pusat, Jengka Triangle

Sulong Mohamad

Introduction

The launching of the New Economic Policy in 1971 marked the beginning of an era of new town building in Malaysia. So far four types of new town, namely new communities within cities, new towns on existing urban peripheries, new towns in rural areas and petroleum-based new towns, have emerged within Malaysia's landscape (Mohd Rosli Buyong, 1978; Sulong Mohamad, 1985).

In this chapter, the third type of new town will be discussed in the context of regional policy in Malaysia. Over nearly two decades, it has become clear that new towns are not developing rapidly, and have failed to play the role that was envisaged in the original conception of their plans. This pessimistic attitude toward spatial planning in the Third World was expressed by Gilbert (1976) in the mid-1970s. In Malaysia, the difficulties involved with spatial engineering have been acknowledged by Higgins (1979; 1982). In this chapter, the problems of one specific new town, Bandar Pusat, which was set up in the early 1970s to function as a growth centre in the Jengka Triangle region in the state of Pahang, will be examined in order to exemplify the issues involved.

The Colonial Legacy and Contemporary Regional Policy

The nature of unbalanced development in Malaysia has been given extensive treatment in the literature (see, for example, Kamal Salih, 1978; Malaysia, 1976; 1986). Therefore, in this chapter discussion is limited to the uneven distribution of major urban centres which favours the states which are already developed. The present pattern of regional inequality is the result of the past concentration of colonial activities before Malaysia achieved independence in 1957.

In 1786, the British established a base in Penang, and later extended it to Malacca and Singapore. These became the Straits Settlements and were the early foci of colonial activities. But the disputes and disorders which occurred in the neighbouring Malay states were a source of concern, and disrupted British trade. As a result, in 1874 the British changed their policy from non-intervention to intervention. The British influence spread first to the Federated Malay States, comprising Perak, Pahang, Selangor and Negeri Sembilan, and later to the Unfederated Malay States of Kedah, Perlis, Kelantan, Terengganu and Johore. All these states of Peninsular Malaysia came under British rule in 1919. The other two states of Sabah and Sarawak came into being when a Federation of Malaysia was formed in 1963 (see Figure 8.1). Two years later, Singapore broke away from Malaysia and became an independent nation.

Under British rule, the tin-rich states of Perak, Selangor and Negeri Sembilan became the centre of economic activities. Tin mines were opened, attracting the Chinese who migrated from southern China to participate in the tin-rush. Tin was an important economic commodity in the history of Malaysia's development. Sites rich in tin ore grew rapidly from mining camps into big villages and then to towns. In the history of urban development, a number of towns and cities grew from modest beginnings (Lim, 1978). These centres include Kuala Lumpur, the national capital; Ipoh, the state capital of Perak; Seremban, the state capital of Negeri Sembilan and other smaller towns such as Bidor, Gopeng and Taiping in Perak. In the late nineteenth century, railways were constructed to link the tin-producing centres with the coastal ports. Later, towns lying in the tin belt were connected with railways (Aiken *et al.*, 1982). At about the same time, roads were introduced, first within the towns and later in order to link up with the other mining settlements. These roads ran almost parallel to the railways. The introduction of railways and roads in the late nineteenth century opened up the country and enabled new land to be developed into rubber plantations, which sprang up on both sides of these transport linkages. More towns grew up at the road junctions to become collecting and distributing centres for this new commodity (Hamzah Sendut, 1962). These developments took place within the tin and rubber belt of the west coast of Peninsular Malaysia, particularly in the states of Perak, Selangor, Negeri Sembilan and, to some extent, Johore. Other states in the north and east were left behind. Penang, being a port, benefited from such developments. Over time, these towns became numerous and grew in size. Some of them, being the chief administrative and transportation centres, acquired locational advantage over the others. Thus they became suitable sites for the concentration of industrial activities.

It is these historical forces that shaped the distribution of major urban

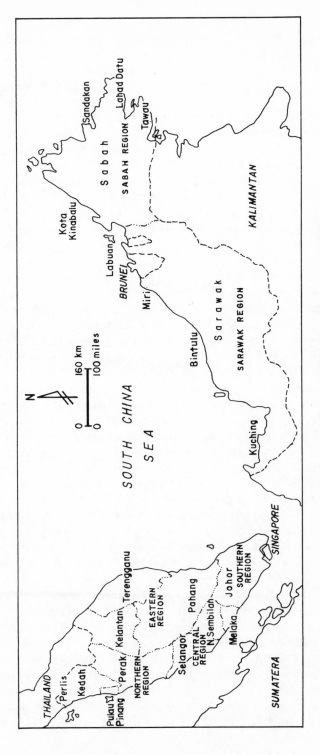

Figure 8.1. The states and development regions of Malaysia.

nodes, leading them to be concentrated in the resource-rich and developed part of the country. Malaysia has never been beset with the problem of urban primacy. The principal urban centres are fairly well-distributed, conforming with the rank-size rule. But there is a clear lack of major urban centres in the resource-poor and less-developed parts of Malaysia, as is emphasized by Figure 8.2. Under these conditions, it is to be expected that the less-developed regions will not be competitive enough to attract industrial activities, which are mainly found in the states of Selangor, Kuala Lumpur and Johore.

The regional distribution of development in Malaysia is complicated by yet another factor. The discovery of tin ore has brought labourers from southern China. In addition, rubber plantations and the construction of railways and roads have resulted in the migration of southern Indians, who supplied cheap labour to the British. The Chinese, again because of historical factors, and reinforced by the British policy of divide and rule, concentrated in the towns, performing various kinds of business and trade. They enjoyed the full benefits of the urban services and amenities provided for the general urban population. The Indians are mostly found on the rubber estates and do not enjoy the urban facilities which the Chinese have. The *Bumiputera* (indigenous) population are found in the rural areas of the developed states, but mostly in the less-developed states of Kedah, Perlis, Kelantan, Terengganu, Pahang, Sabah and Sarawak. Living in rural areas and in the states lacking in major urban centres, many of them are, like the Indians on the rubber estates, deprived of urban services and opportunities in productive urban employment.

The New Economic Policy, which is scheduled to come to an end in 1990, aims to deal with this issue of unbalanced development between regions and ethnic groups. Since 1971, regional development programmes have been implemented in the frontier regions in the states of Johore, Pahang, Terengganu, Kelantan and, recently, Kedah and Penang (Figure 8.3). In these development regions, particularly Kejora, Dara, Jengka Triangle and Ketengah (Figure 8.3), new towns are being built. In other regions, like Kesedar and Keda, the existing towns are being upgraded so that they will become regional centres and play the role of growth centres in their respective regions.

At this point, it is appropriate to summarize the overall objectives of such new towns within the framework of spatial planning policies. The first of these is to urbanize the rural Malays. It is hoped that the employment opportunities being created in these regions will encourage the Malays living in rural villages to migrate into the new towns which are provided with housing, urban facilities and services. In this way, it is intended that the proportion of Malays living in urban centres will not only be increased, but also that their quality of life will be improved. Second, it is intended that the creation of employment will enable rural

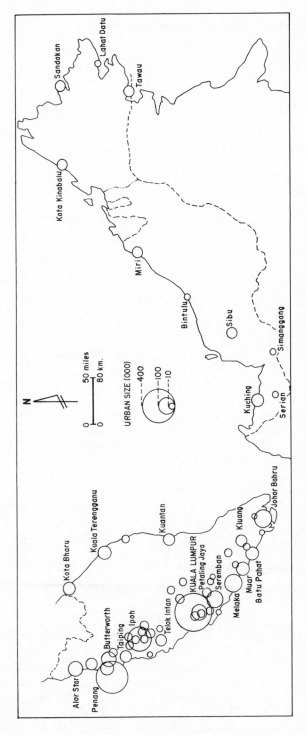

Figure 8.2. The distribution of towns and cites in Malaysia, 1980.

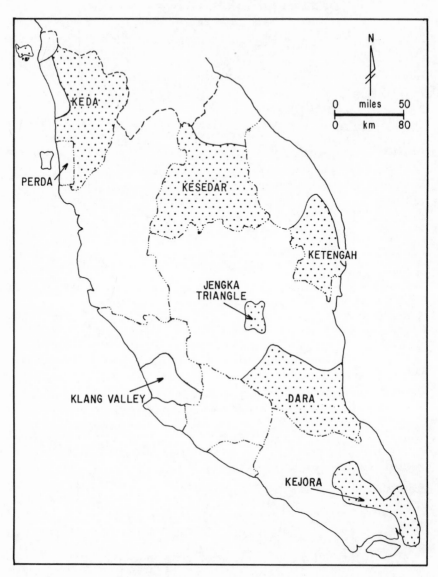

Figure 8.3. Regional development schemes in Malaysia. Adapted from Aiken *et al.*, (1982).

Malays to change their employment pattern from unproductive and traditional pursuits, to productive and modern activities. With this change should come improved earnings. The kinds of employment open to such rural Malays include work in agricultural plantations, factories, government, business and urban services. The last two types of employment lead to the third objective, the creation of Malay business people and entrepreneurs. Thus, it is hoped that the new towns in the rural areas will eventually improve the income of the poor states and reduce the gap between those that are rich and poor. The fourth objective is the creation of a denser distribution of urban settlements in the less-developed regions. It is hoped that these urban centres will facilitate a trickling-down process of development and at the same time help to form corridors of development between them.

The Notion of Rationalized Growth Centres

In Malaysia, the notion of rationalized growth centres was put forward by Kamal Salih in 1975 to ensure the development of an efficient hierarchy of urban nodes distributed evenly in national space (Kamal Salih, 1975). This 'filling the gap' strategy (advocated by Grove and Huszar, quoted in Furnell, 1976) requires that the size of middle-ranking cities be enlarged and their infrastructure and facilities upgraded.

This notion of growth centres implies that Malaysia has not adopted the strategy of uni-level growth nodes as suggested by Appalraju and Safier (1976). Implicit in the notion of rationalized growth centres is a *hierarchy* of growth centres. This is very similar to the notion of a *system* of growth centres, which has been put to the test in a number of countries (Appalraju and Safier, 1976). Since Malaysia has adopted this kind of growth-centre strategy, it becomes imperative that the hierarchy be carefully identified, and the rural new towns placed appropriately within the overall system of growth centres.

Malaysia has been divided into six broad development regions (Figure 8.1). Throughout the country and within the regions there is a hierarchy of growth centres. The first level is the national growth centre, which is represented by Kuala Lumpur. It is also the regional growth centre for the central region. This centre is the most dynamic, and is attracting many activities and in-migrants from within and outside the region (Malaysia, 1986).

The second level consists of the regional growth centres, represented by Georgetown for the northern region, Johore Bahru for the southern region, Kuantan for the eastern region, Kuching for Sarawak and Kota Kinabalu for Sabah (Figure 8.1). Georgetown is the counter-pole to Kuala Lumpur (Kamal Salih, 1978). Looking at the recent rapid development of Johore Bahru, it is not impossible that this centre will be the next, and in fact it is eventually planned to become another counter-pole to Kuala Lumpur (Malaysia, 1986). Kuantan, which has been chosen to be the regional hub for the eastern region, has been the focus of infrastructural investment, by means of which it is hoped that its population will increase from 50,000 in 1970 to 200,000 by the year 2000 (Kamal Salih, 1978). In-migration and structural change in the urban economy have inevitably resulted but, as Higgins (1982) notes, spread effects to the poor states of Kelantan and Terengganu have not occurred. In the Sabah and Sarawak regions, the development impulses are planned to trickle down from Kota Kinabalu and Kuching, respectively, to the lower order centres.

At the third level there are the state-capital growth centres, which include Bandar Melaka, Seremban, Shah Alam, Ipoh, Alor Setar, Kangar, Kota Bharu and Kuala Terengganu. Beside being state administrative centres, they also house planned industrial estates. Some of them, particularly Shah Alam, have become industrial centres of some standing.

The fourth level consists of the local-regional growth centres. They are basically rural new towns or upgraded towns. They are located in the regional development authority (RDA) areas of Kejora, Ketengah, Dara, Kesedar and Keda, and they play the role of regional centres in their respective areas. Although industry is envisaged as the engine of growth of these centres, Appalraju and Safier (1976) felt it appropriate to refer to them as 'service centres'. Bandar Pusat, to which attention will turn shortly, is included in this level of growth centre. The fifth level is made up by the district-capital growth centres. They are mainly service centres supplying their respective local areas. Most of them have planned industrial estates. The local growth centres represent a sixth level. They consist of new and upgraded towns which are to be found in the RDA areas and in other locations throughout the country. They can also be regarded as local service centres, with some industrial activities being planned for them.

This is the kind of urbanization strategy that has been incorporated into Malaysia's regional policy. It is hoped that as urban distribution becomes increasingly efficient, it will facilitate the trickling-down process through a series of urban hierarchical orders, from the highest to the lowest. In the end, it is hoped that a spatially integrated national economy will develop, as suggested by Friedmann (1966).

Bandar Pusat, Jengka Triangle: Planning versus Reality

In the mid-1960s, there was a pressing need to implement development schemes at the regional scale to enable bigger urban settlements to be established in the development regions. This, in turn, made it possible to relocate the rural population in the urban centres and provide them with better services and facilities. There was also a need to channel the flow of rural–urban migration away from the traditional major centres to the other towns. This shift in development thinking represents a contrast to the traditional development approach used by FELDA (Federal Land Development Authority), which built small, concentrated, well-planned villages provided with some urban services and facilities in its development areas (Tunku Shamsul Bahrin and Perera, 1977). Thus, the first regional land development project, the Jengka Triangle scheme, came into being in 1970.

In 1971, the Jengka Development Corporation, a state agency responsible for the implementation of Bandar Pusat and two other urban centres, was set up. Among other things, its master plan proposed the establishment of three new towns. The first was Bandar Pusat, which was to function as the regional centre for the Jengka Triangle region. The remaining two were the Southeast and Southwest towns, which were both established as local service centres (Figure 8.4). Since the last two new towns were meant to be located not far from the existing towns of Maran and Temerloh, the influence of which might be detrimental to their growth, it was suggested that their construction be delayed if not cancelled (Malaysia, 1972).

With this background, the growth of Bandar Pusat can now be examined from its beginnings to the present time. The master plan conceived Bandar Pusat as a regional centre servicing the entire FELDA settlements in the Jengka Triangle region (Figure 8.4). In this region, there are twenty-eight FELDA settlements with a planned total population of 90,000. These settlements have already been established – hence, Bandar Pusat has a fairly large hinterland. It is possible that the population in the region has already exceeded the planned figure, for in 1983 the population was 88,000, and this excluded the Kampung Awah and Sungai Nerek FELDA schemes (Mohd Nawawi, 1983: 20). It is partly for this reason that the master plan's proposal that Bandar Pusat should house a population of 16,000 was rejected by the Jengka Development Corporation. Instead, the Corporation argued that since Bandar Pusat is planned to be the regional centre, its population should be raised from 16,000 to 50,000 on the grounds that, with a larger size, a more varied and higher level of urban services and facilities can be provided, and the creation of more urban employment made possible (Malaysia, 1972). It is argued that this will accelerate urbanism and facilitate the shift of employment among the rural Malays. The planned population, however, is to be achieved by 1990.

But as is often the case, planning and reality are two different things. While it is relatively easy to develop a plan, implementation is frequently fraught with difficulties. Bandar Pusat should now have achieved its target population size, and it should have become a prosperous town from which

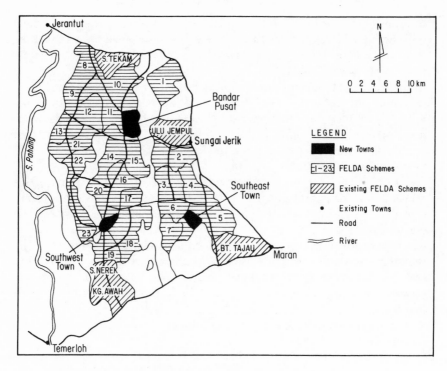

Figure 8.4.   The Jengka Triangle Scheme including Bandar Pusat.
Adapted from Malaysia (1972).

development impulses can spread to the hinterland. However, this notion
of growth and spread effects as formulated in the master plan and development theory has not been realized.

In fact, the population growth of Bandar Pusat has been alarmingly
slow. In 1980, Mohd Suhaimi Mamat (1986) showed that its population
was only 4,129, or 8 per cent of the planned target. By September 1987,
it had increased to 8,000. This slow growth resulted in a review in 1983
by the Jengka Regional Development Authority, a federal government
agency which took over the responsibility of programming and co-
ordinating the development of Bandar Pusat and other projects in the
Jengka Triangle region. The Jengka Development Corporation, after facing
serious financial problems, which in part also contributed to the slow
growth of the regional centre, was dissolved in 1983. The 1983 review
reduced the population target to be achieved by 1990 from 50,000 to 16,000.
This inevitably resulted in some significant changes in the structure plan.
A large portion of land earmarked for residential development is now
either reserved for future development or has been given to the MARA

Institute of Technology, which, when fully in operation, will accommodate some 3,700 students, 308 academic staff and 600 non-academic staff. This new land-use element will be located on a 200-acre site, an area originally planned for the south-east neighbourhood unit. The construction of this tertiary educational institution has not yet started, but the Authority is counting on its early start as a means of accelerating the growth of the town. The target population of 16,000 will only be achieved by 1990 if the planned first student intake occurs as scheduled in July 1989. This is rather optimistic given the fact that the population of Bandar Pusat now barely reaches the 8,000 mark and that the prospect of employment growth is slim under present economic conditions.

The decision to reverse the target population to the original 16,000 was taken in view of the following considerations. First, it was envisaged that development in Bandar Pusat would induce the in-migration of the second-generation groups from the FELDA schemes. But because the growth of employment opportunities was so slow, instead of flowing into the new town, they headed for the other major centres. Second, it was anticipated that FELDA would locate its factories in Bandar Pusat. Again, this did not materialize, and FELDA set up its factories as a part of its own schemes. Third, it was envisaged that FELDA would establish its regional office in the new town. But in the event, FELDA selected a site in Sungai Tekam, about fifteen miles (24 km) away. Lastly, Bandar Pusat was originally planned not only to be the regional centre for the Jengka Triangle region, but also to house a district office for Maran which even at that juncture still did not possess such administrative functions. But, because of political pressure, this district office was later set up in Maran. In this way a considerable volume of job opportunities was lost.

It was stipulated that industry, the main economic activity, should provide 60 per cent of the jobs in Bandar Pusat (Malaysia, 1971). This meant that for a town planned for a total of 50,000 people, about 10,000 jobs needed to be created, of which 6,000 should come from industrial activities. The remaining activities, comprising the government sector and other urban activities, would account for another 40 per cent, or 4,000 jobs.

But industrial development has been very slow. The most important industrial activity is represented by the sawmill run by the Syarikat Jengka Sdn. Bhd. (Jengka Company Ltd), which in 1980 employed some 1,512 workers. Since 1985, owing to the severe economic recession, a large number of workers have been laid off. By September 1987, the industrial sector employed only slightly more than 1,000 workers.

The employment structure of Bandar Pusat in the early 1980s shows that industrial activities actually provided 70 per cent of employment. The next most important source of employment is government services, which accounted for nearly 20 per cent of all jobs. The third most important source of employment is urban activities, accounting for about 8 per cent of the workforce. The level of employment in this sector is rather small in view of the role of Bandar Pusat as a regional centre, having a hinterland population of more than 88,000. This sector requires further expansion because one of the objectives of building the new towns is to encourage the active participation of rural Malays in productive urban activities. The general lack of opportunities existing for the rural Malays will become obvious when the development of the business and service sectors in the new town is examined.

In September 1987 there were about 128 establishments catering for a very limited range of activities and services, a state which reflected the pioneering nature of Bandar Pusat (Tunku Shamsul Bahrin *et al.*, 1986). There is an extremely large number of restaurants, which reflects the structure of the town's population. As reported by Mohd Suhaimi Mamat (1986), a large proportion of those living in Bandar Pusat are bachelors and transient settlers. The latter represent a group of the population who work in Bandar Pusat but leave their families in their place of origin. Bandar Pusat has been perceived as a pioneering town lacking in facilities, particularly in education and health. Because of the nature of the composition of its population, restaurants are in great demand while shops catering for grocery and household items are relatively few in number.

Mohd Suhaimi Mamat (1986) has provided an interesting insight into the town's role as a service centre. In his survey of six FELDA settlements, it was found that Bandar Pusat was only infrequently visited by most FELDA settlers. Two factors contributed to this lack of patronage. First, the settlers could easily obtain supplies from their own settlements, which have their own shops stocked with low-order goods. Importantly, the FELDA settlers could obtain their supplies on credit from shops run by the FELDA Corporation, and such shops are to be found in all FELDA settlements. Second, Bandar Pusat faces keen competition from existing towns, particularly Temerloh, Jerantut, Sungai Jerik, and to a lesser extent Maran. These existing towns have the edge over Bandar Pusat, because the range of goods offered is more varied and relatively cheap. None the less, a fairly high percentage of the people from nearby settlements do come to Bandar Pusat for higher-order goods and services (Mohd Suhaimi Mamat, 1986).

These findings, however, show that the threshold population needed to support urban activities and services is small. This explains why the range of goods and services provided in Bandar Pusat is limited. In fact, the threshold population is limited to its own population and to a few settlers from the nearby FELDA schemes. Looked at from the Christallerian perspective, Bandar Pusat is a central place of a relatively low order. None the less, the prospect of playing a regional role is there, if Bandar Pusat can eventually provide a wider range of higher-order goods and services at much lower prices. Whether or not this can be implemented with few practical difficulties is a matter for debate. But as it is now, Bandar Pusat is losing most of its hinterland consumers to the towns nearby.

There are, however, two regional roles which Bandar Pusat has performed with some measure of success. First, it has become the whole-saling centre for small local businessmen for most of the FELDA settle-ments. In Bandar Pusat, there is a Pernas distribution centre from which local businessmen can obtain their supplies. Second, there is a central market from which traders can buy their perishable goods.

From the outline above, it is evident that the urban activities and services of Bandar Pusat cannot expand fast enough, partly because of a general lack of opportunities created for the Malays to participate in such activities, and also because of the inability of Bandar Pusat to compete efficiently with existing towns.

The last aspect of the planning of Bandar Pusat considered here is the provision of urban facilities which it is hoped will enhance the urban environment for the benefit of the rural population. This in turn, it is argued by the planners, will raise their quality of life. The most important urban facility is, of course, housing.

Housing development has fallen short of that scheduled, and its development phases have been adjusted accordingly since 1983 (Mohd Suhaimi Mamat, 1986). By 1986, two housing areas had been completed, providing a total of 953 housing units. In both areas, various types of house are provided to cater for the needs of different socio-economic groups.

It appears that housing development has kept pace with the growth of population. The number of unoccupied housing units is very small; in fact the total is less than 120 units. The housing units in the three-storey flats in the Rantau Perintis housing area were left vacant because of problems with the water supply. The low preference for the two-room, single-storey, linked houses provided in the Desa Jaya area was due to basic design deficiencies. There has been a change in housing demand, because in the late 1970s Tunku Shamsul Bahrin *et al*. (1986) reported that at least one-third of the housing units were left unoccupied. But the demand for housing is still evidently not expanding fast enough. This, of course, is tied up with the overall lack of employment opportunities in the town.

While the educational facilities provided are sufficient, other govern-ment services are rudimentary. Almost all government services, including the medical, postal, fire and police services, are housed in temporary buildings. The government hospital, which is supposed to service the entire population of the Jengka Triangle region together with that of the Maran district, at the moment has only two medical officers and twenty beds, and has been housed in a wooden building next to the other government offices. In Malaysia, one major problem concerning the provision of government services and therefore the construction of permanent buildings to house them is that decisions as to when these services are to be provided, and the allocation of funds, lie within the jurisdiction of the respective government departments. The regional authority, like the Jengka Regional Development Authority, whose role is primarily one of co-ordination, has no direct influence in these matters.

In the next section an effort is made to provide insights as to why the rural new towns of Malaysia, particularly Bandar Pusat, face such difficulties in attracting the industry which is planned as a catalyst for their accelerated growth. In the planning of Bandar Pusat and the other rural new towns, it was conceived that industry would have a multiplier effect. It was envisaged that it would stimulate or induce growth in other sectors of the urban economy in a fashion similar to Myrdal's process of cumulative causation. It is further postulated that, once this happens, the spread effect, as implied in growth pole theory, will flow from the core to the periphery.

What Lies beyond the Reality?

It has become clear now that the growth of industrial activities has been discouraging. This situation is not confined to Bandar Pusat alone, but to the other rural new towns as well.

There are three major factors which explain the difficulties which rural new towns, particularly Bandar Pusat, are facing in attracting industry (Fu-Chen Lo and Kamal Salih, 1978). The first of these is location. Although the locations of these new towns have been carefully selected and determined, all of them are sited in resource frontier zones, away from existing urban agglomerations and port facilities. This means that they are located at the points where industrial products cannot easily find ready markets or be exported. This places the rural new towns at a disadvantage in relation to the existing urban centres. Although road networks are constructed to link these rural new towns with the existing major urban nodes and ports (Aiken et al., 1982) this, however, does very little to improve their problem of 'industrial isolatedness'. The Locational Incentive Act passed in 1975 was designed to promote industrial dispersal and help the less-developed states. But it has had little effect in encouraging industrialization in the rural new towns.

Second, being plagued with slow rates of population growth, industries cannot expect to enjoy substantial urbanization economies. As discussed earlier, the urban activities and facilities available in Bandar Pusat are limited and rudimentary. It is also important to note that the water supply in Bandar Pusat has never been very satisfactory, and water rationing occurs frequently. Although this shortcoming should be rectified with time, such infrastructural inadequacy is, of course, very important in shaping the perceptions of industrial decision-makers concerning the suitability of places for productive activities. In addition, research centres, which are crucial for the development of new ideas and industrial products, are hard to find in such newly created places. The lack of such facilities and infrastructural elements has had at least two significant implications for industrial growth: (i) if certain industrial concerns do locate in rural new towns of this type, these facilities will in certain cases have to be provided by the industrialists themselves and additional costs thereby incurred; and (ii) it is extremely difficult to attract qualified personnel and industrialists to such locations. The difficulties involved in attempting to raise the level of urbanization economy in a short period coupled with a low level of urbanization planned for the rural new towns raises the issue of optimum urban size. In England, for example, the size of the initial new towns had to be increased in an effort to attract industrial plants.

The third factor is the agglomeration economies, which are noticeably lacking in such rural new towns. One of the conditions for industries to reap agglomeration economies is the presence of industrial linkages, both forward and backward, which as stipulated by Perroux in turn requires a propulsive industry. It is this industry that attracts other industries to locate at a particular location and which thereby leads to self-sustaining growth. In Bandar Pusat and the other rural new towns, the objective is to attract footloose industries. It has never been the intention to set up propulsive industry. This represents a departure from the original growth pole theory, and it is for this reason that these rural new towns find it difficult to attract industries. The absence of agglomeration economies means that industries will have to pay higher costs for certain kinds of services. It is equally true that industries will find it hard to attract and maintain a pool of talented and qualified personnel.

In theory, these locational weaknesses will ultimately be corrected if the existing major urban nodes move into a state of diseconomy or comparative inefficiency, which will lead to convergence. But in Malaysia, such has not been the case. In fact, the highest-order growth centres, Kuala Lumpur, Georgetown and Johore Bahru, are still attractive and continue to receive the highest proportion of industrial activities. But even if the major urban centres had started to experience diseconomy, this will not benefit the rural new towns immediately. The industrial relocation process will first settle for intermediate cities before the process filters down the urban hierarchy. In short, the rural new towns, because of their small size and weak locational advantage, are in the short term, and perhaps even in the long term, unable to compete efficiently for their fair share of industrial activities.

Conclusions

This chapter has been shown how, since the beginning of the colonial period, the processes that have produced uneven development have continued to affect both the space economy as a whole and ethnic groups within the country. This uneven development led to the adoption of clear regional development policies in Malaysia's national development planning when it was realized that the former sectoral approach to national development planning had failed to bring about an equitable distribution of development benefits over space and among the various groups of the population.

Thus, since 1971, with the implementation of the New Economic Policy, regional planning has been rigorously pursued in successive five-year plans. They have emphasized an urbanization strategy which is tied to a policy of industrial dispersal throughout the country. Accordingly, Malaysia has adopted a system of growth centres in order to fill the gap in the urban hierarchy. Several existing urban nodes have been identified for upgrading and new towns are being built. By examining the growth of Bandar Pusat in the Jengka Triangle region, this chapter has highlighted the dilemmas and difficulties which are faced by the rural new towns. The experience of Bandar Pusat suggests two major conclusions. First, the rural new towns have failed to expand fast enough to provide employment opportunities for the rural population. Second, they provide little scope for the rural population to enjoy the full range of urban facilities and services. Thus it is doubtful as to whether rural new towns have the vitality to bring about an equitable distribution of development benefits within Malaysia. Similar doubts have been expressed in many other contexts in recent years.

REFERENCES

Aiken, S.R., Leigh, C.H., Leinback, T.R. and Moss, M.R. (1982) *Development and Environment in Peninsular Malaysia*. Singapore: McGraw-Hill.

Appalraju, J. and Safier, M. (1976) 'Growth-centre strategies in less-developed countries', in: Gilbert, A. (ed.) *Development Planning and Spatial Structure*. London: Wiley.

Fu-Chen Lo and Kamal Salih (1978) 'Growth poles and regional policy in open dualistic economies: western theory and Asian reality', in: Fu-Chen Lo and Kamal Salih (eds) *Growth Pole Strategy and Regional Development Policy: Asian Experience and Alternative Approaches*. Oxford: Pergamon Press.

Furnell, D.C. (1976) 'The role of small service centres in regional and rural development: with special reference to Eastern Africa', in: Gilbert, A. (ed.) *Development Planning and Spatial Structure*. London: Wiley.

Friedmann, J. (1966) *Regional Development Policy: A Case Study of Venezuela*. Cambridge, Massachusetts: MIT Press.

Gilbert, G. A. (1976) 'Introduction', in: Gilbert, A. (ed.) *Development Planning and Spatial Structure*. London: Wiley.

Higgins, B. (1979) *Perils of Perspective Planning: Pahang Tenggara Revisited*. Nagoya: United Nations Centre for Regional Development.

Higgins, B. (1982) 'Development planning', in: Fisk, E. K. and Osman-Rani, H. (eds) *The Political Economy of Malaysia*. Kuala Lumpur: Oxford University Press.

Hamzah Sendut (1962) 'Patterns of urbanization in Malaya'. *Journal of Tropical Geography*, **16**: 114-30.

Kamal Salih (1975) 'Rationalised growth centre strategies in Malaysian regional development', in: Chee, S. and Khoo Siew Mun (eds) *Malaysian Economic Development and Policies*. Kuala Lumpur: Malaysian Economic Association.

Kamal Salih *et al.* (1978) 'Decentralization policy, growth pole approach, and resource frontier development: a synthesis of the response in four southeast Asian countries', in: Fu-Chen Lo and Kamal Salih (eds) *Growth Pole Strategy and Regional Development Policy: Asian Experience and Alternative Approaches*. Oxford: Pergamon.

Lim, H. K. (1978) *The Evolution of the Urban System in Malaya*. Kuala Lumpur: University of Malaya Press.

Malaysia, Federal Department of Town and Country Planning (1972) *The Jengka Regional Centre*. Report submitted to the Chairman of the Jengka Development Corporation. Kuala Lumpur: Federal Department of Town and Country Planning.

Malaysia (1976) *Third Malaysia Plan 1976-1980*. Kuala Lumpur: Government Printing Office.

Malaysia (LKWJ) (1985) 'Pembangunan Kawasan Wilayah Jengka dari segi Kemudahan Asas, Bandar Baru dan Kampung Tradisional'. Briefing given to Minister of Finance, unpublished, Bandar Pusat.

Malaysia (1986) *Fifth Malaysia Plan 1986-1990*. Kuala Lumpur: Government Printing Office.

Mohd Nawawi Arshad (1983) 'Effect of land development on socio-economic growth of region'. *Land Development Digest*, **6**(1): 15-26.

Mohd Rosli Buyong (1978) 'Dasar, Halacara dan strategi bagi Pembangunan Bandar Baru'. Paper presented at a seminar on Development of New Towns, Petaling Jaya, INTAN.

Mohd Suhaimi Mamat (1986) 'Peranan Bandar Pusat Jengka Dalam Pembangunan Wilayah Jengka Tiga Segi: Pandangan dari Kawasan Sekitar', Bangi. Unpublished B.A. graduation exercise submitted to the Department of Geography, Universiti Kebangsaan Malaysia.

Tunku Shamsul Bahrin and Perera, P. D. (1977) *21 Years of Land Development*. Kuala Lumpur: FELDA.

Tunku Shamsul Bahrin *et al.* (1986) *Kemajuan Tanah dan Penempatan Semula di Malaysia*. Kuala Lumpur: Dewan Bahasa dan Pustaka.

Sulong Mohamad (1985) 'Perancangan Bandar Baru, DEB dan Pembangunan Negara', in: Sulong Mohamad and Rahimah Abd. Aziz (eds) *Perbandaran dan Pembangunan Negara*. Bangi: Universiti Kebangsaan Malaysia Press.

Sulong Mohamad and Katiman Rostam (1987) 'Matlamat dan Arah Pembangunan Bandar Baru di Malaysia: Pengalaman Bandar Baru Bangi, Selongor', in: Persatuan Sains Sosial Malaysia (eds) *Pembangunan di Malaysia: Perencanaan, Perlaksanaan dan Prestasi*. Kuala Lumpur: Persatuan Sains Sosial Malaysia.

[9]
Metropolitan Dominance in India: The Demographic Imprint of Colonial Dependency

K. Sita and M. Chatterjee

Overview

In India, as in many other developing countries, the long period of colonial rule has left deep imprints on the organization of economic space. Forty years after the end of colonial domination and the attainment of independence, some of the characteristic features of a colonial space economy persist. One of the aspects in which this persistence is most apparent is the dominance of the three colonial port cities of Bombay, Calcutta and Madras, together with the administrative centre of Delhi. This study focuses on the extent of the contemporary dominance which is exerted by the four metropolitan centres, as witnessed by the spatial distribution of urban population.

The chapter highlights, both statistically and graphically, the sharp distance-decay effect of urban population that occurs away from each of the major metropolitan centres. There is a very high degree of concentration of urban population in the metropolitan centres themselves, and in their immediate vicinity, with a sharp fall over a short distance. Beyond this there is a marked metropolitan shadow-zone in which urban growth appears to have been inhibited by the towering metropolitan centres. Urban population picks up again at greater distances owing to the emergence of a second level of metropolitan centres.

The study suggests that urbanization in India has been a veritable process of *metropolitanization*, the four metropolises dominating the urban scene and reflecting the indelible imprint of the colonial past. However, the work also demonstrates that post-independence trends have begun to have an impact on the organization of space, as witnessed by the emergence of a number of inland urban centres.

Urbanization in India

India has a long tradition of urbanization dating back nearly five thousand years, the Indus Valley civilization being associated with the birth of some of the earliest urban settlements in the world. In successive historical periods, various factors came into play so that the present-day urban pattern of India is the result of processes which have been operating over many centuries. However, as in many developing countries, the long period of colonial domination has left a deep imprint on the system of urban settlements.

The initial impact of colonial rule was the decline of several towns performing traditional activities; this resulted in de-urbanization between the mid-eighteenth century and the mid-nineteenth century (National Institute of Urban Affairs, 1988). Later, with the expansion of British political control, a new dimension was introduced to urban development in India. The British established urban centres with a monetary-based economic system, typical of towns in a capitalist society, which were unlike the consumption-oriented feudal cities of medieval India. The concentration of industrial and commercial investment in and around the port cities of Calcutta, Bombay and Madras led to their development as powerful urban magnets (Alam, 1984). The Indo-British seaports had become the major metropolises of the subcontinent by the end of the nineteenth century and were the focal points of India's modern urban development (Brush, 1977). The peripheral location of these large conurbations reflects the prolonged operation of external factors in the colonial period (Sdasyuk, 1976).

Unlike many developing countries, India does not exhibit the dominance of a single urban centre; this has been interpreted by some as indicating the absence of primacy (National Institute of Urban Affairs, 1988). However, there is no doubt that, at the national level, the economy of the country is spatially organized by the four metropolitan cities of Bombay, Calcutta, Delhi and Madras (Alam, 1984; Raza and Aggarwal, 1986; Sita and Chatterjee, 1989). Hence, a primate-city growth pattern is discernible in all the four elemental regional metropolitan systems of India. This primate pattern is partly the result of the colonial legacy and partly due to sectorally oriented national development policies in the intervening period (Prakasa Rao, 1982). The primate metropolises stand out as 'enclaves', with a sharp distance-decay in levels of development being apparent around them. The failure of the primate cities to diffuse development has been attributed to the overall low level of development and the structure of the wider economic system (McGee, 1971). The process underlying the nonconformity between urban and rural population growth and the imbalanced economic development and social transformation has been labelled 'pseudo-urbanization' (McGee, 1971) and 'dysfunctional

urbanization' (Raza et al., 1979). Since these primate cities differ fundamentally from their counterparts in developed countries, it has been
suggested that it is desirable to describe them as 'satellite primate cities'
(Raza et al., 1979).

Metropolitan Dominance: Methodology

This chapter focuses on the present-day extent of the dominance of the
four metropolitan centres in terms of the spatial distribution of urban
population in India. Owing to constraints of space and time, only the
Class-I designated cities of India in 1981 have been considered. These
cities, which have populations of 100,000 and above, are mapped in Figure
9.1. However, since the Class I towns accounted for 60 per cent of the
urban population in 1981, the conclusions drawn from the analysis are
a good approximation to the urban scenario prevailing in India as a whole.
The analysis was carried out for three time periods: 1951, 1971 and 1981.
The first date was chosen as it represents the situation just after
Independence, while 1971 and 1981 were selected in order to focus on
recent trends.

Of the total of 216 Class I towns existing in 1981, four were the major
metropoles, according to data from the 1981 Census of India. Each of
the remaining 212 cities was categorized according to its distance from
the metropole to which it was nearest. The measure used was not the
straight-line distance, but the travel distance overland as this is more
realistic, particularly in the Indian context. The cities were classified using
50 km distance bands as the spatial units of measurement. For each
metropole, the urban population in each of the decadal years 1951, 1971,
1981, as well as levels of urban growth in 1951–81 and 1971–81 in each
distance band, was determined. A graphical representation of this procedure was carried out to examine the extent to which a distance-decay
effect was operating for the distribution of urban population and of urban
growth with reference to the travel distance from the metropoles. The
data for the individual metropoles were also used in order to obtain the
aggregate picture. The proportions of the urban population and of urban
growth in the hinterland of the metropole concentrated in each distance
band was determined to obtain the relative picture. The occupational structures of the cities were also analysed to determine the characteristics of
the different distance bands. The 1981 Indian Census data do not enable
a differentiation of workers according to the primary, secondary and
tertiary sectors, but this analysis was carried out using data from the 1971
Indian Census.

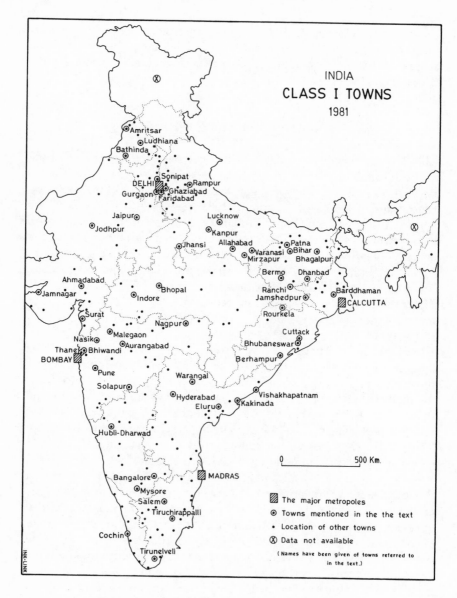

Figure 9.1. India's Class I towns and cities in 1981.

The Distribution of Urban Population

The urban centres considered in this study had a total population of 30 million in 1951, 65 million in 1971 and nearly 94 million in 1981. In the case of Delhi, the concentration in the first distance band increased from 1.5 million in 1951 to approximately 4 million in 1971 and 6.5 million in 1981 (Table 9.1). This growth is due to the Delhi urban agglomeration and towns such as Faridabad, Ghaziabad, Gurgaon and Sonipat. There is a sharp fall in the next distance band and a marked shadow zone extends up to 300 km (Figure 9.2a). There are two subsidiary peaks at 300–350 km and 400–450 km; the first is due to the towns of Ludhiana and Bhatinda, while the latter is, to a great extent, due to the Kanpur urban agglomeration and to a lesser extent to towns such as Amritsar and Jhansi. Beyond there are three minor peaks at 500–550 km, 600–650 km and 700–750 km reflecting Lucknow and Rampur in the first, Allahabad and Jodhpur in the second, Bhopal, Mirzapur and Jaipur in the third.

For Bombay, the concentration in the first distance band is very marked; it increased from approximately 3 million in 1951 to 6.3 million in 1971 and 8.7 million in 1981; Greater Bombay, Thane and Bhiwandi have contributed to it. The fall is very sharp through the second to the third distance band, which had no Class I city (Figure 9.2b). The subsidiary peak is at 450–500 km, and is due primarily to Ahmedabad and to a lesser extent to Solapur and Aurangabad. Two minor peaks occur between 150–200 km and 250–300 km, due to Pune and Nasik in the former case, and Surat and Malegaon in the latter. Another minor peak is visible in the 750–800 and 800–850 bands, this being due to Indore, Hubli-Dharwad, Nagpur and Jamnagar.

Calcutta shows the maximum degree of concentration in the first distance band; the increase has been remarkable – from 2.6 million in 1951 to 7.1 million in 1971 and 9.2 million in 1981. The Hooghly-side conurbation is responsible for this. The extremely sharp fall in the next distance band and the marked shadow effect up to 250 km are noticeable (Figure 9.2c). Minor peaks occur at 250–300 km, 400–450 km, 500–550 km and 650–700 km, these being due to Jamshedpur and Dhanbad in the first case, Ranchi, Cuttack, Rourkela and Bhagalpur in the second, Patna and Bihar in the third and Varanasi and Behrampur in the fourth.

Among the four metropoles, Madras shows the lowest degree of concentration in the first distance band. The urban population in this zone increased from 1.4 million in 1951 to 3.2 million in 1971 and 4.3 million in 1981; a shadow zone extends beyond up to 300 km (Figure 9.2d). The peaks which occur at 300–350 km and 450–500 km are noticeable as they rival and even surpass that in the first distance band, particularly in 1981. The peak at 300–350 km is due primarily to Bangalore and to a lesser extent to centres such as Salem and Tiruchirapalli, while the one at

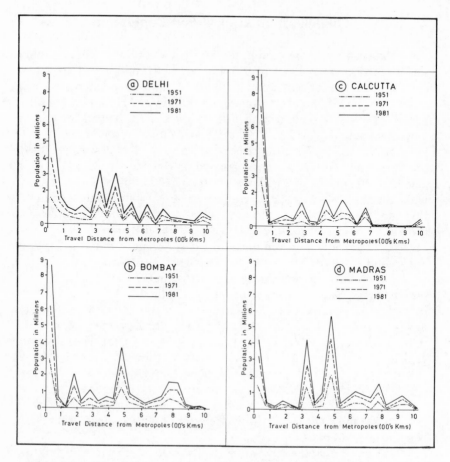

Figure 9.2.   Class I city populations with distance from the four metropoles;
1951–81.

450–500 km reflexes the location of Hyderabad, Mysore and Eluru. Beyond
500 km, there is a very minor peak at 600–650 km due to Warangal,
Kakinada, Tirunelveli and another at 750–800 km due mainly to Visa-
khapatnam and Cochin.

The aggregate situation pertaining with respect to the four metropolises
combined is shown in Figure 9.3. The graph serves to emphasize the overall
urban demographic dominance which pertains in India. It also suggests
that this has increased between 1951 and 1981.

Table 9.1. Population of Class I cities at different distance bands (population in '000s)

Distance bands (km)	Delhi 1951	Delhi 1971	Delhi 1981	Bombay 1951	Bombay 1971	Bombay 1981	Calcutta 1951	Calcutta 1971	Calcutta 1981	Madras 1951	Madras 1971	Madras 1981	Aggregate 1951	Aggregate 1971	Aggregate 1981
Less than 50	1,481	4,000	6,543	2,915	6,257	8,731	2,548	7,125	9,293	1,416	3,170	4,277	8,361	20,551	28,844
50–99	776	1,274	1,717	80	396	648	75	143	167	190	298	392	1,123	2,112	2,925
100–49	470	744	990	–	–	–	185	255	364	25	65	115	682	1,065	1,470
150–99	385	580	765	578	1,407	2,114	82	347	634	81	289	488	1,126	2,623	4,001
200–49	199	678	1,127	122	217	340	76	242	365	170	242	311	566	1,378	2,144
250–99	252	400	584	278	685	1,158	252	875	1,347	37	66	103	820	2,026	3,192
300–49	1,027	2,069	3,173	153	266	451	–	107	261	1,329	2,725	4,285	2,508	5,167	8,170
350–99	333	568	796	211	467	744	43	60	132	90	250	395	676	1,344	2,067
400–49	1,378	2,234	3,036	225	326	607	324	900	1,589	336	735	1,044	2,263	4,195	6,276
450–99	196	343	490	1,265	2,562	3,733	208	349	488	2,381	4,282	5,704	4,050	7,536	10,415
500–99	631	975	1,210	326	709	924	396	733	1,270	100	160	220	1,454	2,577	3,623
550–99	30	82	122	219	399	558	321	611	928	222	435	607	792	1,526	2,216
600–49	513	829	1,136	86	214	300	–	–	–	396	842	1,168	995	1,885	2,605
650–99	45	74	103	153	427	609	482	803	1,067	313	632	980	992	1,935	2,759
700–49	241	555	906	262	504	726	–	–	–	30	439	686	533	1,501	2,317
740–99	209	341	448	645	1,148	1,662	–	–	–	463	1,009	1,583	1,317	2,498	3,693
800–49	162	273	348	554	1,143	1,615	25	71	110	67	87	115	808	1,574	2,188
850–99	121	169	221	101	236	350	202	228	490	196	395	568	438	1,028	1,629
900–49	66	146	207	23	97	130	–	–	–	304	625	825	394	868	1,163
950–99	257	500	758	102	171	239	–	–	–	267	367	515	626	1,037	1,511
1,000 and more	162	289	431	–	–	–	57	223	329	–	–	–	219	512	760

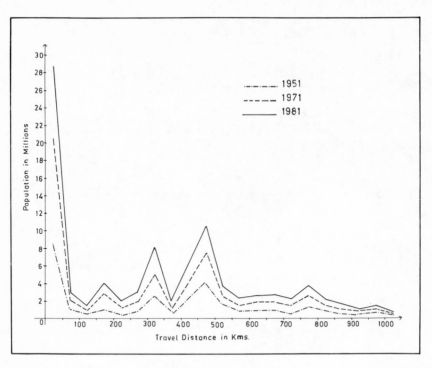

Figure 9.3. Class I city populations with distance from the metropoles: the aggregate situation 1951–81.

Relative Degree of Concentration

The relative degree of concentration in each distance band for each metropole in the three decadal years is represented in Table 9.2 and Figure 9.4. It is evident that, in general, the first distance band had the highest degree of concentration. The share of this distance band of the urban population considered in this analysis increased from 27.2 per cent in 1951 to 31.64 per cent in 1971 and 30.69 per cent in 1981. Among the four metropoles, Calcutta stands out with over 50 per cent of the Class I city population of its hinterland in the first distance band. As mentioned earlier Madras is an exception, since the 450–500 km distance band records a higher degree of concentration than the first.

Another noteworthy feature is that in all the metropoles except Delhi there was a decline in the relative degree of concentration in the first distance band between 1971 and 1981 in spite of the increase in absolute numbers. This is also true of some of the subsidiary peaks. The subsidiary peak

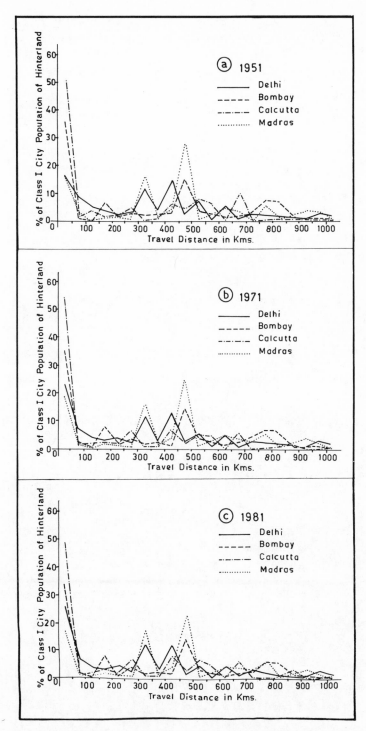

Figure 9.4. The relative disposition of Class I city populations with distance away from the metropoles: the aggregate situation 1951–81.

Table 9.2. Percentage share of urban population of Class I towns at different distance bands from the metropoles

Distance bands (km)	Delhi 1951	Delhi 1971	Delhi 1981	Bombay 1951	Bombay 1971	Bombay 1981	Calcutta 1951	Calcutta 1971	Calcutta 1981	Madras 1951	Madras 1971	Madras 1981	Aggregate 1951	Aggregate 1971	Aggregate 1981
Less than 50	16.58	23.35	26.06	35.13	35.49	34.05	50.02	54.49	49.33	16.83	18.33	17.54	27.20	31.64	30.70
50–99	8.68	7.44	6.84	0.94	2.24	2.52	1.48	1.09	0.88	2.26	1.74	1.61	3.65	3.25	3.11
100–49	5.27	4.35	3.94	—	—	—	3.65	1.95	1.94	0.29	0.38	0.47	2.21	1.64	1.57
150–99	4.31	3.39	3.05	6.97	7.98	8.24	1.60	2.65	3.36	0.96	1.69	2.00	3.66	4.04	4.26
200–49	2.22	3.95	4.49	1.46	1.22	1.32	1.50	1.85	1.94	2.02	1.41	1.28	1.84	2.12	2.28
250–99	2.82	2.33	2.32	3.35	3.88	4.51	4.95	6.69	7.14	0.44	0.39	0.42	2.66	3.47	3.40
300–49	11.50	12.07	12.63	1.84	1.50	1.76	—	0.82	1.39	15.79	15.92	17.58	8.16	7.96	8.70
350–99	3.72	3.32	3.17	2.55	2.64	2.90	0.83	0.46	0.69	1.06	1.46	1.62	2.20	2.07	2.20
400–49	15.42	13.04	12.09	2.71	1.82	2.36	6.36	6.88	8.44	4.00	4.29	4.28	7.36	6.45	6.67
450–99	2.19	2.01	1.95	15.24	14.53	14.56	4.08	2.67	2.59	28.30	25.02	23.39	13.17	11.60	11.09
500–49	7.06	5.70	4.82	3.93	4.01	3.60	7.76	5.60	6.74	1.19	0.93	0.90	4.73	3.97	3.86
550–99	0.33	0.48	0.49	2.64	2.26	2.17	6.30	4.67	4.92	2.64	2.54	2.49	2.56	2.35	2.36
600–49	5.74	4.84	4.52	1.04	1.21	1.17	—	—	—	4.70	4.92	4.79	3.23	2.90	2.77
650–99	0.50	0.43	0.41	1.83	2.42	2.37	9.47	6.14	5.66	3.72	3.69	4.02	3.22	2.98	2.94
700–49	2.70	3.26	3.61	3.16	2.85	2.83	—	—	—	0.36	2.57	2.81	1.73	2.32	2.46
750–99	2.34	1.99	1.78	7.77	6.51	6.48	—	—	—	5.50	5.89	6.50	4.28	3.85	3.92
800–49	1.81	1.59	1.39	6.67	6.48	6.29	0.49	0.55	0.58	0.79	0.51	0.47	2.62	2.42	2.33
850–99	1.35	0.98	0.88	1.22	1.33	1.37	0.40	1.74	2.60	2.32	2.31	2.33	1.42	1.25	1.74
900–49	0.74	0.85	0.83	0.28	0.54	0.56	—	—	—	3.61	3.65	3.38	1.38	1.34	1.23
950–99	2.88	2.92	3.02	1.23	0.96	0.93	—	—	—	3.17	2.15	2.11	2.03	1.60	1.60
1,000 and above	1.82	1.69	1.72	—	—	—	1.11	1.70	1.74	—	—	—	0.69	0.79	0.81

at 450–500 km shows a decline from 13.17 per cent in 1951 to 11.60 per cent in 1971 and 11.08 per cent in 1981. The other subsidiary peak at 300–350 km showed a decrease from 8.16 per cent in 1951 to 7.96 per cent in 1971; however, it increased again to 8.69 per cent in 1981. Since the decrease in the relative degree of concentration has not been accompanied by an absolute decrease, it is probably due to urban spread rather than deconcentration *per se*. The marked shadow zone extending from 50–150 km is noteworthy.

Urban Growth

The cities considered in the present study experienced a total urban growth of approximately 63 million during the period 1951–81, of which 29 million was in the decade 1971–81 (Table 9.3). The first distance band accounted for 20.5 million or 32.38 per cent of the growth in 1951–81 and 8.3 million or 28.6 per cent during 1971–81 (Table 9.4 and Figures 9.5 and 9.6). It is clear that all the metropoles registered a marked growth in this distance band; however, it is particularly noteworthy for Calcutta. Two subsidiary peaks in urban growth are at 300–350 km and 450–500 km. In the case of the 300–350 km band it is primarily due to the growth in the hinterlands of Madras and Delhi of towns such as Bangalore and Ludhiana. On the other hand, the growth in the 450–500 km band has taken place mainly in the hinterlands of Bombay and Madras of towns such as Ahmedabad, Aurangabad and Hyderabad. Minor peaks in urban growth occur at 400–450 km and 150–200 km; the first is due to the growth of Kanpur, Dhanbad and Jamshedpur in the hinterlands of Delhi and Calcutta, the second is due to Pune and Nasik near Bombay.

Occupational Structure of the Distance Bands

The cities considered in the present analysis had a workforce of nearly 19 million in 1971. Of this total, 11.3 million or 59.5 per cent were engaged in tertiary economic activities, 6.5 million or 34.7 per cent in secondary occupations and 1.2 million or 5.8 per cent in primary activities. .

In general there was not much difference in the occupational structure of the different distance bands (Table 9.5). However, in the case of Delhi, tertiary activities are found to be of overwhelming significance in the first distance band, where they accounted for 87.9 per cent of the workforce. It is only in the case of Calcutta that some distance bands show a greater concentration of secondary rather than tertiary activities. Neither the first distance band nor the two bands at 450–500 km and 300–350 km where peaks were present in terms of population and urban

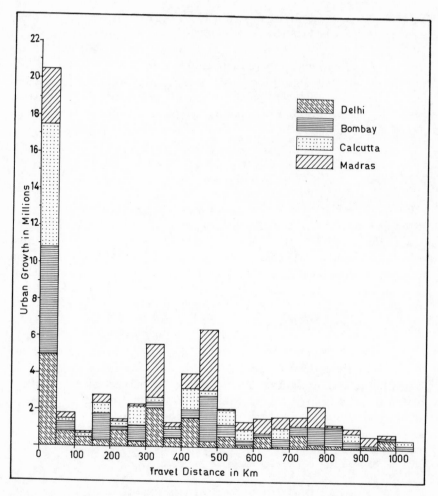

Figure 9.5. Urban growth in Class I cities as a function of distance from the metropoles, 1951–81.

growth show any significant difference as compared to other bands in occupational structure. Thus the difference between the bands cannot be accounted for in terms of variations in their occupational characteristics.

Discussion

This analysis has highlighted the sharp distance-decay effect in terms of urban population with respect to distance from the four major metropoles of India. There is a high degree of concentration in the metropoles them-

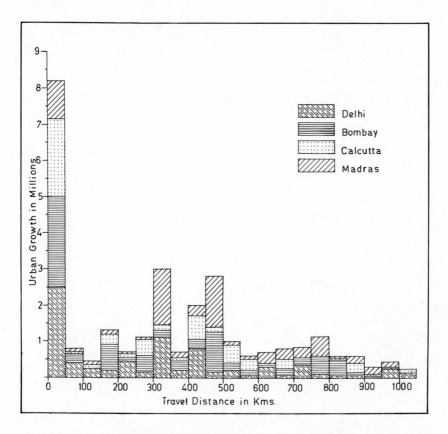

Figure 9.6.   Urban growth in Class I cities as a function of distance from the metropoles, 1971–1981.

selves and in their immediate vicinity; nearly one-third of the Class I city population of India is concentrated within 50 km travel distance of the metropoles. Immediately beyond there is a sharp fall, as is evidenced by the fact that the share of the two successive 50 km distance bands falls to 3 per cent and 1 per cent respectively. This indicates the presence of a marked metropolitan shadow zone where urban growth appears to have been inhibited by the towering metropolitan centres. Urban population picks up again at greater distances due to the presence of the second-level, inland metropolitan centres.

Since Independence, the relative share of the first distance band has registered a marked increase in the case of Delhi. This indicates the explosive urban growth experienced by the union territory where massive investments

Table 9.3. Urban growth in Class I cities from 1971 to 1981 and 1951 to 1981 by distance band

Distance bands (km)	Delhi 1971–81	Delhi 1951–81	Bombay 1971–81	Bombay 1951–81	Calcutta 1971–81	Calcutta 1951–81	Madras 1971–81	Madras 1951–81	Aggregate 1971–81	Aggregate 1951–81
Less than 50	2,543	5,062	2,474	5,816	2,168	6,745	1,107	2,861	8,293	20,483
50–99	443	941	252	567	24	92	94	202	813	1,802
100–49	246	520	—	—	149	179	50	90	495	788
150–99	185	380	707	1,536	287	552	199	407	1,378	2,876
200–49	449	928	123	218	123	289	69	141	766	1,578
250–99	184	331	473	880	473	1,095	37	66	1,166	2,372
300–49	1,104	2,146	185	298	154	261	1,560	2,956	3,003	5,662
350–99	228	463	277	533	72	89	145	305	723	1,391
400–49	802	1,658	281	382	689	1,265	309	708	2,081	4,013
450–99	147	294	1,171	2,468	139	280	1,422	3,323	2,879	6,365
500–49	235	579	215	598	537	874	60	120	1,047	2,169
550–99	40	92	159	339	317	607	172	385	690	1,424
600–49	307	623	86	214	—	—	326	772	720	1,610
650–99	29	58	182	457	264	585	348	667	824	1,767
700–49	348	665	222	464	—	—	247	656	816	1,784
750–99	107	239	514	1,017	—	—	574	1,120	1,195	2,376
800–49	75	186	472	1,061	38	85	29	48	614	1,380
850–99	52	100	114	249	262	469	173	372	601	1,191
900–49	61	141	33	107	—	—	200	521	295	769
950–99	258	501	68	137	—	—	148	248	474	886
1,000 and above	142	269	—	—	106	272	—	—	248	541

Table 9.4. Percentage share of urban growth of the hinterland in different distance bands from the metropoles

Distance bands (km)	Delhi 1971–81	Delhi 1951–81	Bombay 1971–81	Bombay 1951–81	Calcutta 1971–81	Calcutta 1951–81	Madras 1971–81	Madras 1951–81	Aggregate 1971–81	Aggregate 1951–81
Less than 50	31.85	31.29	30.88	33.53	37.37	49.08	15.22	17.91	28.56	32.38
50–99	5.54	5.81	3.15	3.28	0.42	0.68	1.29	1.26	2.80	2.84
100–49	3.09	3.20	—	—	2.57	1.31	0.68	0.56	1.40	1.25
150–99	2.32	2.35	8.84	8.85	4.97	4.03	2.74	2.55	4.75	4.54
200–49	5.63	5.74	1.54	1.26	2.14	2.11	0.95	0.88	2.64	2.49
250–99	2.30	2.05	5.91	5.08	8.19	7.96	0.51	0.41	4.03	3.77
300–49	13.82	13.26	2.31	1.72	2.67	1.90	21.45	18.51	10.34	8.95
350–99	2.86	2.86	3.47	3.08	1.25	0.64	1.99	1.92	2.47	2.19
400–49	10.04	10.24	3.50	2.21	11.96	9.20	4.25	4.44	7.16	6.34
450–99	1.84	1.81	14.62	14.23	2.41	2.04	19.50	20.81	9.92	10.06
500–49	2.94	3.57	2.66	3.44	9.31	6.36	0.64	0.75	3.61	3.45
550–99	0.50	0.57	1.99	1.95	5.50	4.42	2.38	2.42	2.38	2.25
600–49	3.85	3.85	1.08	1.23	—	—	4.48	4.87	2.47	2.55
650–99	0.36	0.35	2.26	2.63	4.59	4.25	4.79	4.17	2.84	2.80
700–49	4.35	4.10	2.77	2.67	—	—	3.39	4.10	2.81	2.83
750–99	1.35	1.47	6.41	5.86	—	—	7.90	7.01	4.11	3.76
800–49	0.94	1.15	5.90	6.14	0.66	0.61	0.39	0.30	2.11	2.20
850–99	0.65	0.62	1.43	1.44	4.55	3.42	2.38	2.33	2.08	1.88
900–49	0.77	0.87	0.42	0.62	—	—	2.76	3.27	1.03	1.21
950–99	3.23	3.10	0.85	0.78	—	—	2.05	1.55	1.63	1.40
1,000 and above	1.78	1.65	—	—	1.11	1.99	—	—	0.86	0.85

153

Table 9.5. Occupational structure of Class I city population at different distance bands, 1971

Distance bands (km)	Delhi			Bombay			Calcutta			Madras			Aggregate		
	P	S	T	P	S	T	P	S	T	P	S	T	P	S	T
Less than 50	2.2	9.9	87.9	1.3	46.1	52.5	1.6	41.1	57.3	4.3	34.6	61.1	2.0	38.0	60.0
50–99	4.2	30.9	64.9	2.2	46.9	50.9	11.0	19.7	69.3	6.7	38.9	54.4	4.6	34.6	60.8
100–49	7.3	29.2	63.5	—	—	—	5.9	24.3	69.8	7.5	21.1	71.4	7.0	27.6	65.4
150–99	5.1	27.7	67.2	5.0	36.6	58.4	8.2	45.8	46.0	11.2	33.3	55.5	6.1	35.7	58.2
200–49	3.2	30.0	66.8	6.6	43.0	50.4	5.7	42.3	52.0	14.0	22.7	63.3	5.9	32.8	61.3
250–99	5.5	25.7	68.8	4.8	60.2	35.0	32.6	35.3	32.1	7.6	22.6	69.8	16.2	44.0	39.8
300–49	4.5	35.2	60.3	7.8	27.0	65.2	22.5	56.7	20.8	4.6	40.8	54.6	5.4	39.2	55.4
350–99	5.8	32.3	61.9	4.4	39.1	56.5	2.5	11.6	85.9	10.6	33.5	55.9	6.4	34.0	59.7
400–49	3.6	32.2	64.2	14.8	27.1	58.1	7.6	29.3	63.1	8.6	27.3	64.1	6.2	30.3	63.5
450–99	5.0	23.1	71.9	3.3	48.8	47.9	13.7	21.9	64.4	6.8	26.4	66.8	6.0	32.7	61.3
500–49	4.4	24.8	70.8	10.7	30.5	58.8	21.5	18.8	59.7	22.7	19.9	57.3	12.1	24.4	63.5
550–99	23.9	32.4	43.7	9.1	25.3	65.6	13.0	20.6	66.4	10.2	31.0	58.8	11.9	25.8	62.3
600–49	6.0	23.2	70.8	9.1	34.4	56.5	—	—	—	12.9	35.4	51.7	9.6	30.1	60.3
650–99	18.5	22.0	59.5	7.1	31.4	61.5	7.8	33.8	58.4	11.7	29.0	59.3	9.6	31.2	59.2
700–49	6.5	31.7	61.8	5.1	36.7	58.2	—	—	—	4.6	27.1	68.3	5.5	31.9	62.6
750–99	8.0	19.1	72.9	6.1	42.1	51.8	—	—	—	11.9	31.4	56.7	8.0	35.6	56.4
800–49	6.3	33.4	60.3	5.5	36.4	58.1	37.3	11.4	51.3	5.3	22.5	72.2	7.2	33.8	59.0
850–99	23.0	36.6	40.4	19.0	20.3	60.7	—	—	—	7.9	36.6	55.5	13.8	32.0	54.2
900–49	7.3	41.0	51.7	10.2	32.3	57.5	—	—	—	6.8	30.1	63.1	7.2	32.2	60.6
950–99	4.5	34.2	61.3	14.0	29.5	56.5	—	—	—	8.9	35.0	56.1	8.0	33.4	58.6
1,000 and above	12.2	27.5	60.3	—	—	—	6.4	24.2	69.4	—	—	—	9.5	26.0	64.5

The figures represent percentage of workers in primary (P), secondary (S) and tertiary (T) activities.

by central government in developmental activities have induced large-scale migration into the area. It also reflects the important role of administrative activity along with its multiplier effects, which cannot be underestimated. As the National Institute of Urban Affairs rightly points out, any urban decentralization policy would be assured of greater success if it were accompanied by an administration decentralization policy (National Institute of Urban Affairs, 1988: 16). In the case of the three port cities, though the relative share of the first distance band increased between 1951 and 1971, there was a decrease in the decade 1971–81; this is very marked in the case of Calcutta. This decrease was not accompanied by a decline in absolute numbers, suggesting that it was due more to urban sprawl than to deconcentration *per se*.

The study lends support to Sdasyuk's conclusion that the dynamics of formation of the territorial structure of India's economy in the post-Independence period reveals the focal role on an all-India scale of the three major port cities and the capital. These four centres form the apexes of a vast quadrangle (see Figure 9.1), which constitutes the basic framework of the territorial structure of the country (Sdasyuk, 1976).

Prakasa Rao has recognized three major facets of Indian urbanization: metropolitanization/industrialization, commercialization, and the urbanization of the countryside (Prakasa Rao, 1982). It is evident that the first of these is still very significant, and the four metropoles dominate the urban scene; this is the indelible imprint of the colonial past. However, there are some signs that post-Independence trends are beginning to have an observable impact on the organization of space. The emergence and growth of inland cities such as Ahmedabad, Bangalore, Hyderabad and Kanpur are resulting in a modification of the earlier pattern that prevailed during the colonial period.

REFERENCES

Alam, S.M. (1984) 'The national settlement system of India', in: Bourne, L.S. et al. (eds) *Urbanisation and Settlement Systems: International Perspectives*. Oxford: Oxford University Press, 453–72.

Brush, J.E. (1977) 'Growth and spatial structure of Indian cities', in: Noble, A.G. and Dutt, A.K. (eds) *Indian Urbanization and Planning*. New Delhi: Tata McGraw Hill, 64–92.

McGee, T. (1971) *The Urbanization Process in the Third World*. London: Bell.

National Institute of Urban Affairs (1988) *State of India's Urbanisation*. New Delhi: National Institute of Urban Affairs.

Prakasa Rao, V.L.S. (1982) *Urbanization in India*. New Delhi: Concept.

Raza, M. and Aggarwal, Y. (1986) *Transport Geography of India: Commodity Flows and the Regional Structure of the Indian Economy*. New Delhi: Concept.

Raza, M., Habib, A. and Kundu, A. (1977) *Spatial Organisation and Urbanisation in India – A Case Study of Underdevelopment*, Occasional Paper No. 9. New Delhi: Jawaharlal Nehru University.

Sdasyuk, G. V. (1976) 'India's urban growth and problems of regional planning', in: Alam, S. M. and Pokshishevsky, V. V. (eds) *Urbanization in Developing Countries*. Hyderabad: Osmania University.

Sita, K. and Chatterjee, M. (1989) 'The economic structuring of India'. *International Journal of Urban and Regional Research*, 13(2): 245–55.

[10]
Urbanization and Spatial Strategies in West Africa

Ademola T. Salau

Introduction

Urbanization is one of the most important and highly visible aspects of the process of change which is taking place in West Africa today. Although the proportion of the total population that is living in cities is still relatively low, the rate of urbanization in West Africa, especially in the past two decades, has been one of the most rapid in the world. The magnitude of the rate of urbanization can be gleaned from the United Nations' projection that by the year 2000 West Africa will be almost 40 per cent urbanized, as compared to less than 30 per cent at present (Riddell, 1980: 26). Of course, there is considerable variation in the level of urbanization across the region, but the fact remains that all West African countries are inexorably caught up in this fundamental process.

In this chapter, the pattern of urbanization in West Africa is examined, focusing in particular on the factors responsible and the policies which have been or are currently being adopted by governments in the region in order to influence population distribution and achieve an orderly pattern of human settlements. The chapter is divided into three main parts. The first considers the historical context of urbanization, while the second provides a general overview of the contemporary pattern of urbanization in West Africa. The third and longest part examines the national urban development policies that are being implemented in West African countries today.

The Historical Context of Urbanization of West Africa

West Africa is different from many parts of sub-Saharan Africa in that it has a long tradition of urban development which predates the arrival of Europeans. In the savannah zone and forest belt important kingdoms and empires such as those of Ghana, Mali, Songhai, Oyo, Benin had emerged which were essentially based on centralized political and economic power located in cities.

The importance of these kingdoms rested to a large extent on their export and import trade relations, and these were predicated on cities such as Kano, Timbuktu, Gao, Benin, Ougadougou, Maradi, Katsina, Segou and Bamako. These were essentially pre-industrial cities performing important administrative and commercial functions. A city like Timbuktu was also a centre of knowledge and intellectual life and was focused on a university (Gutkind, 1974: 13). Thus, before the coming of the Europeans, the northern savannah areas were the major foci of the socio-economic and political activities of the West African region. The slave trade and the succeeding colonial economy effected the redirection of economic activities, population and administration towards the forest belt and the coast. The production of cocoa, oil palm, timber and rubber provided the impetus for migration from the interior to the coast. Other factors accounting for this spatial shift of focus are described by Sudarkassa (1977: 178–9) as follows:

> By the imposition of taxes, the introduction of various goods and services that had to be purchased with European currencies, and the passage of compulsory labour laws, colonial governments virtually and literally forced people to move away from those areas which could not provide them with adequate cash incomes. For most of West Africa, with the exception of Nigeria, the inland areas became virtually labour reserves for the coast. Something of the magnitude of the resultant population shifts is indicated by Samir Amin's (1974) estimate that between 1920 and 1970 there was a net population transfer (including migrants and their offspring) of at least 4.8 million persons from the interior to the coast. This number represented about 21 per cent of the coastal population and 26 per cent of the inland population of West Africa in 1970.

Thus, the present development landscape in most West African countries is in great part the result of these historical forces. Colonialism destroyed the traditional economy based on subsistence and exchange systems, and a modern export-oriented economy was erected in its place. New agricultural commodities such as cocoa were introduced in conjunction with modern production and marketing methods. The pre-existing peasant economies were thereby restructured, though not entirely eliminated, to respond to these external interventions. Underlying uneven spatial development therefore was the colonial objective of achieving the maximum exploitation of resources at minimum costs.

Colonialism also ushered in a new administrative system. Invariably coastal centres were chosen to serve as administrative centres, ports and the commercial nuclei of the colonies. Investment in infrastructural provision and public services in these capitals enhanced their rapid growth into primate cities within their respective countries. The establishment of a modern transportation network imposed a new pattern of spatial integration and generated a new system of cities for the export-oriented economy. Contemporary West African cities thus bear heavy imprints of colonial and European culture and it is not surprising that they have been lumped together under the ideal type 'colonial city'. According to Williams (1970: 236) the colonial city

> developed . . . as a centre of commerce and administration rather than industrial production. It originated as a means whereby the metropolitan rulers established a base for the administration of the countryside, and the exploitation of its resources, and consequently the transfer of the surplus extracted from the countryside to the metropolis. At the same time, the city itself engaged in the parasitical extractions of a surplus from the countryside.

Colonialism thus effected a spatial shift in the focus of West Africa from the inland areas to the coast. Thus, the legacy of colonialism in relation to the modern process of urbanization and the growth of cities in West Africa is reflected in this concentration on, or near to, the coast. For example, the capitals of all countries in West Africa, with the exception of the landlocked nations, are to be found on the coast. There is also a dense concentration of cities within a belt extending some 300 km from the coast. In the case of Ghana, White and Gleave (1971: 283) note that 113 out of 135 settlements with populations of 5,000 and above are located within a broadly defined coastal ·belt. In Nigeria, twelve or more of the twenty largest cities are located on the coast or within 200 km of it.

However, without doubt, the most important and lasting effect of colonialism on urban development and urbanization in West Africa has been the incorporation, albeit as a peripheral part, of these countries into the world metropolitan or capitalist system. Thus, the development and growth of most West African cities is essentially different from that which took place in eighteenth-century western Europe. Whereas in Europe the process was the result of local developments, with modern techniques being introduced in both agriculture and manufacturing, in most parts of West Africa it has essentially been effected by outside powers, the central object of which was economic exploitation. The cities thus did not grow as productive industrial centres from which generative influences could

be diffused into the rural areas. This is the crux of the urbanization process
that is occurring in West Africa today.

The Modern Pattern of Urbanization in West Africa

The rapid rate of urbanization in West Africa is essentially a post-Second
World War phenomenon. On the whole, the region still exhibits one of
the lowest levels of urbanization in the world. However, the process of
urbanization has accelerated considerably since 1950, and between then
and 1970 the annual rate of urbanization was as high as 7 per cent (Davis,
1972: 20). However, as can be seen from Table 10.1, West Africa still
lags behind the southern and central parts of the continent with respect
to its overall level of urbanization.

West Africa has a high rate of overall population growth, about 2.5
per cent per annum, but more important is the fact that this is also accompanied by one of the fastest rates of urbanization in the world. However,
great care must be taken with regard to the cross-country comparison
of levels of urbanization. Countries vary in the criteria they adopt for
defining settlements as urban. Thus, while Ghana adopts 5,000 as the
minimum population for an urban settlement to be so defined, in Liberia
and Senegal the minimum population figures are 2,000 and 10,000 respectively. Nevertheless, the level of urbanization in 1960 for West African
countries ranged from 3 per cent in Mauritania to 23 per cent in Ghana
and Senegal. By 1982, the level of urbanization had more than doubled
in countries such as Mauritania, Côte d'Ivoire (Ivory Coast), Niger and
Togo. The urban population of Mauritania, the least urbanized country,
had increased from 3 per cent to 26 per cent in 1982. There is a clear
indication that larger cities, particularly the national capitals, have been
growing faster than the medium- and small-sized cities. The capital is
the largest urban area in all West African countries except Benin, where

Table 10.1. The pattern of urbanization in different sub-Saharan African regions

Regions	Per cent urban			Urban growth rate % p.a.		
	1960	1980	2000	1960 – 1970	1970 – 1980	1995 – 2000
Eastern Africa	7.4	15.7	29.4	6.42	5.25	6.00
Middle Africa	18.2	34.4	52.2	5.08	5.92	4.46
Southern Africa	42.2	49.2	61.1	2.60	3.65	3.48
Western Africa	13.4	22.8	36.6	5.35	5.91	5.46
Total sub-Saharan Africa	14.9	24.2	37.9	4.93	5.73	5.30

Source: United Nations (1985).

Cotonu is bigger than Port Novo. There are substantial differences in the growth rates recorded by the largest cities on the one hand, and secondary cities on the other. Some countries have more than one-third of their urban population living in the largest city, with Conakry and Lomé, for example, having 80 per cent and 60 per cent respectively of their countries' urban populations.

As pointed out previously, one of the major characteristics of the urbanization process in West Africa, as in other developing regions of the world, is that it has not been accompanied by a concomitant economic transformation from an agrarian to an industrial base. The rapid rate of urbanization is thus taking place in the context of a stagnant economy and a relatively negligible growth of industrialization. Between 1960 and 1979, countries such as Niger, Ghana and Senegal actually recorded a negative rate of annual growth in GNP per capita. Others, such as Sierra Leone, Ghana and Liberia, also recorded a decrease in the average annual growth of their industrial sectors.

Another important characteristic is the explosive nature of the rate of growth of large cities. At the beginning of this century, only one city in West Africa, Ibadan, had a population in excess of 100,000. By 1950 there were eight such cities and this had increased to forty-three by 1970. In 1960 there was no city with a population of a million or more. In 1980 there were four such cities and it is estimated that by the end of this century they will have increased to nineteen or twenty (Table 10.2). In 1980 metropolitan Lagos was estimated to have reached the 4.5 million level, and this is projected to increase to 12.9 million by the year 2000 according to the 1980 Lagos Master Plan.

The most urbanized country in West Africa seems to be Côte d'Ivoire, which had 42 per cent of its population living in urban areas in 1980. However, it must be emphasized that even though Nigeria has a relatively

Table 10.2. Number of cities by size group in West Africa, 1950 – 2000

Size group (in 000s)	Number of cities					
	1950	1960	1970	1975	1980	2000
5,000 +	0	0	0	0	0	0(1?)
2,000 – 4,999	0	0	0	1	1	5
1,000 – 1,999	0	0	1	0	3	14
500 – 999	0	2	3	4	6	14
200 – 499	3	5	11	24	22	20
100 – 199	5	19	28	21	19	16
Total	8	26	43	50	51	69

Source: United Nations (1985).

Table 10.3. Comparison of urban/rural investment in the Nigerian Second National Development Plan 1970–74

Selected sectors	Total planned investment (million of nairas)	Urban investment		Rural investment	
		Millions of nairas	Per cent	Millions of nairas	Per cent
Education	277.8	196.8	70.9	81.0	29.1
Industry	172.2	155.4	91.2	16.8	9.8
Water and sewage	103.4	84.4	71.6	19.0	18.4
Electricity	90.6	80.6	89.0	10.0	11.0
Social welfare	24.0	22.0	91.7	2.0	8.3
Health	107.6	90.4	84.0	17.2	16.0
Town and country planning	38.2	36.0	94.3	2.2	5.7
Total	813.8	665.6	81.8	148.2	18.2

Sources: Nigeria, Second National Development Plan 1970–74, Lagos: Federal Ministry of Economic Development, 137–265; Aluko (1971).

low level of urbanization, with a total population of about 100 million, its urban population is greater than the combined urban population of all other West African countries combined from in-migration. The World Bank (1979) found that in-migration contributed an average of 49.5 per cent to the urban growth of Senegal, Niger, Burkina Faso and Mali in 1975. Perhaps more important is the fact that capital cities have a higher proportion of their growth directly attributable to rural–urban migration (Dakar, 73.7 per cent; Niamey, 73.2 per cent; Ouagadougou, 67.51 per cent; and Bamako, 65.4 per cent). Between 1955 and 1963, 76 per cent of the total population increase of Abidjan was due to migration, while for Lagos, the figure was 75 per cent for the period between 1952 and 1962 (World Bank, 1972: 60). Thus, it seems clear that the single most important factor contributing to the rapid rate of urbanization which is occurring in West African countries is rural-to-urban migration. The question then is why, especially in view of the appalling conditions which await most of the unskilled and semi-literate migrants in the cities, do they continue to flock to them? According to many commentators, the explanation for this is to be found in the apparent 'urban bias' of the policies which have been followed by most governments in developing nations (Lipton, 1977). In West Africa, this bias is manifest in the location of industries, the provision of infrastructure and social amenities and the subsidized price of food for the urban residents, and the low income accruing to the farmers due to agricultural pricing policies. Government policies and investment programmes, especially as exhibited by the national development plans of most countries, clearly indicate the priority which is placed on cities in the national development process. For example, in Nigeria over 80 per cent of the non-agricultural public capital investment was devoted to the urban areas in the 1970-4 National Development Plan (Table 10.3). The 1975-80 Third National Development Plan did not deviate radically from this overall pattern. The concentration of administrative infrastructure and public-sector employment is especially biased in favour of the national capitals.

The Factors Responsible for Accelerating Urbanization in West Africa

West Africa as a whole has one of the highest levels of fertility in the world. The crude birth rate ranges from 52 per 1,000 in Niger to 41 per 1,000 in Guinea Bissau. The mean crude birth rate for all countries in the region is 47.8 per 1,000, which can be compared to the prevailing rate of 15 per 1,000 in North America and Western Europe (United Nations, 1979: 58). Even though the mortality rate at 19.7 per 1,000 is also one of the highest in the world, the rate of natural growth is very high. The question is whether the urban areas have a higher rate of natural increase than the rural areas in West Africa. Surveys in Nigeria, for example, have tended to suggest that this is the case. The reason is that while there is little difference in the fertility rate of women in urban and rural areas, the mortality rate is generally far lower in the urban areas (Salau, 1987).

Many studies have indicated that rural–urban migration contributes substantially to the rapid rate of urbanization which is occurring in Africa. For example, it was calculated that 49 per cent of the total urban population increase experienced in sub-Saharan Africa between 1970 and 1975 was attributable to rural–urban migration. The difference between the national population growth (the mean natural increase of population) and observed rates of urban population growth theoretically reflects migration to and from urban centres. The mean annual population growth rate for West Africa is 2.8 per cent, in contrast to the mean annual growth rate of urban population, which stands at 5.5 per cent. A substantial portion of the difference between the two can be attributed to net rural–urban migration (World Bank, 1979a: 18).

Another factor is the lopsided nature of the concentration of government investment, and this in turn is reinforced by the location of manufacturing activities in the largest cities. This is well exemplified by the data contained in Table 10.4. Thus, it is not surprising that one of the most famous models attempting to explain rural–urban migration in developing nations is based on the idea that the process reflects urban–rural differentials which are discounted by the probability of employment

Table 10.4. The proportion of national manufacturing to be found in various West African cities, *c.* 1972

City	Percentage share of national manufacturing
Dakar	87
Bathurst (Banjul)	100
Conakry	50
Freetown	75
Moonrovia	100
Abidjan	63
Accra	30
Cotonou	17
Lagos	35

Source: Mabogunje (1973: 11).

(Todaro, 1969). According to this model, the (estimated) real wage or income differential and the (estimated) probability of getting a job determine an individual's propensity to migrate. A number of studies, however, have stressed that migration into the cities of West Africa is continuing even in the face of declining job opportunities, high unemployment and declining real income differentials. Failure to find a job in the cities, which might conceivably lead migrants to return to their areas of origin, is not generally happening because of the opportunities which are presented by the informal sector. Thus, other factors must be effective over and above income differentials and job opportunities.

In fact, the most important factor is education (Peil, 1966; Caldwell, 1969). There are many ways in which education affects migration. One of these is that the level of education attained seems to be associated with the migration decision. It is in some senses rational for an educated person to want to leave the rural area, since the higher his or her educational attainment, the bleaker the prospect of finding the type of job for which education has prepared them. Thus, even in the face of high unemployment rates, it is still rational for some to migrate to cities where there is a chance, no matter how small, or the period of time it takes, of eventually finding a job. Further, the process of acquiring education itself in West Africa frequently entails migrating from rural areas to cities. For example, all of Nigeria's federal universities in 1981 were to be found located in cities with a population of 50,000 or more (Table 10.5).

Table 10.5. The location of universities in Nigeria, 1981, according to city size

City size	Number of universities	Percentage of total
Small (20,000 – 50,000 population)	0	0
Medium-sized (50,000 – 250,000 population)	10	58.82
Large (above 250,000 population)	7	41.18
Total	17	100.00

Source: Salau (1987).

Spatial Strategies and Policies in West Africa

According to Renaud (1981: 38–9) there are three major elements in any national urbanization strategy. First, there are the implicit spatial policies which are created when national economic plans are formulated. Secondly, there are policies which are developed at the regional scale in order to reduce spatial inequalities and increase the degree of national socio-economic integration. Finally, there are normally a range of intra-urban policies which deal with the problems of congestion and pollution that affect large cities. The principal implication is, of course, that spatial policies generally reflect wider national economic and social objectives.

The spatial policies which have been adopted by the countries of West Africa have taken many different forms. Among the most notable are overall national settlement policies which endeavour to curb the accelerated growth of primate cities, promote sub-national capitals and relocate national capitals. Other approaches have depended on the growth-centre strategy or on the establishment of rural-based planning programmes (Salau, 1988). These three broad policy options are considered below with regard to West Africa.

National settlement policies

National settlement policies include a variety of programmes which are adopted in an effort to influence population distribution and achieve a more orderly spatial distribution of human settlements and development within a country.

The most notable aspect of this policy involves the attempt which has been made by most West African countries to reduce or slow down the accelerating rate of growth of the capitals and major cities. The most potent method of achieving this is by curtailing migration to cities. Some countries have tried to curb in-migration to the capital by upgrading a limited number of cities which lie at a considerable distance from it, and which will act as counter-magnets. It is hoped that these will develop into destination points for rural–urban migrants who might otherwise proceed to the capital cities. In Senegal, there are plans for a number of regional centres to be upgraded in order to serve as counter-magnets to the Dakar–Thies axis. Another method is to encourage private investment in cities other than the capital. Attempts to accomplish this are normally made through the provision of incentives such as lower taxes, the provision of industrial estates, public services, infrastructure and facilities. Most West African countries have tried this approach in one form or another.

One of the most important instruments for slowing down the growth of primate cities, and for changing the regional distribution of population and restructuring the national space economy in general, is the relocation of the national capital. This has generally involved a move from the coastal zone to an interior part of the country. New capitals located in the lagging region are seen as a viable opportunity for decentralization and as a means for reducing perceived regional inequalities at the national level. In 1976, the Nigerian government announced its intention to transfer the national capital from Lagos to Abuja in the central and relatively underpopulated part of the country. The movement from Lagos had started with the relocation of some government ministries to Abuja in 1986. Côte d'Ivoire is also developing a new national capital at President Boigny's village of Yamoussoukro. This is located in the interior at a distance from Abidjan, the present capital.

A variant on the strategy of relocating the national capital is the promotion of a few medium-sized cities as the capitals of sub-national units such as the states or provinces making up a country. This approach is associated with measures to strengthen planning at the regional level and the provision of administrative decentralization. The designation of a town as a state or provincial capital generally confers tremendous benefits on it in terms of the provision of infrastructure and key social services. For example, the creation of more states in Nigeria in 1967 and 1976 entailed the designation of some formerly neglected medium-sized cities as state capitals especially those in the peripheral areas such as Calabar, Maiduguri, Sokoto, Yola, Minna and Makurdi.

Growth centre strategy

Growth centre strategies have been one of the most popular types of regional development policy in West Africa. However, enthusiasm for such strategies has waned over the years in most developing nations owing to their failure to achieve the desired objectives. Commonly, the application of the strategy involves the selection of a limited number of cities which are supposed to function as the locations for new industries or the decentralization of existing ones. The hope is that with limited investment in infrastructure and public services, the economic structure of the urban centres can be transformed by new industries which are attracted there by other fiscal incentives, and thus that the cities develop into alternative destination points for rural–urban migrants.

In Senegal, the planning of growth centres is supposed to aid the process of decentralization of economic activities from the core area, to provide employment opportunities in the interior and to alleviate the congestion of Dakar. Kaolack, Zinguichor, Saint Louis and Tambacounda have been designated as growth centres to serve as counter-magnets to Dakar. In Côte d'Ivoire, the port of San Pedro in the south-eastern region was constructed to serve as a growth centre. Construction started in 1968 and was completed in 1971. The goal was to create a growth centre in the south-east that would enhance the development of this lagging region, which is characterized by abundant natural resources. A regional development authority was created in 1971 and charged with the co-ordination of development plans for the south-west. The project necessitated the construction of some 400 km of major roads and feeder routes in the region. It was hoped that the congestion of the Port of Abidjan would be eased, with San Pedro becoming a new destination point, especially for the rural migrants from the region.

The approach has been implemented in a number of other West African countries. In Ghana, for example, the plan was to create new growth centres in the country so as to slow down the growth of Accra and cities such as Kumasi and Takoradi. Tamale in the north, as one of the designated cities, is expected to function as the industrial hub of the north. In Sierra Leone, the objective is to curtail the growth of Freetown and achieve a more balanced population distribution and a more orderly pattern of regional development through the establishment of selected cities as regional growth centres. Three major and nine medium-sized cities located in the eastern, northern and southern regions, excluding the most urbanized and developed western region, were identified, and thus selected as growth centres (Manly-Spain, 1977: 93–9).

Rural development policies

The increasing rate of rural–urban migration and the resultant explosive growth of major cities in particular has been ascribed largely to the wide imbalance in the level of living which exists between the urban and rural areas. Thus, numerous rural development programmes have been implemented in all West African countries in an effort to redress these imbalances. The idea is obviously that if the rural areas are improved and made attractive by the provision of employment opportunities and public services and infrastructures, there will be less incentive for the rural dwellers to migrate to the cities.

There are many variants of rural development policy adopted by West African countries. Mali is implementing a 'villagization' scheme based on the regrouping of rural population in organized settlements with the objective of expanding agricultural production and improving the access of rural dwellers to basic infrastructure and facilities. In Côte d'Ivoire Burkina Faso, Benin and Senegal, rural housing and rural settlement upgrading schemes are being undertaken. Ghana is attempting to promote rural development and expand agricultural productivity through the development of a hierarchy of settlements. This is expected to result in the improvement of housing infrastructure and services and better access to urban markets. In Guinea integrated rural development policy involves changes in land tenure, mechanization of agricultural and the use of work bridgades and co-operatives. In Senegal, the government is attempting to regroup the dispersed rural population in central villages where the people will be provided with essential services and infrastructure. The plan is to resettle some 100,000–200,000 persons from the overpopulated groundnut-producing region in the 'newlands' of eastern Senegal and the Upper and Middle Asamance regions (Brennan and Richardson, 1986).

Conclusion

In this chapter, an attempt has been made to examine the pattern of urbanization in West Africa, the factors responsible and the policies adopted or being adopted by various governments to influence population distribution and achieve an orderly pattern of human settlements. While West Africa is one of the poorest and least urbanized regions of the world, it currently has one of the highest rates of urbanization. One of the factors responsible for the present pattern of human settlement and the high rate of urbanization is historical in nature. Colonial policies reinforced by the pattern of national development investments and public expenditures have accentuated differences in income and living conditions between rural and urban areas. As Gugler and Flanagan (1977: 274) contended,

West African countries with greater economic resources tend to channel them into the urban sector, especially into the bureaucratic apparatus and public works. The (relative) wealth of Liberia, Ivory Coast, Senegal and Ghana is not manufactured in the urban areas but derived from the extraction of iron ore and phosphates, the production of rubber plantations, and the labour of peasants growing cocoa, coffee and peanuts.

It is in recognition of this fact that a variety of programmes and projects have been and are still being formulated and implemented by governments across the West African region. However, the results to date have been rather disappointing. The efforts to slow down the growth of primate cities and to redirect it toward counter-magnets have failed to yield great dividends. Although net migration is still a major component of the rapid rate of urbanization, there are indications that it is becoming less important. High rates of natural increase in the cities are emerging as the dominant factor ensuring continuing rapid urbanization and the growth of urban areas, particularly major cities. As can be seen from Table 10.6, rural–urban migration is accounting for less and less of the urban growth in all parts of Africa. The implication of this is that undue attention on rural–urban migration alone will be inadequate to curb urban growth. The policies adopted must be realistic and they need to be based on a careful appraisal of national resource endowments and constraints. Policies such as the relocation and building of new capitals in the interior are expensive and could be potentially harmful to the overall rate of national economic growth, so may constitute a wasteful and inefficient way of spending a nation's limited revenue.

Table 10.6. Average annual rural–urban population transfer as a percentage of urban population growth for sub-Saharan Africa

	Rural urban transfer as a percentage of urban growth		
	1950–60	1970–75	1975–80
Africa	56.3	45.2	38.7
East Africa	61.5	51.7	45.5
Middle Africa	78.7	61.1	48.8
North Africa	45.5	58.0	32.9
South Africa	36.2	28.3	28.0
West Africa	57.8	48.7	43.1

Source: Findley (1977), cited in World Bank (1979b: 73).

There is need for policies to be implemented in a sustained manner over a long period of time. Spatial structures are generally rigid, and policies designed to influence them may not show any result over a short time period. The frequent changes of government are political instability which characterize many developing nations are inimical to the formulation of sound spatial policies, which must be implemented over a long period of time in order to achieve results. For example, Richardson (1978) has argued that the disillusion with growth centre strategies is really not justified as they are not usually implemented with sustained political·will over a reasonable period of time.

Most of the spatial policies are solely national or regional in focus and thus fail to address the problems engendered by urbanization which are expressed at the local level, such as environmental degradation, housing shortages and overcrowding, and the skewed intra-urban distribution of social services. Such problems must also be addressed directly on a metropolitan or local level.

As has been argued previously, the present settlement pattern in West Africa is a result of both the explicit and the implicit policies which have been adopted over the years. There is thus the need for policy-makers to be sensitive to the potential spatial outcomes of their decisions. The present author agrees with Renaud (1981: 129) that the most crucial prerequisites for effective national spatial policies are political commitment at the highest level and the appropriate adjustment of governmental structures and modes of operation.

REFERENCES

Aluko, S. A. (1971) 'Resource allocation and overall strategy in Nigeria, Second Development Plan 1970–74. A symposium'. *Quarterly Journal of Administration*, 5(3), 267–84.

Brennan, M. E. and Richardson, H. W. (1986) 'Urbanization and urban policy in sub-Saharan Africa'. *African Urban Quarterly*, 1(1), 20–42.

Caldwell, J. C. (1969) *African Rural–Urban Migration: The Movement to Ghana's Towns*. New York: Columbia University Press.

Davis, K. (1972) *World Urbanization 1950–1970*, Vol. 2: *Analysis, Trends, Relationships and Development*. Berkeley, California: Institute of International Studies, University of California.

Findley, S. E. (1977) *Planning for Internal Migration*. Washington, DC: Department of Commerce, Bureau of Census.

Gugler, J. and Flanagan, W G. (1977) 'On political economy of urbanization in the Third World: the case of West Africa'. *International Journal of Urban and Regional Research*, 1(2), 272–92.

Gutkind, P. C. W. (1974) *Urban Anthropology*. New York: Barnes and Noble.

Lipton, M. (1977) *Why People Stay Poor: Urban Bias and World Development*. Cambridge, Massachusetts: Harvard University Press.

Mabogunje, A.H. (1973) 'Manufacturing and the geography of development in West Africa'. *Economic Geography*, 49, 1–20.

Manly-Spain, P.F.V. (1977) 'Urbanization and regional development in Sierra Leone', in: Mabogunje, A.L. and Faniran, A. (eds) *Regional Planning and National Development in Tropical Africa*. Ibadan: Ibadan University Press.

Peil (1966) 'Middle school leavers: occupational aspirations and prospects'. *Ghanaian Journal of Sociology*, 2, 7–16.

Renaud, B. (1981) *National Urbanization Policy in Developing Countries*. New York: Oxford University Press.

Richardson, H.W. (1978) *Region and Urban Economics*. Harmondsworth: Penguin.

Riddell, J.B. (1980) 'Is continuing urbanization possible in West Africa?'. *African Studies Review*, 1, 69–79.

Salau, A.T. (1986) 'River basin planning as a strategy for rural development in Nigeria'. *Journal of Rural Studies*, 2(4), 321–35.

Salau, A.T. (1987) *Nigerian Cities: The Evolution and Dynamics of an Urban System*. Oguta: Nigeria Zims Pan African Press.

Salau, A.T. (1988) 'National development and regional planning in West Africa'. *Regional Development Dialogue*, special issue (United Nations Centre for Regional Development, Nagoya, Japan), 89–113.

Sudarkassa, N. (1977): 'Women and migration in contemporary West Africa', in: Wellesley Editorial Committee (eds) *Women and National Development*. Chicago: University of Chicago Press.

Todaro, M.P. (1969) 'A model of labour migration and urban unemployment in less developed countries'. *American Economic Review*, 59, 138–48.

United Nations (1975) *Trends and Prospects in the Population of Urban Agglomerations 1950–2000 as Assessed in 1973–75*. New York: Department of Economic and Social Affairs.

United Nations (1979) *Patterns of Urban and Rural Population Growth*. New York: Department of International Economic and Social Affairs.

United Nations (1985) *Estimates and Projections of Urban, Rural and City Populations 1950–2025: The 1982 Assessment*. New York: United Nations.

White, H.P. and Gleave, M.B. (1971) *An Economic Geography of West Africa*. London: Bell.

Williams, G. (1970) 'The social stratifications of a neo-colonial economy', in: Allen, C. and Johnson, R.W. (eds) *African Perspectives: Papers in the History, Politics and Economics of Africa*. Cambridge: Cambridge University Press.

World Bank (1972) *Urbanization*, Sector Working Paper. Washington, DC: World Bank.

World Bank (1979a) *Urban Growth and Economic Development in the Sahel*, Staff Working Paper No. 315. Washington, DC: World Bank.

World Bank (1979b) *Policies for Efficient and Equitable Growth of Cities in Developing Countries*. Washington, DC: World Bank.

World Bank (1981) *Accelerated Development in Sub-Saharan Africa: An Agenda for Action*. Washington, DC: World Bank.

[11]

Dependent Urbanization and Retail Change in Barbados, West Indies

Robert B. Potter
and
Graham M. S. Dann

After a brief introductory section stressing the neglect of retail change in the geographical literature on urbanization and development, the commercial history and recent experiences of Barbados, West Indies are considered in his chapter. In contemporary Barbados, approximately 97 per cent of the total retail floorspace is to be found located within the south-western coastal strip, which also serves as the urban–tourism–manufacturing belt. This is a quite staggering overconcentration relative to the area and population of the zone.

The chapter first considers the historical genesis of this core–periphery structure, relating it to the mercantile-capitalist periods. In this connection, the objectives of national urban development strategies since the 1960s are also considered. An analysis of both the traditional and modern components of the present-day retail system of Barbados is then provided. The former consist of rural rum shops, local markets and street hawkers and vendors. The modern component is represented by a series of supermarkets developed in the 1960s. Although these large stores are owned and managed by Barbadians and not outside interests, it can still be argued that they are primarily the outcome of external agents of development in the guise if tourism, expatriates and imitative elites. It is concluded that, in the twentieth century, change in retailing, especially the trend toward large supermarkets, appears to be leading to further social and spatial inequalities within the country. Both structurally and spatially, such patterns may be viewed in relation to Santos's (1979) concepts of the *shared space*.

Retail Change and Development

Given the interest that human geographers have traditionally shown in the structure of commercial activities on the one hand and patterns of economic change and development on the other, it seems surprising that so little research has sought to explore the structure and disposition of commercial activities in Third World countries. What little work has been undertaken in this generally neglected area has, by and large, been carried out by development specialists rather than commercial geographers. In this respect it is perhaps the work of Santos (1979) and, in particular, his concept of the *shared space* that has been most influential in the field.

In a conference paper, Guy (1986) has stressed that studies of economic activities in Third World countries have come to be dominated by the consideration of small-scale traders, these normally being viewed in the context of the role and structure of the informal sector or the lower circuit of the urban economy. Thus, relatively little work has endeavoured to examine the structure of the retail systems of developing countries as a whole. This is a valid observation, and Guy goes on to argue that in 'those few sources where the whole spectrum of retail activity in considered (e.g. Beaujeu-Garnier and Delobez, 1979; Santos, 1979), most of the attention is given to "informal" trading and "formal" retail activity tends to be summarised in a rather trivial manner' (Guy, 1986: 1). While this judgement might perhaps seem somewhat dismissive of the detailed chapter that Beaujeu-Garnier and Delobez provide under the title 'Commercial organisation in poor countries with a free economy' (ch. 2: 64–79), which does contain a good deal of material on upper-circuit or formal retail concerns, the general point is well made. Certainly, there is a burgeoning literature on periodic central place systems which basically sees these as market responses to low levels of effective demand, poor transport facilities, poor storage and handling operations and the need for many individuals to remain as both the producers and marketers of commodities. The same type of argument can, of course, be applied to explain other forms of petty commodity trading such as street hawkers and vendors in Third World commercial systems. Here also the principal characteristics of the urban informal sector can be noted, expressly its labour-intensive nature, limited capital, direct and personalized contact with consumers and the negligible fixed costs of operations.

But it is perhaps equally important to observe that few Third World cities are to be found today which do not possess modern retail developments to some degree or another (see, for example, Mabogunje, 1964; Gwynne, 1978; Paddison, Findlay and Findlay, 1984). These principally take the form of supermarkets and other large stores and also planned shopping malls along Western lines. It is this modern and capital-intensive component in juxtaposition with vestiges of traditional retailing that the present chapter seeks to emphasize in relation to one small developing country, namely Barbados. Indeed, the central theme is that it is the wide diversity of retail forms and the essential combination of traditional and modern facilities that currently represents the most salient characteristic of the retail systems of many middle-income developing countries. In fact, it is the central argument of this account that such diversity can be seen as a further expression of a core–periphery type of patterning that typifies economic change and development in the majority of developing nations under capitalism. This argument is not only exemplified in terms of the spatial manifestation of retailing patterns in Barbados, but equally with regard to the social implications of the development of large retail stores in the period since 1960.

In the next section the context is provided by considering the wider historical development of settlement and commercial patterns in Barbados since its original colonization. The overall present-day macro-structure of retailing is then considered. Subsequently, the chapter focuses first on the nature of traditional forms of retail practice in Barbados, and then on the development and social impact of modern supermarketing operations. Finally, the wider implications of these developments are considered.

The Development of the Urban Commercial Pattern of Barbados under Mercantilism and Capitalism

In the Caribbean, the legacy of colonial settlement and subsequent orientation to West European economics is witnessed in a large number of shared socio-economic characteristics, foremost among which are open economies with agricultural orientations and marked tendencies toward monoculture. In a spatial sense, the realities of such patterns of dependent development are witnessed most forcefully in the highly skewed and spatially uneven settlement patterns that are to be found throughout the Caribbean region (Potter, 1985; 1986a; 1986b; 1989).

The key agent in this historical development was that of mercantile trade, the progress of which served to focus settlement growth from the first on the sheltered leeward coasts of the various islands. Thus, throughout the Caribbean region, linear coastal settlement patterns are strikingly evident and present a graphic illustration of the appropriateness of the 'mercantile model' of settlement evolution suggested by James Vance (1970) as a socio-historical corrective to the traditional theory of central places (see Potter, 1989). In summary, Vance argues that the central place model is one which considers only *endogenic* demand – that is, needs and wants that arise exclusively *within* an area – thereby rendering what is effectively a closed settlement system. In this sense, Vance maintains that the classical central place model is positively 'feudal' in its conception. In contrast, the mercantile model seeks to stress the vital role that has been played by *exogenic* forces, for the source of change for developing countries was *external to* the evolving settlement system. The outcome is the remarkable linearity of settlement patterns that is mapped into the Vance model. The first component of this linearity is the alignment of urban and commercial fabrics along continental coasts, and the second component the development of linear settlements along the routes which over time come to extend into staple-producing areas. The model has been reviewed in detail elsewhere (Potter, 1985), and it can be argued that its principal merit is that it emphasizes that the high degree of urban primacy and the littoral orientation of settlement which are so characteristic of the Caribbean region are the direct products of a form of *dependent development* and associated urbanization (Robert, 1978), and not the reflection of a *lack* of development *per se*. Hence, pattern of spatially unequal or polarized growth emerged several hundred years ago with the strengthening of this symbiotic relationship between the colony and colonial power.

The basic mercantile model can, of course, be related to John Friedmann's (1966) four-stage core–periphery model which, at least initially, envisages the transition of spatially undifferentiated pre-industrial economies to ones dominated by a single strong core, which siphons off factors of production and results in the draining of the peripheral regions. In the sequence originally envisaged by Friedmann, a spontaneous trend toward inter-regional convergence occurred during the last two stages of the model. However, Friedmann subsequently re-evaluated this view, arguing that historical evidence supports continuing divergence and disequilibrium rather than convergence.

This type of patterning fits well the realities of the historical development of the macro-spatial commercial and settlement systems of Barbados (see Potter, 1985). The island was discovered by the Portuguese in 1536, but was not settled until 1627. In 1625, an English ship returning home from South America came upon the island fortuitously. On return the master reported his find to his employer, a rich merchant, Sir William Courteen. Courteen regarded the island as a potential location for a tobacco plantation. Accordingly, in 1627 settlers arrived and became established at present-day Holetown. A year later a rival group had settled in the vicinity of Bridgetown. Subsequently, the west-coast settlements of Speightstown in the north and Oistins in the south were established. In fact, this early pattern of settlement, geared to the mother country, still characterizes the country today (Figure 11.1), and developments in the twentieth century have all served to bolster the west-coast urban zone. No matter which index of socio-economic structure is selected, a sharply divided map characterizes this nation of only 430 sq km. The parishes of St Michael, Christ Church and St James constitute the thriving core of the island, and the remaining areas its unmistakably periphery. This pattern cannot be interpreted as the outcome of chance or haphazard processes operating in space, however, but the direct outcome of the original pattern of unequal growth which has been constantly bolstered and intensified during the last 200 years of capitalist development.

In particular, the encouragement of enclave light manufacturing and the tourist industry as principal pillars of postwar economic policy has resulted in continued polarization within this coastal linear urban zone.

The avowed intention of physical development planning in Barbados since its holistic inception in 1965 has been to reduce such inequalities in development, principally by means of the decentralization of economic and commercial activities away from the Bridgetown core. The first national physical plan was drawn up in 1970 and suggested the development of a four-tier national hierarchy of urban commercial centres. The 1970 plan was clearly inspired by classical central-place theory, and was Utopian in its advocacy of a widely dispersed national hierarchy of settlements by the end of plan year 1980. The amended version of this plan was produced somewhat belatedly in 1983. Its aim is to rationalize and therefore plan *with* the emerging linear urban corridor and to promote the growth of certain urban and suburban sub-cores within it. In this light the plan is to expand Oistins and Speightstown and the Warrens–Cave Hill area, which is situated close to the university in the northern part of the parish of St Michael. In fact, in the last ten years, both Speightstown and Oistins have already been the sites for a number of commercial developments, including modern shopping plazas. Whether these developments and the current measures adopted in the Amended Physical Development Plan will succeed remains to be seen, but certainly there is a real danger that the policy, in seeking to rationalize the existing situation of spatial polarization, will merely serve to spread development within the existing core area in a form of concentrated deconcentration. This particular argument is important in that the present chapter basically suggests that recent changes in retailing in Barbados are leading to the intensification of a strong core–periphery patterning of life-chances and lifestyles in Barbados, and not their amelioration.

The Present-Day Retail Pattern of Barbados

Surprisingly, little research has been carried out on either the development of retail marketing in Barbados or present-day patterns of retailing in the country, and the present authors are not aware of any comprehensive study that has been published on this topic. Curiously enough, the 1970 Physical Development Plan included little on retailing, despite the fact that its primary objective was the decentralization of infrastructure and activities, including services, away from the primate core region of metropolitan Bridgetown. The absence of a Geography or Planning Department at the Cave Hill Campus of the University of West Indies and the relatively low regard with which geography is held within the Caribbean in general means that an overtly spatial approach to the analysis

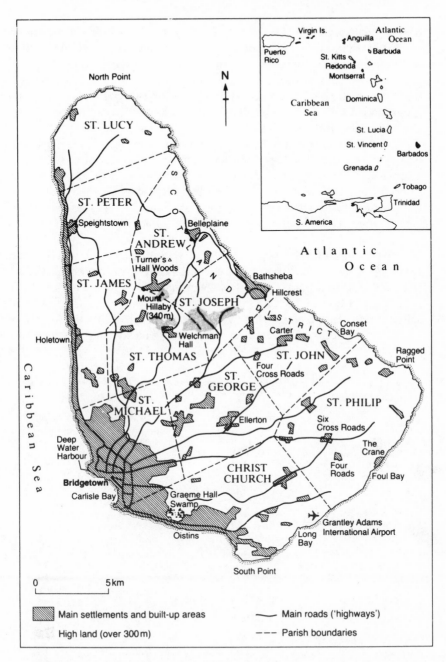

Figure 11.1.   Barbados: principal built-up areas and administrative zones.

of socio-economic issues is conspicuous by its absence. It is tempting to conjecture that this lack of a spatial orientation is also in part attributable to the influence of living in a small island community where the geographical realities of location seem very much to be taken for granted. Such circumstances have also led to a situation where the types of basic geographical survey that one might expect to have been carried out during the late 1960s and 1970s have not, in fact, been undertaken.

As a result of this dearth of information, the Barbados Department of Town and Country Development Planning carried out a number of basic retail surveys in connection with the publication of the survey section of their amended version of the Physical Development Plan, which as noted in the previous section was published in 1983. In the absence of other, more detailed data, the first half of the account which follows is in great part based on the data collated in that document.

The results of this survey of the distribution of retail facilities in Barbados reveal the massive degree of spatial concentration that characterizes the island in this sphere, as well as in many others (Table 11.1). The basic distribution of such facilities is depicted in Figure 11.2. The most salient fact is that a staggering 97 per cent of the total retail floorspace of the entire country is located on the western and southern linear urban

Table 11.1. The size and functional composition of the principal retail centres in Barbados, 1980

Centre	Floor space (m²)	Percentage floorspace	Percentage range of goods
Central Bridgetown	69,259	62.6	100
Speightstown	8,861	8.0	62
Holetown	5,056	4.6	67
Oistins	2,964	2.7	62
Eagle Hall	4,181	3.8	28
Worthing	2,787	2.5	38
Sargeants Village	2,323	2.1	28
Hastings	1,394	1.3	38
Shoppers Centre	1,589	1.4	33
Rockdundo	1,477	1.3	28
Carlton	1,338	1.2	24
Gertz	1,113	1.0	33
Wildey	911	0.8	28
Six Cross Roads	799	0.7	28
Pandoras	557	0.5	14
Stanmore Crescent	539	0.5	14
Totals	105,148	95.0	—

Source: *Barbados Physical Development Plan Amended 1983*: 44, Table 5.5.

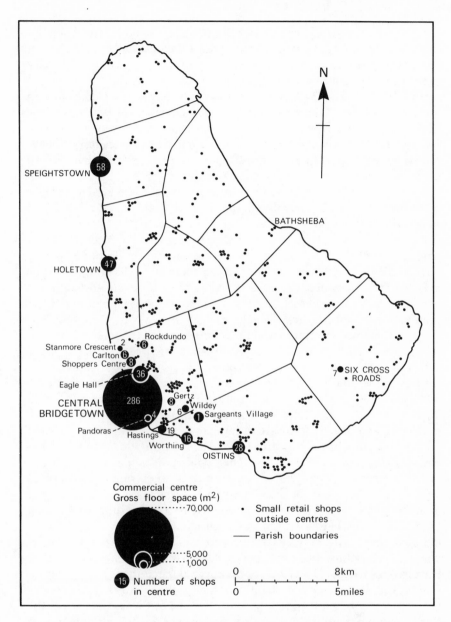

Figure 11.2.   The location of retail facilities in Barbados, 1980.

corridor, while this area accounts for 77.93 per cent of the national population and only 54.02 per cent of its land area. Obviously, the single greatest concentration of floorspace is found in central Bridgetown, with the city centre alone accounting for 69,259 sq m, or 63 per cent of the estimated national floorspace. The city centre dwarfs the remainder of the nation's retail centres. The other urban areas of Speightstown, Holetown and Oistins house the next greatest concentrations of shops, but these contain only 8.0, 4.6 and 2.7 per cent of the national estimated floorspace respectively. The next most important retail areas tend to re-emphasize the importance of the primate capital, for they comprise the nine suburban commercial areas which are located in outer Bridgetown, and these are shown and named in Figure 11.2. Virtually all the suburban centres have developed since 1965, and they are generally based on relatively large-scale supermarkets which have effectively created new commercial centres. A noticeable feature of the distribution of retailing facilities in Barbados is that outside these principal centres, although there is a scattering of shops in isolated locations or small clusters (Figure 11.2), there are no significant concentrations in any of the district centres that were designated as growth points in the 1970 Physical Development Plan.

The structure of retailing facilities in Barbados is such that we can talk about a typology of centres, as shown in Figure 11.3. At the upper end of the retail system, central Bridgetown is primate and, together with the three other major urban centres located at Speightstown, Holetown and Oistins respectively, accounts for nearly 80 per cent of the total retail infrastructure of the nation. But the most salient fact perhaps is that the middle ranks of the national retailing hierarchy are entirely accounted for by the nine suburban centres located in Bridgetown, thereby further stressing the capital's importance. This typology is perhaps best appreciated if a measure of functional importance is taken rather than one of absolute size. As a part of their survey work, the planning team looked at the frequency of occurrence of some twenty selected functions among the retail centres. The key functional traits identified in this analysis were: market, supermarket or minimart, grocer/bar, other food sales, footwear, pharmacist, furniture or office supplies, vehicle sales, stationery and books, travel agents betting and gambling, beauty salon, clothes cleaner, photographic supplies, photocopying, florists, and gifts or crafts. The percentage occurrence of these functions in each of the centres is denoted in the final column of Table 11.1. Central Bridgetown is the only location at which all these goods can be obtained, while the other major centres supply between 24 and 38 per cent of them. Although quite small in terms of its overall size, the centre at Six Cross Roads, in fact, provides as many functions as its suburban counterparts, reflecting its rural central-place importance within the south-east of the country.

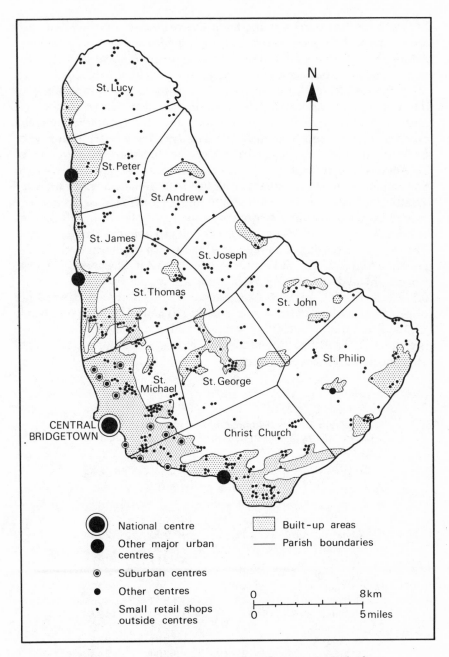

Figure 11.3. A classification of retail centres in Barbados.

However, the most striking feature revealed by the above analysis is the disparity between the urban core of Barbados and the rural periphery. Although the Amended Physical Development Plan argues that the four principal urban centres of Speightstown, Holetown, Oistins and Bridgetown each have 'east-ward service areas which as an aggregate cover the entire country, thus reflecting the complete dependency of the rural areas on the western/southern centres for the higher-order commercial services' (p. 45), this statement underplays the overall primacy of Bridgetown. Certainly, it is hard to believe that the rural residents of St Andrew parish will not be more drawn to Bridgetown than to Speightstown given the radial nature of the national transport network and the geographical realities of community belonging in Barbados. The overall disparity within the country is well exemplified by calculations of floorspace provision per capita for the eleven administrative parishes. The level of provision is as high as 0.8 sq m per capita in both metro-politan St Michael and St Peter and drops to 0.3 in St James and Christ Church. In all the remaining parishes, however, this figure is well below 0.1. The same disparity is also suggested if we look at the average number of persons per shop in the eleven parishes. The results shown in Table 11.2 indicate that a level of provision well below the national average is characteristic of the rural parishes of St Lucy, St Andrew, St Joseph, St John, St Philip and St George.

Table 11.2   The distribution of retail outlets in Barbados by administrative parish and person–shop ratios, 1980

Parish	Number of shops	Population 1980	Persons per shop
St Michael	442	99,953	226
Christ Church	159	40,790	256
St James	95	17,255	181
St Peter	78	10,717	137
St George	42	17,361	413
St Thomas	48	10,709	223
St Philip	46	18,662	405
St John	21	10,330	492
St Joseph	19	7,211	379
St Andrew	18	6,731	374
St Lucy	27	9,264	343
Totals	995	248,983	250

Traditional Retailing in Barbados

Before turning to a fuller analysis of the nature and development of modern capital-intensive retailing in Barbados, it is necessary to consider briefly traditional forms of retailing. There are two main components to this sector, referred to respectively as the rum shop and the hawker or street vendor. The former have been considered from a primarily sociological viewpoint by Stoute and Ifill (1979: 146), who define a rum shop as 'a retail outlet for that intoxicating by-product of sugar, well known the length and breadth of the Caribbean'. As the authors of this piece stress, the rum shop does much more than sell liquor, acting as a meeting place and an informal community centre and catering to the leisure and social needs of the local population. In fact, in many instances, the proprietors of rum shops also possess licences to sell foodstuffs, normally tinned meats and vegetables and other frequently demanded provisions. Thus, Stoute and Ifill note that the front section of rum shops often represent villages' sole retail outlet for groceries, kerosene, oil and other general provisions. They also stress the operation of gender segregation between the front shop and the exclusively male preserve of the backroom bar. It is these types of establishment which make up the bulk of the isolated stores that form the fifth level of the retail hierarchy supplying the rural areas of Barbados (Figures 11.2 and 11.3). In this study, published in 1979, the total number of rum shops in Barbados was given as 897, of which over half were located in the metropolitan parish of St Michael (52.8 per cent), and a further 11.5 per cent in Christ Church. The remaining eleven parishes each contained between 2.5 and 6.2 per cent of the country's total. Clearly, if the data on which Figure 11.2 is based are to be trusted, then only a relatively small proportion of all rum shops also possess grocery licences. Such establishments are still very much a part of the Barbadian national scene and must be viewed as very important components of the lower-circuit retailing system of the country.

The other major component of traditional retailing practice in Barbados is that of street hawking, which even in the 1920s was second only to the occupation of seamstress in the national employment league table. In a review of one type of street hawker, the nutseller, Crichlow (1979) has stressed how at a time of poor transport infrastructure it was the hawker who retailed foorstuffs in rural environs. But with an inadequate number of retail outlets, the hawker was equally to be found in the city streets selling her merchandise. The author records how, during the 1930s, the generic occupation of hawking did much to ameliorate the worst effects of unemployment for many. Traditionally hawkers have been poor black folk, while their suppliers were prosperous and white. Crichlow records how the development of more extensive forms of fixed retailing during the twentieth century resulted in compensatory changes in hawking. With regard to the nutseller, for example, the original focus of her operations was normally schools, but later, owing to increasing competition among vendors, fairs and cricket matches became favourite haunts. The major change in strategy came, however, with the development of the modern retail sector, for the ensuing competition necessitated not only a change in location, but also in product range. Thus, the hawker diversified her product to include consumer goods thus far not to be found in the stores, and changed location from the school to the bus terminal in order better to serve the commuting public.

It is important to stress here that the traditional retailing system of Barbados cannot be seen as entirely separate from the formal sector, a general point which is emphasized by Beaujeu-Garnier and Delobez (1979). This is so for two reasons. First, as the foregoing account demonstrates, the two systems have evolved side by side through the twentieth century. Secondly, although it is true that rural areas are largely dependent on supplies obtained through rum-shop grocery stores, the urban areas are characterized by all types of retail organization, both formal and informal, modern and traditional, petty-commodity trading and capital intensive. Functionally, the operation of a true shared space between the formal and informal sectors can be identified, whilst at the broader spatial scale this is dovetailed with an intranational core-periphery pattern. Indeed, on such a small island the trips of consumers and producers serve to interlink the various components of the retail system (Potter, 1989b), the price being paid in terms of the time, effort and expense of overcoming the friction of distance, the salient point to which we shall return shortly.

The Development and Social Impact of Supermarketing in Barbados

The advent and popularity of one-stop supermarket shopping in Barbados can be said to coincide roughly with the expansion of mass tourism to the island in the early 1960s. Whether the association was causal is debatable, but it seems to be no coincidence that, with few exceptions, the location of such modern forms of retailing outlets is to be found in metropolitan Bridgetown and alongside the southern and western strips of coastal development, as previously stressed. While it can also be argued that this pattern of consumerism is derived from tourism's demonstration effect, at the same time, it should be realized that with approximately 70 per cent of all households currently possessing a television set, Barbadians have long since been exposed to this facet of metropolitan life. Others, of course, have experienced the phenomenon directly by travelling to the United States and Europe on a regular basis.

The mercantile community in Barbados, which historically merged with white-planter interests through the processes of corporatization and intermarriage, has been prepared to satisfy (some would say to create) this new consumer demand. The upper layer of Barbadian commercial interests comprises a complicated network of interlocking directorates, which together form what is often still referred to as the 'Big Six' group of companies. All are in the main white-dominated, and thus representative of 4 per cent of the national population and from a position of virtual monopoly have a stranglehold on the import sector of the economy. Indeed, much of their power is derived from the general process of amalgamation and the sheer size of their operations when compared with the small businesses of the local black entrepreneurs, whose limited success some would argue they generally try to stifle.

A brief consideration of the control of the major supermarkets confirms the foregoing analysis. One retail chain, known as Supercentre, has five strategically located outlets. One of these is in the city centre, close to the new central bus terminal, while another is situated in a retail centre serving a middle-class residential area, that of Rockdundo to the north of Bridgetown (see Figure 11.2). Two supermarkets are to be found in malls adjacent to the tourist belt, while the latest, the result of a takeover bid, is located close to the new highway which serves to link the airport and Deepwater Harbour. Supercentre is a subsidiary of Da Costa's, one of the Big Six, which also controls the Gardiner Austin Company. Another commercial group, Goddard's Enterprises, has two supermarkets, one located on the south coast, another in the rapidly expanding northern outskirts of Bridgetown. This highly successful family business has its offices in C. F. Harrison's, one of the original major departmental stores to which it is linked commercially. Goddard's is also involved in the tourist business through the ownership of hotels and control of the Barbados Flight Kitchen, the sole supplier to the Grantley Adams International Airport. The group has additional interests established in several Caribbean islands. As with Da Costa's, the composition of the board of directors and management is predominantly white. R. L. Seale is another successful white businessman, who operates from a large dry-goods warehouse situated to the north of the city and who until quite recently represented the island's commercial interests in the Senate. He has just sold his two supermarkets to a former executive of another store, J. B.'s. One of these stores is called Carlton, the other A1. Both are located in the parish of St Michael.

While the above cater to an expanding lower-middle-class to middle-class clientele, two other large concerns seek to promote a distinctly up-market image. One is known as Big B and is located on the Worthing section of the south coast, whilst the other is J. B.'s Master Mart at Sargeants Village, Christ Church. The former establishment looks after the interests of the Bourne family and is run by a Mr Edwards. The latter, before being sold to Supercentre, used to belong to Mr J. B. Simpson (hence the initials) who, unlike some of his 'redleg' competitors, can trace his ancestry back to the original English settlers.

The case of J. B.'s[1] is particularly fascinating as it serves to highlight the complex interconnections which exist among commercial interests in Barbados. Back in the early 1960s, before Independence, the Simpson, Bourne and Goddard families decide to open a supermarket on the Worthing tourist coast and christened the store with the name of the first-mentioned family. The three-way partnership endured for some years, after which time J. B. Simpson decided to sell his interest to his remaining two colleagues. Bourne later followed suit and with the proceeds was able to establish Big B. The Goddards held on for a while longer, but with another outlet just a few hundred yards away eventually saw little sense in retaining Simpson's as a supermarket. The store was therefore converted to a hardware and variety-goods emporium under the name Star Discount. In the meantime, Mr Simpson had bought and sold a hotel and became a significant shareholder in the largest Broad Street store of Cave Shepherd. However, it was still his ambition to be the owner-operator of a supermarket. Eventually an opportunity arose and J. B. Simpson was able to lease a suitable property, which became the A1 supermarket. Some four or five years afterwards his ultimate dream became a reality and he was able to sell A1 to R.L. Seale and set up his own Master Mart on three acres of land, the store itself comprising half an acre of floor-space. Today, at some 22,000 square feet, this is the largest of all the island's supermarkets and there are plans for continued expansion.[2]

One other type of operator may briefly be alluded to, and that is the discount business based on bulk purchase. At the present time there is one such establishment in Barbados, which offers supermarket-type items at reduced prices. This establishment is known as General Traders Company and is mentioned here because it falls under the financial wing of another influential member of the Big Six group of companies, Plantations Trading Limited.

The aforementioned concerns operate modern and relatively large supermarkets which cater for the upwardly mobile, and, as we have stressed, control of them all rests in the hands of the elite minority commercial group. Such rivalry as exists is generally of a quite friendly nature, for many of the proprietors are related by kinship and otherwise share the same outside interests, such as horseracing. They also have the opportunity for meeting socially at embassy receptions, for instance, as their hosts on such occasions are frequently their customers.

By contrast, the older, smaller concerns managed by black entrepreneurs tend to cater to the lower end of the market. Even chains such as Excel, Budg-Buy, Basix, Buy-Rite, Shamrock and Ricks are largely patronized by working-class black consumers. Such retail establishments tend to be located in the poorer urban areas of Bridgetown and Speightstown, with their customers travelling to them by bus or on foot from nearby depressed housing areas. In contrast to the more sophisticated supermarkets, they tend not to possess car parks. Their few rural outlets are not much more than village stores, although they do carry more than the basic provisions that are customarily offered by rural rum shops. Closely allied to these chains are the medium- to small-sized family-operated black businesses. Although these are even to be found in the tourist zones and rural districts, they most closely resemble minimarts and indeed many are so named. Usually their prices are no cheaper and are frequently far more expensive than the large modern establishments which regularly feature loss leaders and specials as a result of bulk purchasing and high turnover.

Dependent Commercialization and the Journey to Shop

It may be suggested, therefore, that retail change has basically served to intensify the socio-spatial polarity which characterizes so many features of everyday life in Barbados. The very smallness of the country has been taken as a justification of centralizing even quite basic and frequently required commercial and social facilities. It is in this sense that Bridgetown is frequently referred to as 'central', when its geographical location is clearly anything but. Indeed, the retail and commercial developments described in this chapter have led to the continual need for rural denizens to commute into the primate capital for all manner of commercial purposes.

This point has recently been exemplified with respect to a whole series of activities in an essay on the nature of rural–urban interaction within Barbados and the southern Caribbean states (Potter, 1989). Part of this work was based on a social survey carried out during the summer months of 1980. The principal aim of the field research was to explore the daily commuting and transport activities of Barbadians located in different parts of the island. In total, 207 individuals were interviewed. The respondents were drawn in almost equal numbers from the five settlements of Bridgetown, Speightstown, Oistins, Six Cross Roads and Belleplaine (see Figure 11.1).

The relatively frequent nature of visits to Bridgetown by rural residents is well illustrated by the data contained in Table 11.3. For example, the respondents from suburban Six Cross Roads reported that they travel there on average every thirteen days. Even denizens of rural Belleplaine visited the city centre once every month or thereabouts. Only the inhabitants of Speightstown showed that they are relatively immune to the attractions of Bridgetown. The principal reason for individuals' travelling to the city was, in each case, in order to shop (Table 11.3). An interesting confirmation of such trips was provided by Mr Simpson, who noted that any casual observation of rural garbage would quickly reveal the ubiquitous presence of his supermarket's brightly coloured yellow plastic bags. He even went on to suggest that a study based on unobtrusive measurement would actually pinpoint the exact spatial distribution of his customers.

The survey respondents were also asked where they normally shopped for three categories of merchandise: bread, main provisions and clothing (Table 11.4). The most interesting feature is the heavy dependence of the rural Belleplaine sample members on Bridgetown for purchases of even quite low-order goods such as bread and main provisions, with the city accounting for 39.02 and 46.34 per cent of purchases in these two categories respectively. Although lower, saliently, 17.78 and 11.11 per cent respectively of the Six Cross Roads sample shopped for bread and provisions in Bridgetown. The dependence of residents of these rural and suburban areas of Barbados on the Bridgetown metropolitan area for purchasing clothes is clearly revealed, being over 90 per cent in the case of inhabitants of Six Cross Roads in St Philip.

This analysis is effective in giving some impression of the dependence of rural Barbadians on the metropolitan core for quite humble, everyday purchases. The rural–urban flows thus generated reflect uneven social provision in a small dependent country. Evidence suggests that this imbalance is currently getting worse and not better. In the recent past, the branch banks which existed in small rural service centres such as Four Cross Roads and elsewhere have been closed. Thus, to go to the bank in Barbados today is entirely synonymous with going to town.

Conclusions: Core–Periphery and the Shared Space in Barbados

The consequences of retail change in the post-1960 period in Barbados seem quite clear, in that the process has generally served to intensify the core–periphery structure that characterizes so many aspects of social and economic life in the country. The outcome has been a highly polarized map of shopping opportunities. Although there are functional and spatial linkages between them, in terms of both the movement of produce and consumers, it is correct to talk of the modern and traditional sectors of the Barbadian retail system, and, further, to acknowledge that these types are at least in part spatially defined, although, as stressed earlier, it would be erroneous to regard them as comprising quite separate systems. Thus, the urban and tourist zones are characterized by modern supermarkets, which generally sell a very high proportion of imported goods, especially foodstuffs. These stores, or more accurately suburban retail centres,

Table 11.3. Frequency of visits to Bridgetown among residents of five areas of Barbados and the principal reason for making such trips

Survey loation	Mean no. of days between visits to Bridgetown	Stated reasons for making trip								
		Shop (%)	Business/ employ't (%)	Shop/ entertainment (%)	Shop/ other (%)	Pay bills/ shop (%)	Pay bills (%)	Collect pay (%)	'Lime' (%)	Other/ NR (%)
Bridgetown	11.20	55.56	24.44	0.00	6.67	0.00	4.44	0.00	0.00	8.89
Speightstown	51.68	51.61	9.67	22.58	0.00	3.23	0.00	0.00	0.00	12.91
Distins	18.67	60.00	13.33	6.67	0.00	4.44	4.44	0.00	2.22	8.90
Six Cross Roads	13.44	33.33	20.00	0.00	17.79	13.33	0.00	0.00	4.44	11.11
Belleplaine	28.03	41.46	21.95	7.32	9.76	2.44	4.88	7.31	0.00	4.88

Source: Authors' survey, 1980.

Table 11.4. Shopping patterns among residents of five areas of Barbados

(a) Shopping for bread

Survey location	Percentage of respondents shopping in:		
	Bridgetown	Home parish	Other/NR
Bridgetown	88.89	88.89	11.11
Speightstown	6.45	67.74	25.81
Oistins	11.11	68.89	20.00
Six Cross Roads	17.78	60.00	22.22
Belleplaine	39.02	43.91	17.07

(b) Shopping for main provisions

Survey location	Percentage of respondents shopping in:		
	Bridgetown	Home parish	Other/NR
Bridgetown	88.89	88.89	11.11
Speightstown	9.68	67.74	22.58
Oistins	22.22	53.34	24.44
Six Cross Roads	11.11	60.00	28.89
Belleplaine	46.34	26.83	26.83

(c) Shopping for clothes

Survey location	Percentage of respondents shopping in:			
	Bridgetown	Home parish	Overseas	Other/NR
Bridgetown	75.56	75.56	11.11	13.33
Speightstown	54.84	32.26	12.90	0.00
Oistins	66.67	2.21	15.56	15.56
Six Cross Roads	91.12	2.22	4.44	2.22
Belleplaine	78.06	2.43	9.76	9.75

Source: Authors' survey, 1980.

cater to expatriates, tourists and the indigenous upper-middle and upper classes. But the metropolitan area of Bridgetown is also, of course, the locus for the street vendor, attesting to the complex interrelation of the two sectors. The rural areas of Barbados are, however, characterized by a much more homogeneous pattern of retail provision, consisting principally of the rum-shop grocery, a few minimarts and small chain supermarkets.

In recent publications, both of the present authors have pointed to the strong and continuing social and spatial inequalities which pervade Barbadian social and economic life. For example, Dann (1984; 1986) has looked at various aspects of the quality of life of people in Barbados and the provision of health services and has stressed their inequality. Here a basic divide is made in terms of four types of area: urban (St Michael), suburban (St James, St Peter, Christ Church), rural 1 (areas of growth: St Philip, St George), and rural 2 (areas of decline: St Lucy, St Thomas, St Andrew, St Joseph and St John). In a remarkably similar vein, but using the results of social-psychological surveys, Potter (1986a) produced the following classification of Barbadian administrative areas: highly developed/non-agricultural: St Michael, St James, Christ Church; intermediate 1: St Peter; intermediate 2: St George, St Thomas, St Philip; and finally, less developed/agricultural: St John, St Joseph, St Lucy and St Andrew.

As might be expected, the salient point is that developments in retailing correspond almost exactly with these socio-economic divisions. In particular, those who live in the most disadvantaged parts of the island, the parishes of St Lucy, St Andrew, St Joseph and St John, are faced with something of a dilemma. Either they can travel by public transport in search of bargains from large supermarkets, at the expense of time, physical effort and a two-way bus fare, or else they can shop locally and face inflated prices for items which are not government-controlled. In such a manner, the already existing social disparities in Barbados are further reinforced, with the poor having to pay proportionately more than the affluent for the necessities of life. It is primarily in this regard that we can talk of the existence and operation of a strong core–periphery pattern of retailing in Barbados, and one which will require much change for even a basic improvement to occur.

NOTE

1 The material for this section is largely derived from a personal interview with Mr Simpson on 20 April 1986, for which the authors express their gratitude.
2 In December 1989 Plantations Limited opened a superstore in Six Cross Roads with a retail floorspace of 46,292 square feet, including lumber sales.

REFERENCES

Beaujeu-Garnier, J. and Delobez, A. (1979) *Geography of Marketing*. London: Longman.

Crichlow, W. (1979) 'The nutseller', in: Dann, G. (ed.) *Everyday Life in Barbados: A Sociological Perspective*. Leiden: Royal Institute of Linguistics and Anthropology, 124–43.

Dann, G. (1984) *The Quality of Life in Barbados*. London: Macmillan.

Dann, G. (1986) *Some Observations on the Nature of Barbadian Society, and*

Its Capacity to Cater to the Needs of the Mentally Ill and Elderly. Report prepared for the Pan-American Health Organization.

Friedmann, J. (1966) *Regional Development Policy: A Case Study of Venezuela*. Cambridge, Massachusetts: MIT Press.

Guy, C.M. (1986) 'Retail distribution in Third World cities: some research issues'. Paper presented to the annual conference of the Institute of British Geographers, Reading.

Gwynne, R.N. (1978) 'City size and retail prices in less developed countries: an insight into primacy', *Area*, 10, 136–40.

Mabogunje, A.L. (1964) 'The evolution and analysis of the retail structure of Lagos, Nigeria'. *Economic Geography*, 40, 304–23.

Paddison, R., Findlay, A. and Findlay, A. (1984) 'Shop windows as an indicator of retail modernity in the Third World city: the case of Tunis'. *Area*, 16, 227–31.

Potter, R.B. (1985) *Urbanisation and Planning in the Third World: Spatial Perceptions and Public Participation*. London and New York: Croom Helm and St Martin's Press.

Potter, R.B. (1986a) 'Spatial inequalities in Barbados, West Indies'. *Transactions of the Institute of British Geographers*, 11, 183–98.

Potter, R.B. (1986b) 'Physical development or spatial land use planning in Barbados'. *Bulletin of Eastern Caribbean Affairs*, 12, 24–32.

Potter, R.B. (1989) 'Rural–urban interaction in Barbados and the southern Caribbean: patterns and processes of dependent development in small countries', in: Potter, R.B. and Unwin, P.T.H. (eds) *The Geography of Rural Interaction in Developing Countries: Essays for Alan B. Mountjoy*. London: Routledge.

Roberts, B. (1978) *Cities of Peasants*. London: Edward Arnold.

Santos, M. (1979) *The Shared Space*. London: Methuen.

Stoute, J. and Ifill, K. (1979) 'The rural rum shop: a comparative case study', in: Dann, G. (ed.) *Everyday Life in Barbados: A Sociological Perspective*. Leiden: Royal Institute of Linguistics and Anthropology, 146–67.

Vance, J.E. (1970) *The Merchant's World: The Geography of Wholesaling*. Englewood Cliffs, New Jersey: Prentice-Hall.

[12]
Cities and Development: Conclusions

Robert B. Potter

The chapters included in this volume have provided empirical evidence of the need for new perspectives concerning the relations between cities and development in Third World countries. Specifically, some of the case studies have exemplified how the rejection of simplistic forms of modernization theory has promoted more positive and optimistic perspectives on the role of the urban informal sector in providing both gainful employment and housing in sufficient quantity. This reevaluation in thinking has brought with it a more circumspect assessment of the effects of introducing new consumerist trends and productive techniques in a largely indiscriminate manner. As a corollary, it is increasingly coming to be accepted that regional and national-level planning imperatives which are based on the acceptance of basically top-down and centre-out systems of development administration must be viewed with caution. Effectively, these are the legacy of an era during which concentration was equated directly with development. Today, therefore, growth-pole and growth-centre strategies are viewed with some suspicion and planning efforts are increasingly mindful of the fact that they must serve basic needs. Further, development projects must be based on principles of sustainability in the long run.

Taken together, the chapters serve to stress the salience of a further point which has started to receive much attention during the past ten years, namely the crucial role played by both the national and local state in affecting patterns of urban development. This is particularly true with respect to low-income housing in Third World cities. Main, in his overview of changing attitudes to squatting in Kano, Nigeria, during the past twenty years, points to the role of the state and the national government in both creating and maintaining existing illegal residences. The presence of such housing serves class interests and explains the apparently ambiguous, ambivalent and often contradictory actions of the state. Squatter settlements serve the functional needs of peripheral capitalism, offering a location for the continuing reproduction of a cheap urban labour supply. Thus, despite a long history of periodic forcible action by government against squatters in Kano, periods of economic upturn have resulted in a policy of non-action. At the same time, cheap accommodation itself reduces pressures for real wage increases. Thus, government may well be loath to see an end to squatting, either by eviction, public-housing schemes or appropriate and inexpensive forms of self-help.

The examination of the low-income housing system or urban Barbados provided by Potter also serves to highlight the hegemony of the state in controlling the degree to which a longstanding spontaneous self-help housing system has resulted in a satisfactory level of housing upgrading. Despite a fully articulated vernacular architectural system based on an expandable modular design, full upgrading has not occurred owing to the insecure system of land tenure which has been maintained by state legislation right from emancipation through to the beginning of 1980s. The resultant firm upper limit placed on what has been achievable by self-help has meant that the poor have been forced to expend much time, effort and money in maintaining the condition of their homes. This case also serves to stress the need to appreciate indigenous culture, in this instance the syncretism which occurred between West African and English vernacular architectural forms.

The salience of the informal sector of the urban economy is also highlighted by Bryant in her preliminary report on a survey recently carried out in Labasa, and in Suva, the capital city of Fiji. Here between 12 and 20 per cent of all residents are to be found in low-income settlements. The account shows how as a response to the economic pressures of the 1980s, the residents of such areas have sublet space to tenants in order to increase household incomes. Another response has been the diversification of the employment of the family unit. It is concluded that both the poor and the not so poor have acted in a logical and responsive manner to the economic circumstances they face.

The less than progressive effects of top-town paths to planning and development are chronicled in Salau's overview of the provision of housing in Nigeria. He shows how the benefits of the wealth generated by oil have not been equitably distributed. The increasing shortage of housing that is documented in the chapter shows quite clearly that this basic need is not being provided for those who so desperately need it. In explaining the reasons for this underachievement, Salau points an accusing finger at urban bias in recent national economic development planning and the stream or rural-to-urban migration which has resulted. The findings of a field survey of government housing in several Nigerian cities suggest that the needs of residents have not been taken into account. As is so often the case, the average household could not afford the typical dwelling being built by the government at the present time. Thus, state construction has resulted in the building of a few over-expensive dwellings. In addition, it is suggested that planning and building regulations have been predicated on upper- and middle-class values, and have thus been elitist. There is the clear need to accept the veracity of the Turnerian argument that the government must not build houses. Rather, it should do all within its powers to facilitate the efforts of those who can and wish to build for themselves. The author returns to another of the themes set out in the introduction to the present volume, namely that any such programme of aided self-help must stress indigenous methods and resources, rather than accepting Western standards as an act of faith.

The indigenous versus endogenous theme is taken up in a somewhat different context by Cumming, where she stresses the need for Third World academics to study their own environments. Within urban areas, the housing market is in the normal course of events quite resistant to change. After independence in Zimbabwe, uncharacteristically rapid residential neighbourhood change occurred in some areas. The colonial, tenure system of Rhodesia had separated the major racial groups, a situation which had no legal backing after Independence. Cumming looks carefully at the movement of the black population into one area of the city of Harare between 1980 and 1986, the first seven years of independence in Zimbabwe.

The importance of providing basic needs is also emphasized by Drakakis-Smith's chapter, which discusses changes in the system of food distribution in Third World urban areas. This is a topic which has received far less attention than shelter, especially from the radical school of development experts. One theme stresses the tendency of imported food to replace local foods in the diets of indigenous populations. As a process, of course, this follows the rise of urbanization itself, being first reflected in the rise of populations in early colonial entrepôts, and more recently in the restruc-turing of diets along Western lines. The role of multinational corporations in this must be stressed, especially in relation to the rise of fast-food retailing and mass supermarketing. Thus, the penetration of Western capital and the Westernization of dietary preferences are both factors which are giving rise to a growing dependency in urban food-supply systems in Third World countries.

These are some of the forces which are leading to a convergence on global norms of consumption within the towns and cities of developing countries, a theme which received attention in the first chapter. This is further illustrated by Potter and Dann's examination of recent change in the retailing system of the small island economy of Barbados. It is noted how in that country a staggering 97 per cent of the total retail floorspace is to be found within the narrow urban–tourist coastal strip. Although based on indigenous capital and commercial groups, new supermarket-based centres have been established since the 1960s basically catering for the demands of tourists and the elite and middle classes. Several of these new stores premise their activities on the sale of imported food items. The chapter illustrates how the mercantile community and planter interests have served to control the formal retail sector. Meanwhile, the rural areas of the country are almost exclusively supplied by informal-sector rum shops and hawkers. The net outcome is that ordinary citizens must either accept relatively high prices and a very limited range of goods in their locality, or must expend both time and money in travelling to the urban and suburban zones. Such effort must be seen as comprising part of the unequal exchange which occurs between the rural periphery and the urban–suburban–tourist core.

Sita and Chatterjee demonstrate just how clearly the colonial imprint is still to be witnessed in India, in terms of the continuing dominance of the three colonial port cities of Bombay, Calcutta and Madras together with the administrative centre of Delhi. The chapter highlights, both statistically and demographically, the sharp distance-decay of urban population which occurs away from these four major metropolitan centres. Using data for the years 1951, 1971 and 1981 for cities with a population of 100,000 or more, Sita and Chatterjee show that nearly one-third of all the Class I city population of India is concentrated within a 50 km travel distance of these four metropoles. The implicit failure of these major nodes of the urban system to diffuse and spread development is clearly revealed.

In a similar vein Salau shows that although urban development predated the arrival of the Europeans in West Africa, the process of colonialism still saw a massive spatial shift in the then existing urban system from the interior to the coast, such was the strength of imposed externally oriented 'development'. It is argued that these colonial cities engaged in the parasitical extraction of social surplus product from the countryside. This is seen as the crux of the development problem: the cities did not grow as productive industrial centres from which generative influences would inexorably be diffused into the rural areas. Recent urban bias in the provision of educational facilities, manufacturing industry and government investment have all exacerbated this historical condition. In looking at the four major policy approaches to national urban development planning that have been put into practice by the states of West Africa, Salau notes that a waning interest now characterizes growth-pole strategies.

This theme is further developed in Mohamad's consideration of the establishment of new towns in the rural areas of Malaysia as a part of regional policy since 1970. These new settlements were charged with the task of instigating the trickle-down process. A six-level hierarchy of urban growth centres was envisaged, giving rise ultimately, it was hoped, to a spatially integrated national economy in the manner envisaged by John Friedmann. The aim has been the frequently repeated one of filling the missing gap in the urban hierarchy. But, as Mohamad shows, it has become only too clear that the imposed urban growth points are not developing rapidly and have failed to play the role intended in the original conception of their plans. The efforts to urbanize the rural Malays and to change their employment from traditional pursuits to what are seen as more productive ones appears largely to have failed, at least in great part because of the top-down and centrist mode of planning connoted by the growth-pole mechanism.

As noted in the introductory chapter, we have reached the end of an era of direct association between urbanization and Western ideas of development. This change is involving a thorough ongoing reappraisal of the role that cities play in the overall process of development. The new approaches which are emanating from these deliberations are not anti-urban as such, but by and large involve a more positive evaluation of rural areas and ways of life. Basic needs, selective regional closure, agropolitan development, bottom-up and periphery-in planning are all associated with the socio-economic and administrative efficacy of small and medium-sized urban places. Practical implementation of policies involving these approaches needs to run the full test of time, but there are indications that the new paradigm is likely to meet with greater success than those adopted in earlier periods. This is particularly likely to be the case if the country-specific nature of the process of urbanization and development is fully appreciated by theoreticians and practitioners alike.

Index